Not Turning Away

NOT TURNING AWAY

The Practice of Engaged Buddhism

EDITED BY SUSAN MOON
FOREWORD BY JOANNA MACY

Introduction by Alan Senauke

SHAMBHALA
Boston & London
2004

Shambhala Publications, Inc.
Horticultural Hall
300 Massachusetts Avenue
Boston, Massachusetts 02115
www.shambhala.com

9 8 7 6 5 4 3 2 1

First Edition
Printed in the United States of America

⊗ This edition is printed on acid-free paper that meets
the American National Standards Institute z39.48 Standard.

Distributed in the United States by Random House, Inc.,
and in Canada by Random House of Canada Ltd

Library of Congress Cataloging-in-Publication Data

Not turning away: the practice of engaged Bugghism/edited by
Susan Moon; foreword by Joanna Macy; introduction by Alan Senauke.— 1st ed.
p. cm.
ISBN 1-59030-103-x (pbk: alk. paper)
1. Buddhism—Social aspects. 2. Religious life—Buddhism.
I. Moon, Susan Ichi Su, 1942-
BQ4570.S6 N6 2004
294.3'37—dc 22
2003025037

Contents

Foreword ‣ Joanna Macy   vii

Preface ‣ Susan Moon   ix

Introduction ‣ Alan Senauke   xiii

PART ONE: Practicing in the Home and in the Heart   1

Introduction   3

On Beggars ‣ Susan Moon   5

Crawling ‣ Gary Snyder   12

Money and Livelihood behind Bars ‣ Fleet Maull   15

Bad Dog ‣ Lin Jensen   22

Imperfection Is a Beautiful Thing ‣ Joan Tollifson   28

Dealing with the Anger Caused by Racism ‣ Robin Hart   38

Making Peace with Myself ‣ Jenna Jordison   46

Healing and Empowerment ‣ Sally Clay   53

Shadows of War and Class ‣ Annette Herskovits   58

Dead Man's Coat ‣ Jarvis Jay Masters   67

The Breakfast Club ‣ Michael Acutt   71

PART TWO: Taking the Practice into the World   77

Introduction   79

Seeking Evil, Finding Only Good ‣ Melody Ermachild
Chavis   81

Being Arrested ‣ Maylie Scott   90

Landmines of the Heart ‣ Bob Maat   98

Journey of a Broken Heart ‣ Marianne Dresser   103

Impossible Choices ‣ Maia Duerr   108

Nowhere to Run ‣ Tony Patchell   115

There Was a Gun in the House ‣ Lynn Dix *interviewed by*
    Susan Moon   124

Just Trust Yourself ‣ Wendy Egyoku Nakao   130

Becoming the Landscape ‣ Nanao Sakaki *interviewed by*
    Trevor Carolan   138

PART THREE: Food for Thought   143

    Introduction   145

The Practice of Peace ‣ Thich Nhat Hanh   147

Wellsprings of Engaged Buddhism ‣ Kenneth Kraft   154

Buddhist Resources for Despair ‣ Joanna Macy   162

Nourishing Freedom ‣ Mushim Ikeda-Nash   168

About Money ‣ Robert Aitken   174

Impossible Possibilities ‣ Norman Fischer   179

Buddha's Mother Saving Tibet ‣ Robert Thurman   186

Caring for Home ‣ Jack Kornfield   197

Speed ‣ Diana Winston   202

Can This Practice Be Saved? ‣ Jan Chozen Bays   209

Imagine Living in Your Bathroom ‣ Diana Lion   217

Vowing Peace in an Age of War ‣ Alan Senauke   220

    Resources ‣ Donald Rothberg   229

    Contributors   234

Foreword

This is the kind of teaching I prefer nowadays. Axioms from a single wise authority may benefit me greatly, but I turn more quickly and gratefully to testimony from lives being lived in the crosscurrents of our world. Precious to me are the words of my sisters and brothers as they tell of their efforts to embody the dharma, to make it real in their encounters and actions. Even when they stumble and fail, the discoveries they make feed my soul. They show me what an ordinary person can do and learn. And I am once more reminded of the irreplaceable value the Buddha put upon *kalyana mitra*, spiritual friends.

This book, like the journal from which it draws, widens my circle of spiritual friends. The companionable voices it brings would be welcome at any historical moment, but one is especially grateful for them right now. For this is a dark time. As preemptive wars become the order of the day, as more and more poisons are pumped into air, seas, and soil, as jobs and civil rights are decimated as fast as the forests and farms, we need each other. We need the kind of counsel and courage that spiritual friends can give. In this darkness, we can be lamps to each other.

My *kalyana mitra* in the Buddhist Peace Fellowship, a good number of whom appear now in this volume, have been lamps for me. It is good to remember the wisdom I have found in their lives and words. And I'm happy to have so much of that wisdom gathered together here, so that I can return to it for encouragement. Three of their teachings stand clear in my mind.

The first is on the cover of this book: don't turn away. Stay present. Our full presence is the greatest gift we can give to our world and to ourselves. This is the First Noble Truth and this is the boundless heart of the bodhisattva: not to be afraid of the suffering, but to let it be known and touched. That takes courage in a society addicted to comfort, but until that happens there is no healing. So trust your own experience of grief and distress. As the voices in the book attest, acceptance of these feelings transforms them and lets them reveal how closely we are all interwoven in the web of life.

Secondly, watch out for the schemes and ambitions of the ego-centered self. Even our most noble efforts can get hooked by them. See if, instead of that, you can open into big mind, sky mind, the vast Buddha-nature in which pettiness dissolves. My friends show me the kind of resilience this brings: swift recovery from failures and embarrassments, and a sweet, persistent capacity to begin again and again. I see in them, too, the freedom that arises, as they stop comparing themselves with others and become less and less dependent on the visible results of their own actions. As they stop computing their personal chances of success, it seems that nothing stops them. Despite discouragements and fears, they keep on keeping on, for the sake of all beings.

And a third teaching coming through to me is to use a wide-angle lens. See the big picture: a whole society in travail. In our corporate profit-driven, consumer society, the roots of suffering—greed, hatred, and delusion—have taken powerful, institutionalized forms. We share collective karma, and, to the extent that we recognize it, we begin to change it. As these spiritual friends have helped me see, we are fully capable of accepting responsibility for our common condition—and in ways that don't cripple us with guilt, but empower us to act. For in this dance of dependent co-arising, every thought, word, and deed has ripple effects we can barely perceive. Therefore, to live in genuine awareness of our mutual belonging in the web of life is, in itself, good, strong medicine for the healing of our world.

Other teachings as well are to be found in these pages—teachings that will encourage and inspire. For this is a book that offers us many examples of how each one of us can step forward into a world that needs our help. May these voices gladden us with gratitude for having companions on the way, with whom to share both the challenges of this time and our love for the Buddha Dharma.

—JOANNA MACY

Preface

During my years as editor of *Turning Wheel*, my heart has been opened like a door, over and over, by the field reports people bring to us from their lives. It's a privilege to work with people who have gone into the trenches of suffering, whether in their own hearts, in the woods, or in the streets, and who want to let us know what they found there. Grace Paley, one of my writer-heroes, says, "The world is a better place for having its stories told." So, in *Turning Wheel*, we encourage each other by telling these stories, by bringing the news of what it means to be a human being in the world today.

My work as editor is a form of midwifery, helping people bring forth what they have to say. It's a pleasure to work with experienced writers, but most satisfying for me is to attend the birth when someone has a compelling story to tell but is not sure she can tell it, and to help her see that she can. "Breathe! Push! You can do it! I see the head!" I exclaim.

Many editors are also writers, but as an editor you have to forget about your own longing for recognition, and help the writer find his voice. You suggest ways for him to clarify his message while keeping your own mouth shut. Your work, when it's successful, is invisible.

Some of the challenges of my job include: Critique without discouraging. Don't take forever to answer queries and submissions. For heaven's sake, don't lose people's manuscripts! Don't be afraid to reject a piece when it doesn't work out, but do so with compassion. Choose what to print, knowing there is never room for everything you want to include. And somehow get writers to meet your deadlines—even though you can't pay them a darn thing—so that you can get it all done on time.

We are all swamped with words. And so I ask myself sometimes: "Why should I be causing even more trees to be cut down (we use recycled paper, but it isn't 100 percent)? And why should I be producing more material for people to read when they already have too much, and not enough time in which to read it?" I hold myself accountable for making the magazine worth both the paper and the time.

Turning Wheel, and therefore this anthology, offers a particular perspective. As editor, I bring to *TW* a bias for the personal narrative. I have a great curiosity about how other people meet suffering. What do they do when they are afraid? What gives them the strength to reach out, again and again, to people who have turned their backs in anger? What gives them the courage to ask a soldier to put down his gun?

Readers will find in these pages accounts of how ordinary people bring together in their own lives their dharma practice and their work for peace and justice. Their courage gives me courage. It takes courage to speak up, now more than ever, as fear-mongering and war-mongering are systematically stifling the human voice and the human imagination.

Along with the work of recognized teachers, elders, and writers, we print a high proportion of unsolicited material, which helps to give *Turning Wheel* its grassroots flavor. As Mister Rogers used to sing, "These are the people in your neighborhood," and in this case, your neighborhood is the planet. Whether the words we print come to us in e-mail attachments or handwritten from prison cells, all of them come from the heart.

I've enjoyed the relationships I've developed with writers over the years. It's surprising how intimately an editor and a writer can get to know each other through working together, even if they never meet face-to-face. We share a commitment to telling it like it is.

Making the selection for this anthology was painfully difficult. There simply isn't room to include many of the pieces we would have liked to present here. I hope this sampling of twenty-five years of *Turning Wheel* and the *BPF Newsletter* brings you some of the hope, inspiration, and encouragement I have felt myself.

Creating the anthology has been a collaborative effort. Special thanks go to the people who helped to make the selection: Marianne Dresser, Maia Duerr, Mushim Ikeda-Nash, Melanie Phoenix, Alan Senauke, and Diana Winston. In addition, countless others have helped to produce *Turning Wheel* over the years. I particularly want to thank the following longtime consulting editors: Denise Caignon, Annette Herskovits, Shannon Hickey, Albert Kutchins, Rachel Markowitz, Christopher Martinez, Karen Payne, Terry Stein, Jon Stewart, Meredith Stout, Larry Watson, and Lewis Woods.

In the lineage of editors, I received transmission from David Schneider, who received it from Arnie Kotler. Thanks to them and the others who went before them, for their turnings of the wheel.

Thanks to my two editors at Shambhala: Dave O'Neal, who suggested the book in the first place and shepherded it through the early stages, and Beth Frankl, for her patient and careful editing.

—SUSAN MOON

Introduction

After his great awakening, Shakyamuni Buddha arose from his seat under the bodhi tree on the banks of the Neranjara River. He took to the dusty road and came upon five old friends in the Deer Park at Isipatana. Right away they could see the glow of enlightenment and they asked him for a teaching. The Buddha offered his friends a discourse on the Four Noble Truths, his great dharma discovery. They became his first disciples. There, among good friends, the Buddha turned the dharma wheel for the first time.

Elsewhere in the Axial Age—that extraordinary, pivotal era of Socrates, Plato, Aristotle, Homer, Zarathustra and Zoroastrian -ism, Mahavira, Confucius, Lao Tzu, the Buddha, and the Jewish prophets—the world experienced the simultaneous flowering of rationalism, monotheism, science, social justice, and standards for ethical behavior. The prophet Ezekiel had a vision of a wheel within a wheel, our world spinning like a gyroscope within the divine itself.

We are heir to all these turnings. The wheel of life turns continuously. Beings are born and die. Dharmas arise and fall away. The Buddha awakened to the reality of impermanence. He (or she) is still helping us wake up to suffering and the end of suffering. The Biblical prophets saw a different vision of the wheel, one that turned by faith and justice. Gary Snyder wrote about these two turnings in his seminal 1960s essay on engaged Buddhism, "Buddhism and the Coming Revolution." He says, "The mercy of the West has been social revolution; the mercy of the East has been individual insight into the basic self/void. We need both."

These two mercies turn together in the heart of the Buddhist Peace Fellowship—honoring and learning from our Asian roots, while not forgetting the teachings of Judaism and Christianity in which many of us were born. Each of us cultivates our dharma practice in meditation and faith. We also cultivate a common vision of peace and social harmony. We become attuned to the ways we create suffering for ourselves as individuals, and we learn how we cocreate structures of oppression and privilege that generate the various "isms" and wars that plague the world. We need stories of transformation as much as we need theories of social change.

In the summer of 1991, as the Gulf War was ending and oil wells were still smoldering in Kuwait, the first issue of the newly named *Turning Wheel* rolled off the presses. Editor Susan Moon recalled Ezekiel's vision in a song we both remember from childhood.

> Ezekiel saw the wheel,
> Way up in the middle of the air.
> And the little wheel turns by faith,
> And the big wheel turns by the grace of God.

Her editor's column closed with these words:

> A wheel doesn't have a top or a bottom. You keep turning it, but you can't tell where one revolution ends and the next one begins, unless the wheel is calibrated, and I don't think the dharma wheel is. So you can't tell whether you've made "progress" in turning the wheel, you just have to go on faith. You just have to keep forever turning the wheel of dharma, way up in the middle of the air.

Turning Wheel has a noble pedigree. From BPF's founding in 1978, it had a *Newsletter* that linked engaged Buddhists and BPF chapters with each other and with the world. Buddhist Peace Fellowship and *Turning Wheel* are rooted in a kind of international Buddhist ecumenism. BPF has eschewed identification with any particular school or sect of Buddhism (although some might legitimately complain that there are too many Zen types hanging around the office). The earliest issues of the *BPF Newsletter* featured first-person reports on liberation struggles in Tibet, Vietnam, and Bangladesh. It made connections between these seemingly distant conflicts and the policies of U.S. corporations and militarism. There were teachings from Thich Nhat Hanh, Joanna Macy, Robert Aitken, and other well known teachers. And, as with BPF itself, there was an emphasis on grassroots activism that called for individuals and groups to look for truth in their own experience rather than in institutions and hierarchies.

Over time, the look and content of the *BPF Newsletter* evolved. By the middle 1980s, with Fred Eppsteiner as editor, the *Newsletter* developed a serious and professional look. This was matched by the quality of material between the covers. Arnold Kotler was editor from 1986 to 1989. At the same time that he was getting Parallax Press off the ground and editing Thich Nhat Hanh's books, Arnie poured his considerable editorial and networking skills into making the *BPF Newsletter* an essential resource for Buddhist activists. I remember some of those days. I worked at Parallax and recall Arnie putting in long days and nights in front of his Macintosh screen while the telephone rang ceaselessly and computers crashed even more frequently than they do today.

As Parallax and the newly established Community of Mindful Living (an organization founded to support individuals practicing in the Thich Nhat Hahn tradition) took more and more of Arnie's attention, he put the *Newsletter* into the hands of David Schneider. David had been a fellow Zen student at San Francisco Zen Center, and was an excellent writer and editor. He had already helped out with the *Newsletter* for a year, so it was a natural fit. As I read through old issues, it becomes clear to me that David's editorial vision and Larry Watson's design eye created a look that we are still working with in *Turning Wheel*—a magazine that is at once attractive and serious, aimed at engaged Buddhists rather than scholars or dharma tourists.

In the autumn of 1990, as the United States and allies were girding their loins for the first war with Iraq, Susan Moon took the *Newsletter*'s editorial reins from David Schneider. Larry Watson, then working as art director at *Yoga Journal*, stayed on as our designer. Larry had earlier designed BPF's "lotus in hand" logo. Now, many years later, he is still tending to our covers, graphics, and design. Sue's first issue featured our first-ever color cover, a brush painting by Kaz Tanahashi with blood red splattered across a jagged black stroke, and the words "if we go to WAR . . ." In her first editor's column, Sue wrote, "Engaged Buddhism is about the bodhisattva's understanding that no one is really free until everyone is free. Let's listen to each other's stories, so we can help each other."

During this period I became increasingly involved with BPF, and began, in January of 1991, to serve as BPF's executive director. By the end of that year, it became clear to all of us at BPF that we had something more than a "newsletter" on our hands. Susan Moon's vision was of a journal that was linked to BPF's work and mission, with its own editorial identity. It needed a name of its own. We thought up many possibilities: two that I remember are *Attention* and *This Is It*. At last we settled on *Turning Wheel*. And it has been turning ever since, four issues a year, regular as clockwork.

Turning Wheel and *Not Turning Away* are impossible to imagine apart from the clear editorial vision of Susan Moon. She has been at it for nearly fourteen years now, going back to the time when each issue was carved on stone tablets in cuneiform. Actually, one of the things I most admire about Sue is how she has steadfastly maintained the human scale of *Turning Wheel*, while having to reckon with the ceaseless march of technological complexity in the world of publishing. In the midst of cyberspace she has kept an eye on the words and the story.

Sue has the dubious honor of being BPF's longest extant employee. It has always been a great pleasure to work together, through life's various ups and downs—health crises, arrests, child-rearing, and hairstyles. As friends and practitioners, we see eye to eye. Our common love for the work of BPF goes very deep.

As an editor, she has a gift for seeing which words are extra. She subtly (and sometimes not so subtly) helped me polish columns and reviews in every issue of *TW*. As a writer, Sue is attuned to stories. Stories, like people, embody "emptiness," which is a Buddhist way of speaking about the interdependent nature of all being. This kind of everyday storytelling, as much as anything, sets *Turning Wheel* apart from other Buddhist publications.

I took part in the selection process for *Not Turning Away*. We looked at many wonderful pieces and struggled to distill twenty-five years of the *BPF Newsletter* and *Turning Wheel* into one manageable volume. Sue and her eager corps of readers have tried to select pieces that both stand the test of time and illuminate the life and practice of socially engaged Buddhism. We had an embarrassment of literary riches to choose from. The hardest part was having to narrow it down to the final selection—not just because there were so many excellent articles, but because each piece speaks of and from a whole world of suffering and liberation. If, as the sutras preach, there are 108,000 sufferings and 108,000 doors of liberation, only a handful can be represented here. But this is part of our dharma practice as well: recognizing and accepting that things in life are necessarily incomplete, and continuing to turn our lives toward freedom in spite of incompleteness.

Turning Wheel is what most people know best about BPF. Like many of you, I read the *BPF Newsletter* for years before becoming involved in the organization's work. I felt a little guilty about my lack of involvement, but this reading planted many seeds. I learned about actions and practices and places I never would have known about without these writers' and editors' efforts. We hope the same will be true for many of you as you read this anthology.

Zen Master Dogen, our thirteenth-century Japanese Soto Zen ancestor, offered this commentary on the bodhisattva precept of telling the truth: "The Dharma Wheel turns from the beginning. There is neither surplus nor lack. The sweet dew saturates all and harvests the truth." Truth, or dharma, has many faces, many forms. We sense that our own age is what Joanna Macy calls the "Great Turning." Joanna explains, "The Great Turning is a name for the essential adventure of our time: the shift from the industrial growth society to a life-sustaining civilization." If we and our planet are to survive, we will have to make this shift. Sometimes it feels like a race against time. Which will come first? Will we save the world or will we turn it into a barren rock? Truth-telling is the necessary essence of this turning, the essence of life. From beginning to end of *Not Turning Away*, countless faces shine through the pages. These are beings, like ourselves, dedicated to turning the wheel. We are encouraged by their actions and inspired by their lives. We turn again to the hard and joyous work of liberation.

—ALAN SENAUKE

Introduction

PART ONE

Practicing in the Home and in the Heart

INTRODUCTION TO PART ONE

In our eagerness to work for the alleviation of suffering, for peace and justice in the world, we sometimes try to leapfrog over our own situation—as if the pickle we ourselves are in doesn't count—and go straight on to saving the world. I think of a character in Dickens' s *Bleak House*, a Mrs. Jellyby, who has many children of her own, but who spends all her time working for the education of the natives of "Borrioboola-Gha, on the left bank of the Niger," while her own children fall ill from neglect.

If Buddha has told us once he's told us a hundred times: our own suffering is inextricably connected with the suffering of others. Not only is it the case that "When you suffer, I suffer, too." The reverse is also true: "When I suffer, so do you." And we can't be very helpful to the wide world if we can't be helpful to ourselves. We can't stand up for justice for sentient beings if we can't stand up for justice for this particular sentient being.

So in Part One, we start with our own experience. Here we have included pieces in which the authors write about the suffering in their own hearts, in their own families, and in their own living situations. We hear from a woman who meets and forgives her father's murderer; we hear from people dealing with negative projections from society because of skin color, physical disability, and mental illness. We hear from people practicing in prison, and on the street, homeless. They are not complaining or feeling sorry for themselves. They are finding ways of working with the difficulties life has brought them. And they are passing these findings on to us, the readers, on the chance that we, too, may encounter some difficulties along the way, and that we might benefit from their experience. So don't say, "What's the use in hearing about just one earthling's personal struggle when we've got a whole world to change?" If you want to learn how to make full use of this precious human birth, ask an expert—a human being! Ask a human being who is in training to save all sentient beings.

—S.M.

ON BEGGARS

Susan Moon

When I was ten, on a family vacation, my father and I took a walk through the narrow, cobbled streets of Quebec City. A band of barefoot children danced along beside us, chanting in French. Was this an invitation to play? My father, blushing slightly, ignored them. After they were gone, I asked him what their song meant, and he said they were poor children begging for money. I was ashamed for him, that he had not given them any—I knew he had money in his pocket. But I said nothing, sensing discomfort on my father's part.

For Buddhist monks in Asia, begging is honorable. They may not till the soil—lest they break the first precept by killing insects—so they beg for their food from the villagers, and in exchange they offer prayers and meditations for them. They must beg each day, as they can't keep food overnight. Begging makes them intimate with the people around them. Everybody gets merit. Everybody is giving something to somebody else, in accordance with their situation in life.

In California we don't call it begging, we call it panhandling.

Years ago I had a boyfriend, an alcoholic in recovery, from whom I parted when he went back to drinking. He soon became jobless and homeless. I'd come out of the Safeway and practically trip over him sitting at the edge of the parking lot. Or he'd be on the sidewalk by the drugstore, his upside-down blue beret beside him, smelling so strongly of alcohol that I didn't even have to lean over to notice it.

Sometimes he played the flute, if he hadn't pawned it, but mostly he sat and waited, and when someone gave him money he would say,

"God bless you," as if he was giving something back. He told me begging was his way of earning a living. It was hard work, he said. Just like everybody else, he was making the money to buy what he needed to get through the day—in his case fortified wine and a muffin. And like a Buddhist monk, he was not hoarding anything overnight. He shared his spoils with his friends on the street. Still, when I passed him on my way to the drugstore, I felt angry at him, knowing he'd traded a job and a comfortable rented room for this besotted life on the sidewalk.

I didn't put any money in his blue beret—I didn't want his blessing—but I knew he slept under some boards behind the bakery, and once, that rainy winter, when nobody was looking, I left a blanket there for him.

One December, I was fortunate to be part of a "Buddhist-Christian Pilgrimage" to India. The centerpoint of our trip was a meeting in Bodh Gaya, where His Holiness the Dalai Lama and Benedictine monk Father Laurence Freeman engaged in a dialogue for several days, in a small Tibetan meditation center.

Before I left for India, an American friend who had lived in Bodh Gaya advised me to make up my mind ahead of time as to whether I would give to beggars or not, so that I wouldn't have to make a decision every time. She told me about parents who maimed their children to make them better beggars, about lepers walking away from a cure for the same reason, about gang leaders who took the most crippled people they could find, put them down to beg in the middle of a busy intersection in town, and then took away their earnings, à la *Oliver Twist*. She said that if you gave to one beggar, you were immediately surrounded by dozens more. She told me begging was an industry she had decided she didn't want to support. So before I left for India I decided I wouldn't give to beggars.

On the way to Bodh Gaya, our group stopped in the holy city of Varanasi. On the steps by the river, there were many lepers. I'd never seen a leper before. The way the flesh is gone is not the clean cut of an amputation, but a gradual eating away, like a worn-down pencil stub. Leprosy is a scary reminder of impermanence: time eats the victim alive, too impatient to wait until death for the body's meat. The invisible truth is made visible. This body of mine will also be disassembled.

A woman walked along beside me, sideways, as I went down the steps to the river. Her dark face was framed by a bright pink sari, her mouth looked moth-eaten, and on the hand that reached out to me were little bumps where her fingers used to be, not long enough to grasp anything. She stuck right with me, thrusting her hand in front of me all the way to the river. "How contagious is leprosy?" I wondered, and was ashamed to catch myself wondering. "Good morning," I said to her, looking into her eyes. This became my three-part vow: to look into the eyes of every beggar who approached me, to speak to them, and to remember that I could be in their bare feet instead of my shoes.

There are more beggars in Bodh Gaya than in most parts of India, because it is a Buddhist pilgrimage site, and pilgrims often give money to beggars in order to gain merit. During our dialogue meeting in Bodh Gaya, questions were invited, and Venerable Santikaro Bhikkhu, an American monk and teacher in Thailand, commented that being confronted by so many beggars was a disturbing experience for visiting Westerners, and he asked how we might respond to them.

The Dalai Lama spoke of the importance of social programs that can provide education, health care, job training, and a sense of personal dignity for people, so that they don't have to become beggars. He mentioned intentional communities formed to help disabled people. He said that he gave some of his Nobel Prize money to a self-help community of lepers. He said that politicians lack a sense of responsibility for poor people. There is too great a gap between rich and poor, he said, not only in the state of Bihar, but in the world, between rich nations and poor ones, and this is the cause of many problems. He said there is something morally wrong when there is that much of a gap, and that giving money to beggars does not change the situation.

At first this came as a relief, seeming to get me off the hook. It was okay for me not to give to beggars! But really, it's a big hook, and we're all on it. Each time I meet a beggar, we demonstrate, in street-theater form, the global economy. As Buddha said: Because there is this, there is that.

But interconnectedness is complicated. There's not having enough, there's having what you need, and there's having more than you need. You can guess which category I fall into. There's also the fact that poverty is relative, and there's the truth—a truth that shouldn't keep on surprising us, but does—that material wealth doesn't bring happiness.

When the teachings were over, my friend Diana and I sat on our suitcases on the platform of the Gaya train station, waiting for our train to Varanasi. It was three hours late. We were the only Westerners in the crowded station. A small ragged boy with the face of a teenager dragged himself toward us on hands and knees along the filthy platform. His bare legs were twisted like a pretzel. When he reached Diana, he put his hand firmly on her shoe. We remained in this silent tableau for a moment, and then he gripped her ankle with both hands and laid his head against her thigh. "Hey," Diana said. "No."

He pushed his face into her, the way a cat rubs its nose against your leg, but unlike a cat, there was no affection in his movements. No feeling other than: I'm here. Give me something. He made no appeal to pity. He was not cute. Perhaps the attempt to bury his head in Diana's lap was a misapplication of something he'd seen, his version of a gesture of supplication.

Diana looked frightened, and this worried me further. An experienced traveler, she'd been living in Asia for a year and a half, and I took my cues from her. She stood up, but he still held on to her ankle. He made a strange, sharp, sipping noise with his lips and tongue, over and over—a hissing, kissing, sucking noise, like a blind baby goat looking for the nipple. She moved her foot, but he wouldn't be dislodged. She moved her foot more vigorously. He let go and grabbed my ankle instead, in the same viselike grip, and buried his face in my thigh. I stood up, too, but he didn't let go.

Suddenly I noticed that a dozen Indian men stood in a semicircle on the platform in front of us, watching with amusement. Their stares were neither hostile nor friendly. I moved my foot, tentatively. The boy held on.

Diana offered him a banana from our bag of food for the train. He shook his head almost angrily, and nodded at the whole bag. Diana addressed the staring men. "Can you help us?"

One of them stepped forward, shouted at the child, and raised his arm to threaten a beating. As the boy scrambled away he took the banana after all. He split the peel with one hand and squeezed the whole banana into his mouth like toothpaste, then hurled the peel down onto the train tracks, and retreated, crablike.

"I've spent years in India," said Diana, "and I've never had that happen. I completely left my body."

Afterward, at a safe distance, I wondered: Was he an orphan? Did he live in the train station? Did he have a relationship with anybody at all? How did he keep warm on cold nights?

A week later, on Christmas Day, I sat on another train platform, by myself, in Varanasi, waiting for the train to Delhi. The train was late and I had a long wait. There were many beggars in the crowded station, and as the only Westerner in sight, I was the most obvious target. I had just two small coins in my purse, and if I gave to one beggar, the others would all surround me in a crescendo of requests, and I'd have to fend them off till my train came, which could be another two or three hours.

An old woman, bent over at almost a ninety-degree angle, hobbled over to me, leaning on a stick. Her brown hand reached out from the folds of a brown shawl. Her brown face twisted into mine, and the gaping hole of her mouth opened wider and wider, so that I felt I was looking straight into the mouth of hunger. She was so wrinkled and toothless, so archetypal, she could have walked out of a Shakespeare play, a dream, a dharma talk by the Buddha. She wasn't dead, but she looked like she might keel over in front of me at any moment.

And it was Christmas, the birthday of the man who said, "Inasmuch as you have given unto the least of these, you have given unto me." My wallet in my pocket was full of bills, and I shook my head. The old woman looked again into my face, pleading, then faded back and disappeared down the platform.

"God forgive me!" I said out loud.

Then a boy of six or seven came up to me, not visibly disabled but with a glazed look. He stood before me, held out his hand, and waited, without aggression. His eyes were dull. In his face I saw no anger, no hope, no despair, no disappointment.

I shook my head and he walked dazedly on down the platform. I saw him stop in front of a food cart. The vendor handed him a samosa. Perhaps he lived in the station and survived on what he was given by the food vendors. He walked on, eating his samosa. There didn't seem to be anyone with him.

A woman in a bright sari squatted before me with her two children, a boy and a girl. These children, about four and five, were very cute. The woman's sari was pretty—bright purple and orange—but dirty at the bottom. She pointed to my water bottle. Afraid of germs, I didn't want to share it with her, so I bought her a bottle of water from a nearby cart. She tucked it under her shawl, and she and her children continued to squat before me and stare and smile at me. She didn't seem to be asking me for anything more, though I wasn't sure. I smiled at the kids, pointed to myself, said my name, pointed to them, asked their names. They didn't say anything, but seemed to enjoy my meaningless antics.

I heard a charming sound of wooden clackers, and a man walked by carrying a big tray on his head piled high with colorful wooden toys and noisemakers. I went after him, and bought two brightly painted wooden dolls that nodded their heads: a soldier and a fat woman. I gave them to the two children according to their sex.

"Merry Christmas," I said.

They grinned, examined the toys, showed them to their mother, clutched them. This was how I celebrated Christmas.

My blanket decision not to give money to beggars while I was in India was supposed to save me from "dealing with it" every time. But it saved me from nothing. A pilgrimage is a double journey: inner and outer. Each time I looked into a hungry face, I felt my own longing. Each time I turned away from a beggar, what was that turning? Now it seems to me that my decision not to give to beggars brought me face-to-face with their poverty in a way that giving wouldn't have done. I don't say this to justify it, but in saying no, I felt their situation more keenly. I entered into the NO that their lives were made of.

Whether I give to a beggar or not, the moment of turning away still comes, and the beggar is still in need. My own longing is still unsatisfied. The beggars are everywhere, inside and out, real and metaphorical. I can't feed them all. What can I do?

Seven years ago, when my father died, I took a vow. According to Tibetan Buddhist beliefs, for forty-nine days after death, the departed are in a sort of limbo state called the *bardo*, and they need all the help they can get from the living. So for forty-nine days after my father's death, I gave money to every person on the street who asked me for money. This was no small matter in Berkeley, though it would have been a much bigger commitment in Varanasi or Bodh Gaya. I tried always to have change in my pocket. Usually I gave a quarter. But if I didn't have change, I'd have to give something bigger in order to keep my vow. I dedicated the merit of my giving to my father. It made me feel better, even though he might not have wanted this kind of merit. He would have agreed with the Dalai Lama that poverty has to be addressed at the systemic level; he worked for social justice all his life. Only now, as I write, does it occur to me that there could be a connection between my vow and the beggar children in Quebec to whom my father gave nothing. Because there is this, there is that.

(1999)

CRAWLING

Gary Snyder

I was traveling the crest of a little ridge, finding a way between stocky, deep red, mature manzanita trunks, picking out a route and heading briskly on. Crawling.

Not hiking or sauntering or strolling, but crawling, steady and determined, through the woods. We usually visualize an excursion into the wild as an exercise of walking upright. We imagine ourselves striding through open alpine terrain, or across the sublime space of a sagebrush basin, or through the somber understory of an ancient sugar pine grove.

But it's not so easy to walk upright through the late-twentieth-century, mid-elevation Sierra forests. There are always many sectors regenerating from fire or logging and the fire history of the Sierra would indicate that there have always been some areas of manzanita fields. So people tend to stay on the old logging roads or the trails, and this is their way of experiencing the forest. Manzanita and ceanothus fields, or the bushy groundcover and understory parts of the forest, are left in wild peace.

My crawl was in late December, and although the sky was clear and sunny, the temperature was around freezing. Patches of remnant snow were on the ground. A few of us were out chasing corners and boundary lines on the Bear Tree parcel of the Inimim Forest with retiring B.L.M. [Bureau of Land Management] forester Dave Raney, who had worked with that land many years before. There is no way to travel off the trail but to dive in: drop down on your hands and knees on the crunchy manzanita leaf-cover and crawl around between the trunks. Leather work gloves, a tight-fitting hat, a long-sleeved denim work jacket, and old Filson tin pants make a proper crawler's outfit. Face right in the snow, I came upon my first of many bear tracks. Along the ridge a ways, and then down a steep slope through the brush, belly-sliding on snow and leaves like an otter. You get limber at it—and see the old stumps from early logging surrounded by thick manzanita, still-tough, pitchy limbs from old wolf trees, hardy cones, overgrown drag-roads, four-foot butt logs left behind, webs of old limbs and twigs, and the periodic prize of a bear scat.

One of our party called us back a bit: "A bear tree!" And sure enough, there was a cavity in a large old pine that opened up after a fire had scarred it. A definite black bear hangout, with scratches on the bark. To go where bears, deer, raccoons, foxes—all our other neighbors—go, you have to be willing to crawl.

So we began to overcome our hominid pride and learned to take pleasure in turning off the trail to go directly into the brush to find the contours and creatures of the pathless part of the woods. Not really pathless, for there is the whole world of little animal trails that have their own logic. You go down, crawl swift along, spot an opening, stand and walk a few yards, and go down again. The trick is: have no attachment to standing, find your body at home on the ground, be a quadruped, or, if necessary, a snake. You brush cool dew of a young fir with your face. The delicate aroma of leaf molds and mycelium rises from the tumbled humus under your hand, and a half-buried young boletus is disclosed. You can smell the fall mushrooms when crawling.

I began to fantasize on the larger possibilities of crawling. Workshops in Power Crawling? Crawling to Achieve Your Goals? Self-Esteem Crawls? Well, no. But at least: Crawl Away into the Wild. The world of little scats and tiny tracks. And self-esteem—no joke! "I feel finally liberated. I have overcome my aversion to crawling, and I can go anywhere!"

It's not always easy, and you can get lost. Last winter we took a long, uphill cross-country transect on some of the land just above the Yuba Gorge that soon turned into a serious crawl. We got into denser and denser old manzanita that had us doing commando-style lizard crawls to get under their low limbs. It became an odd and un-familiar ridge, and I had no idea where we might be. For hundreds of yards, it seemed, we were scuttling along, and we came on a giant, to-tally fresh, worm-free boletus. It was a *Boletus edulis,* the prize of all the boletes mushrooms. That went into the little day pack. A bit further the manzanita opened and there we were! Suddenly we had arrived at the opening below a friend's cabin, which is built partially on B.L.M. land, near a dirt road that led toward home.

Get those gloves and a jacket and a hat and go out and explore California.

(1993)

MONEY AND LIVELIHOOD
BEHIND BARS

Fleet Maull

One of my early bunkmates in federal prison was a cook in the prison kitchen, and when I moved in above him, he started working on me right away, trying to sign me up on one of his "dinner contracts." He had three or four prisoners paying him several hundred dollars a month each to provide them with a good restaurant-quality meal every evening: steak, chicken, deluxe hamburger and the like, with salad and dessert, served alongside their bunk, with a tablecloth and dinnerware. He was making serious money by prison standards. I suppose I still had the air of money about me from the street, but I was actually completely broke and already committed to avoiding that kind of prison hustling as much as possible, so he gave up on me after a few days.

Before coming to prison, I didn't think much about the practice of Right Livelihood or the lay precepts. Like many Westerners, I was more interested in the practice of meditation and the Buddhist teachings on the nature of mind. Unfortunately, from early on it seemed my spiritual yearnings had run a parallel course with alcohol and drug abuse, and by the time I began to get serious about Buddhism, I was already an alcoholic and addict. My denial was so strong that I was blind to the jarring incongruities in the life I was leading as an active Buddhist practitioner and a part-time drug smuggler.

Even after taking refuge and bodhisattva vows in 1979 and 1981, I continued to engage in criminal activity for another two years, without ever really experiencing any sense of the wrongness of what I was doing. I did begin to sense the precariousness of my situation at a certain point and tried to extricate myself from that way of life, but I still wasn't able to see the harm I had been causing until that first cell door slammed shut on me in May 1985 and my life unraveled completely.

In the weekly recovery meetings I began to attend in prison, I listened to the stories of other addicts and realized the harm I had been doing to others by bringing cocaine into the country. When the crack epidemic hit a few years later, I saw what a devastating effect cocaine, in this new form, was capable of having on whole communities. It became very clear to me that I needed to make the practice of Right Livelihood, with its underlying basis in the five lay precepts, a central focus of my training from that point on.

In federal prison the authorities try to equalize prisoners as much as possible and to keep a lid on all the smuggling and black-marketeering that goes on by limiting what people can spend. There is a prison commissary store where you can shop once a week for postage stamps, ink pens, notebooks, toiletry items, laundry soap, beverages and snack foods, athletic shoes, and sweat suits. You can also buy a small, Walkman-style radio with headphones, an inexpensive watch, or a small fan to provide some relief during the hot summer months. You pay for your purchases with a plastic, magnetic-strip account card, which also serves as a picture I.D.

While there is no limit on the amount of money you can have in your commissary account, you're only allowed to spend up to $125 a month. You can also purchase up to $15 a week in coins to use in the washing machines, dryers, and vending machines in the residential units, but you're not allowed to have any more than $20 in coins in your possession at any time. If you're caught with more than that, you'll lose the money, and you may do some time in the hole, or segregation unit, as well. At the very least, you will lose your room seniority, which means starting out again on a top bunk in one of the large, noisy dormitories. Men who use a lot of coins find ways to hide them, though, or they stash them with other prisoners who are below their limit.

The $125 a month spending limit mainly serves to limit an individual's use of outside resources. Most prisoners have no money coming in from the outside. Wages range from eleven to sixty dollars a month for full-time prison jobs, but most of the prisoners make less than twenty-five dollars a month. Many, especially the medical and psychiatric patients who account for two-thirds of the population at this institution, earn only five dollars a month for part-time work, or nothing at all. Some prisoners look to some kind of honest but gray market work like washing and ironing clothes, cleaning rooms, or cutting hair for other prisoners. Some also make greeting cards, draw portraits, or produce other arts and crafts work for sale to augment their income; but many more resort to food smuggling or some other hustle to get money. Some men even manage to send money home to their families.

One can get by with no money in prison. The institution provides you with three meals a day, work clothing, and basic toiletry items. You can throw your prison-issue clothing, which is stamped with your name and bin number, in the laundry cart, and it will reappear several days later in your clothing room bin. Dirty socks and towels, which don't get tagged, can be exchanged daily in the clothing room for clean ones.

Being broke in prison is kind of a drag, though. You feel somehow disempowered, not being able to "buy something," which in our culture seems to be the ultimate mark of personhood. But you are not looked down upon for being broke in prison, as long as you don't become a mooch, always borrowing or asking for things from others. Some men do adjust to living with very little, even some who were doing quite well on the street. Most, however, try to get some money somehow.

I've lived very simply in the past, especially during my early traveling years, when all my earthly possessions fit quite easily into a backpack. That's actually one aspect of prison life that has been enjoyable for me, just learning to live simply again. From the beginning, I had some notion of taking at least a modified monastic approach to prison life, and when I took temporary novice vows for the duration of my sentence in 1989, that further reinforced the idea of keeping things simple. I'm not rigid about it, but I always try to question myself as to whether I really need something. My small locker space, almost entirely taken up with books and correspondence files, provides a built-in limitation.

I haven't really had to struggle about money myself; my family has sent me funds since my fourth month here, so I can't speak for being destitute in prison. I probably spend about 75 percent of what I earn and what my family sends on postage for my extensive correspondence, and on phone calls to my sixteen-year-old son in South America. The rest goes for toiletries and a few food items. Once a year or so, I'll buy some new athletic shoes. At Christmas I buy a lot of holiday food items in the commissary and throw an extended party for friends and neighbors. It's become kind of a tradition.

For those who have the money, there is a flourishing black market in food smuggled out of the prison kitchen and in stolen prison clothing, especially new socks, underwear, and towels. Also, if you have the money, you can eat better in your residential unit than you can in the dining hall. You can buy three-inch-thick, deli-style sandwiches, real hamburgers, omelet sandwiches, and sometimes burritos for seventy-five cents to a dollar; or you can buy tomatoes, green peppers, onions, and cheese to cook up a batch of classic, prison-style nachos. They sell the chips in the commissary.

Last year they were even smuggling homemade pizzas out of the kitchen and selling them for five dollars. They would precook the dough in the kitchen, and then finish cooking the pizza with toppings to order in the microwaves that were installed in the residential units a few years back, when they put in vending machines. Before that, all cooking in the units was done with stolen heat lamps. A friend used to run a grill in his room every night, preparing hamburgers to order with a cookie tin and a heat lamp.

Prisoners are not permitted to give each other anything of value, so all the business that goes on violates policy and is subject to punishment. But it's impossible to control, and prisoners routinely buy and sell anything of value, barter goods and services, loan each other money, and gamble on sports and card games. The medium of exchange is coins, books of postage stamps, cigarettes, or commissary items.

Larger debts, primarily from gambling or jailhouse lawyer fees, are settled outside the prison by having family or friends send funds back and forth and into prisoners' commissary accounts. Gambling is the major evening entertainment in prison, and for some it's a livelihood. At about 7:00 P.M. the gambling enthusiasts transform the TV rooms into casinos, where they play poker until lights out.

Despite all the hustling, the efforts made by prison authorities to keep prisoners on relatively equal footing, both socially and economically, are largely successful, and I think this is a very good thing. Even a prisoner with unlimited financial resources can't really live much better than any other prisoner in federal prison. You can only wear so many athletic shoes and jogging suits, and you can only eat so many black market sandwiches.

Shortly after arriving here in 1985, I found a job in the prison education department where I felt I would be able to earn an honest wage while using some of my talents and education to help other prisoners. I have worked full time ever since, teaching other prisoners to read and helping them to prepare for the GED exam, and it's something I both enjoy and feel really good about doing. As the senior tutor, I earn about sixty dollars a month for my efforts.

Knowing I'm extremely fortunate for the help my family gives me, I have never felt judgmental toward those who hustle to get by, and I have a lot of respect for the men who find ways to earn and send money home to their needy families. But it saddens me greatly that the system is set up in such a way that prisoners are actually encouraged to become proficient at hustling and thievery while in prison, skills that will only lead to more crime and more prison time down the road.

I try, but it's difficult to avoid participating in the black market completely. Like it or not, this convict world is my community, and I often find myself trying to balance my commitment to the precepts with the Mahayana vows I have taken to extend myself to others. Something as simple as a birthday party for a friend is bound to involve some black-market food. Prison-style nachos are the usual fare. I must confess to buying a few of those black-market pizzas last year, and they were pretty good, too. I split them with a hospice patient, probably so I wouldn't feel so guilty.

At work I sometimes assist some of my students with very simple legal work, like writing a letter to the parole board, but I steadfastly refuse payment. I decided very early on that I didn't want to profit from dealings with my fellow prisoners. Other prisoners often ask me for help with legal work, probably because they think I'm well educated or something, and there have been times when my son and his mother's living situation in South America has been really bad. This has tempted me to get into the jailhouse lawyer business to help them. Each time, though, after considerable agonizing and pride swallowing, I have instead reached out to my parents and friends in the *sangha* [spiritual community] for help. This meant breaking a deeply ingrained pattern of refusing to ask for help and of looking for a way to make a quick buck instead. So this has been a positive change for me, and I know it's been better for my son, too. My family and friends have been incredibly generous. My family provides my son with ongoing support, and a group of *sangha* friends even raised the money for him to visit me here last summer and then go on to Nova Scotia to participate in a Shambhala youth program called Sun Camp.

Another important part of right livelihood practice for me involves the way I relate to the people I work with, both the prisoners and the staff. Prisoners and staff generally have a very adversarial relationship. The staff expects the prisoners to steal and lets a certain amount of it go, in many cases as a kind of job perk in order to keep good workers, especially in the kitchen and on the hospital wards.

I've always tried to be honest with my work supervisors, as far as my own behavior is concerned, and I try to do a good job. I also try to be supportive to my coworkers and sensitive to the needs of my students. The education staff respects that and so do many of the prisoners. Even though many try to get by with as little work as possible, they do respect someone who does a good job, as long as you are careful to be a prisoner first and never act like a staff person. The fact that my job involves helping other prisoners also earns their respect.

Sometimes other prisoners ask me to steal office supplies for them. My bosses generally give me whatever I need for my own use, so if it's not much and I have it, I usually just give them something from my own supplies. When they press me for bigger quantities that would have to be stolen, I just tell them I don't do that. I usually explain that it isn't worth risking my job for, but sometimes if the person seems open to it, I will share something about my monastic commitments.

Hardly anyone sees stealing from the institution as immoral. Prisoners see it more as liberating things from the enemy, or just trying to get even a little. Even some of the more religious Christian prisoners I know don't regard stealing from the institution as a problem. For me, though, it's not so much a moral issue as it is a question of discipline, having to do with the qualities I would like to cultivate in myself, and thievery and smuggling are just not among those qualities.

I understand why many prisoners feel almost obligated to fight back in any way they can against the injustices of our prison system, and how they see stealing as part of that struggle, but unfortunately this approach is mainly self-destructive. I've given a lot of thought to how prisons could be set up differently, to build self-esteem and encourage the development of ethical principles like Right Livelihood, rather than just cultivating bitterness and thievery. Maybe one day I will get the chance to implement some of those ideas. But sometimes I would just as soon see all the prisons torn down, since in their present form they are horrible places, hardly fit for human habitation.

(1993)

BAD DOG
From Shame to Compassion

Lin Jensen

Within all light is darkness:
But explained it cannot be by darkness
that one-sided is alone.
In darkness there is light:
But, here again, by light one-sided
It is not explained.
Light goes with darkness:
As the sequence does of steps in walking.

—Sekito Kisen, *Sandokai*

I'm eight years old; my brother, Rowland, ten. We follow our father up the steep, wooden stairs to the second-story bedroom. He doesn't talk. Our steps echo in the hollow of the stairway enclosure. Father holds the lath stick by its end. It's stiff and splintery and it hangs from Father's hand almost to the floor. I'm sick with dread. I'm swallowing the words that would beg Father, once more, not to do this.

In the upstairs bedroom, Father shuts the door behind us. A ceiling light hangs from a cord. It lights the surface of the bed, leaving the corners of the room in shadows. Father stands by the bed. He turns to face us. Rowland and I stand together, backed up against the shut door. We don't move. Outside in the hall, Laddie, our farm dog, scratches at the bedroom door. Father looks sad and serious, like he wishes we didn't have to do this. He points toward us with the lath stick, and I hear him ask, "Which of you goes first?"

Rowland goes to the bed. He wants to get it over with. It's worse to go last, but I can never bring myself to go first. Rowland unbuttons his jeans and pulls them down to his knees. He does this without being told. He knows he has to pull his jeans and underwear down, and then lay himself naked, facedown on the bed. He pulls his underwear down at the very last because he doesn't like to show himself, and waits for the first blow. I look away. My body shivers as though it were cold. I hear Laddie snuffling and scratching at the door and then I hear the crack of the lath stick. Rowland doesn't cry out. He holds his breath. He's told me that this is the way to do it.

I hear the lath again, and then again. Still Rowland doesn't cry out. Laddie scratches at the door. I don't know why we are being whipped. Rowland teased me and punched me behind the barn, and I called him bad names. Did Mother hear us? I had some bad thoughts. Did Mother know this? Mother was angry, and then she was sick and lay on her bed and put a wet cloth over her eyes and told us that we would be whipped when Father got home. I got scared and tried to talk to her and make it okay again, but the cloth was over her eyes and she wouldn't talk to me.

Rowland's whipping is done. I pull my shirt up and tuck the end of it under my chin to keep it from falling. I pull my pants and underwear down. My penis feels rubbery where I try to hide it under my hands, and Rowland is watching me. I'm holding my breath. The first blow comes. It hurts more than I can stand. My hands are stretching back to cover my buttocks, and I hear myself whimpering, "Please, Father. Please."

"If you do that, you'll only make it worse," my father warns.

When it's over, Father goes out. Rowland is in the dark near the wall. I'm under the ceiling light. Rowland can see me wiping at my runny nose with my shirt, but he looks away. We have something wrong with us. We both have it. We don't like to look at one another. It makes us too sorry.

In a moment or two, Rowland goes out. The door shuts behind him and I hear him going down the stairs.

Later, when I go out, Laddie is waiting. He's glad to see me and wags his tail and pushes himself against me. "Go away, Laddie," I say. Later, in the dark of a sleepless night, I slip from my bed and open the door onto the hall where Laddie waits and, clutching him to me, I tell him how sorry I am.

I'm eleven years old. Laddie has done something bad and Father has seen him do it and I don't know what is going to happen. Rowland says that Laddie killed a turkey. When the neighbor's dog killed a turkey, Father shot it. I saw him do it. The neighbor's dog whined and went round and round in circles until it fell down. Blood was coming out of its nose when it breathed, and pretty soon it died.

In the barn, Father has a rope around Laddie's neck. When Laddie tries to pull away, Father jerks the rope, making Laddie cough. Laddie's fur is tangled and dirty like he's been drug on the ground. A young turkey, about the size of a chicken, is dead on the barn floor. It's torn and bloody and its feathers are wet. "Oh, Laddie," I cry out. "What have you done?" I squat and put out my hand. Laddie wags his tail and starts toward me.

Father jerks him away with the rope. "Don't be good to him, Linley," Father says. "We can't have a dog that kills poultry. Don't you see that?" Father looks angry but his voice sounds kind of sad. "Once he's tasted blood it's not likely he'll ever quit."

"He doesn't know, Father." I'm trying to keep from crying, but I can feel my face screwing up and my voice is going high. "Please, Father, please."

"That doesn't help," Father says. He sounds impatient now. "If he kills again, that's it. He goes." Father hands me the rope that's tied to Laddie's neck. "He's your dog. If you want to save him, you must do exactly what I say."

Laddie is tied by the rope to a post in the barn. I have gathered the baling wire and wire cutters and the roofing tar that father told me to get. I have to wire the turkey around Laddie's neck and paint it with tar so that Laddie can't chew it off. Laddie has killed the turkey and now he has to carry it around his neck until it rots away. Father says we have to do this because we only have one chance. I am not supposed to be good to Laddie. He must learn not to kill.

The dead turkey is covered with flies. Tiny yellow eggs are already stuck to the places where the blood has dried. I take a stick and dab tar on the turkey until its feathers are all plastered down and the torn places are filled and its eyes are stuck shut. I punch the baling wire through its body and around both legs.

I take the rope off Laddie. He's glad and wags his tail and tries to lick my face. "Bad dog," I tell him, "Bad dog." I tie the turkey around his neck. The tar sticks to his fur. "Bad dog," I repeat.

After three days, Mother won't let Laddie near the house anymore. We are told to keep the yard gates shut. "It's intolerable," she tells Father. "I can smell him even here in the house."

"Lucy, it's our one chance for the dog. I owe it to the boy to give it a try."

"It's not just the smell, you know," she says. "I can't bear the thought of it."

"That doesn't help any," is all Father says.

At the end of the week, Laddie quits coming for the food I have been carrying out to him. I find him where he has crawled back into a space under the floor of the storage shed. I call to him but he won't come. I push the food under to him. I bring a basin of water and push it under too. I do this for two more weeks. Sometimes a little of the food is eaten and some water taken, but often, both are untouched.

Once, during this time, I see from a distance that he has come out from under the shed. The turkey around his neck drags on the ground when he walks. Even from far away, I can see that the turkey is slimy and bloated from rot. "Laddie," I call. I run to him, but before I can get to him, he crawls back under the storage shed. I see him there in the darkness. "Laddie, I'm sorry." I try to crawl in but it's too tight and I can't reach him. The smell of him gags me. "Laddie," I say again.

And then one day, he's out. I find him in the barnyard, the baling wire still wound around his neck where the turkey has rotted off. I take the wire off, but he doesn't wag his tail or try to lick me. He doesn't do anything at all. I take him to the washroom and fill the washtub with warm water. I lift him into the tub and wash him with soap. I scrub him and rinse him and draw more water and wash him again. I dry him with a towel and brush him, and I keep telling him that it's okay now, that it's all over. I let him out on the lawn by the house where the sun shines through the elm tree, and go back to clean up the washroom.

When I come for him, he's gone. I find him under the storage shed.

I am sixty years old. Father is ninety-three and he's in the hospital with pneumonia. It's not at all certain that he will survive this illness. My brother Rowland and I take turns watching him through the night. Rowland has gone to get rest. It's nearly two in the morning. Father is fitful. He's suffering from diarrhea, and it awakens him frequently in such a state of urgency that I do not dare to doze off myself. Father is embarrassed to use a bedpan, but because he's too weak to reach the toilet by himself he needs me to get him there in time.

I watch him there on the hospital bed where he labors in his sleep to breathe, his thin chest struggling with the effort. Father has lived long and is much softened with age and with grandchildren and with great grandchildren who have coaxed him out of his darkness and fear.

A quarter past three. Father calls, "Linley, I need to go." He is trying to sit up and get his feet to the floor even before I can get to him. I help him up. He has so little strength, and yet he uses every bit he has to walk himself to the bathroom. I support him as we walk around the foot of the bed and through the bathroom door, and then I realize we are too late. His hospital gown is pulled open in the back and diarrhea is running down his legs and onto the linoleum where he tracks it with his bare feet.

He looks at me with the most urgent appeal. He is humiliated by what he has done and his eyes ask of me that it might never have happened. I back him up to the toilet and sit him down. A neon ceiling light glares down on us. In the hallway beyond these walls I can hear the voices of the night nurses on their rounds. I shut the bathroom door and, when the latch clicks shut on the two of us, the sound of it sends a shiver through me. This old man, sitting soiled in his own filth, disgusts me; and then, suddenly, there rises in me an unutterable tenderness.

"It's okay, Father," I tell him. "It's okay." I find clean towels and a washcloth and soap. I run water in the basin until it's warm. I take off his soiled hospital gown and mop the floor under his feet with it and discard it in a plastic bag I find beneath the sink. I wash Father carefully, with soap and warm water, removing all the diarrhea from around his anus and the hair on his testicles and down the inside of his legs and between his toes. I wash him as though I were washing my very own flesh, until all the awful, rotten things are cleansed away.

In the morning, Father is breathing easier, and he survives another year before dying on the eighth of December, 1993.

I have written of these things out of gratitude, so that others might know, as I have come to know, that pain summons its own healer. You do not have to seek outside yourself for deliverance. If shame is all you have, embrace what you have, honor it, and care for it with all your attention and kindness. In your own grief you will find the power to convert shame to compassion.

(1996)

IMPERFECTION IS A BEAUTIFUL THING

Joan Tollifson

I dream about being in a world where being disabled is no big deal. No one considers it a tragedy. No one thinks you're inspiring. No one feels sorry for you. No one stares at you. What an amazing relief it would be to be seen every day as perfectly ordinary.

But in fact, I'm not seen as perfectly ordinary, because I'm missing my right hand and half of my right arm, and my life, as a result, has been different. I was born that way, and the question "what happened to your arm?" has followed me through my life like some *koan* or mantra that the universe never stops asking me. Total strangers come up to me on the street and ask me. Children gasp in horror and ask. People tell me with tears in their eyes how amazingly well I do things, like tie my shoes. Or they tell me they don't think of me as disabled (which is like telling a woman she's doing the job as well as a man, or like telling a black person that they don't really seem black). Sometimes I think that if I have to deal with one more question or statement like this, I'm going to get violent.

But the opposite response is even deadlier. Most well-trained adults have been so conditioned not to mention disability that they try desperately to pretend that they don't even notice. They don't say a word. People swallow their natural curiosity, their socially unacceptable feelings, reactions, and questions, and pretend that the Great Dream of Normalcy is still intact. One of the central memories of my childhood is of children asking me what happened to my arm and their parents instantly silencing them: "Shhh!" Don't talk about it.

We are all in so much pain, trying to do the right thing, trying to pretend everything is okay, trying not to be bad, trying not to ask the wrong questions. If we need anything in this world, it's honesty: honest looking, honest seeing, honest speaking. The ability to be with the actual truth is what love really is, and that—to me—is the heart of what Buddhist practice is all about.

But people think Buddhist practice is about all kinds of other things. When I first went to *zazen* instruction at San Francisco Zen Center, there was great concern about what to do with a single hand, since I couldn't form the traditional Zen *mudra* [formal hand position] while sitting. It was suggested that I talk to Baker Roshi about it; perhaps he would know. This strikes me as ridiculous now, but at the time it seemed reasonable enough. I never did talk to him about it, though. I sat for years with my single hand suspended in midair, forming half of the official mudra, with chronic shoulder pain as a result, until I arrived at Springwater Center in New York, where no one cares about mudras anymore and I discovered the possibility of using a small cushion to rest my hand on. How simple!

My intention in writing this article is to encourage people to make Buddhist practice accessible to the disabled community, to be with their actual feelings about disability, and to begin to break the silence.

Disability is usually regarded as a personal tragedy, not a political problem. A friend who heard I was writing an article about disability and Buddhist practice said that she expected it to be about "how practice helps a disabled person cope with disability." But if I had told her I was writing about women and Buddhist practice, I don't think she would have imagined an article on how Buddhist practice helps women cope with being female.

I do sometimes feel angry about some of the things that have happened to me and other disabled people involved in Buddhist practice. I'm going to speak from my own history because it's what I know, but I certainly don't want to single out any particular lineage, Zen center, or teacher for criticism. Angry fanaticism is not the way to make changes; that's an important part of what Buddhist practice is always teaching me. If we start with honest seeing, then the right kind of changes will naturally evolve. Nor do I wish to ignore all the ways people have been wonderful. Despite all of our intense condi-tioning to be otherwise, people have again and again demonstrated honesty, humor, and love.

The various Buddhist practice communities I've been involved with, like the great majority of people I've come across in my life, have for the most part been very accepting of me and trusting of my capabilities. The Zen centers taught me to eat the *oryoki* meals [the meal ritual in the Zen tradition] and made me a food server at *sesshins* [Zen retreats], which entails carrying big pots of food and serving everyone. I held positions of responsibility in running the zendo, and people seemed to regard me as a capable person who could do whatever job needed doing.

When I decided to be lay ordained at Berkeley Zen Center and began sewing a *rakusu* [a bib-like garment symbolic of the Buddha's robe], I wasn't sure whether or not I'd be able to do all that micro-scopic stitching together of tiny pieces of cloth. One of the women who was sewing hers at the same time told me that if I couldn't do it, she'd give me hers, and if you know what kind of labor goes into these things, you'll understand that that's no trifling offer. As it turned out, I was able to do most of the sewing myself, and what I couldn't do, people generously helped out with. Later, I watched as various people in the sangha sewed a *rakusu* for Judy Smith, a quad-riplegic member of the zendo, while she practiced a mantra with every stitch. That kind of quiet generosity was always there.

On the other hand, there was considerable opposition to ramp-ing the zendo. I think people thought it would ruin the aesthetics and there wouldn't be any call for it (this was before Judy came, al-though there had been others in wheelchairs who had tried to prac-tice there in the past and given up). It was painful to me that people felt that way, that they seemingly cared more about a certain idea of aesthetics than about including disabled people in the practice. But there was also a persistent and outspoken group who pushed for ac-cessibility over many years, and who finally brought it about with the help of Judy Smith.

The long struggle at the Berkeley Zen Center over wheelchair accessibility is an excellent example of how this struggle typically unfolds, so I think it's worth looking at as a way of examining frequently held attitudes and assumptions. The changes that have happened (and are happening) there have ultimately been very positive, and can in fact serve as a model for other practice centers.

People at BZC wondered if a ramp was really needed, if there would really be people in wheelchairs wanting to practice in the zendo, and if there were, why they couldn't simply be carried in and out. These are the questions that always seem to come up.

Why don't most people in wheelchairs want to be carried? First of all, it's dangerous to the person in the chair, to the carrier, and to the equipment. Electric wheelchairs in particular are very heavy; it would be quite a feat to carry a large man in an electric wheelchair up and down a flight of stairs. Finally, imagine how you would feel if every time you wanted to go outside for a breath of air, or visit the bathroom, you had to find three or four strong people with good backs to carry you downstairs, and then hang around until you were ready to come back in. It would be pretty inhibiting, wouldn't it?

After much explaining, people finally understood that, but they still felt there was no call for accessibility at BZC. They decided to wait and see if someone appeared. If a wheelchair-user turned up who wanted to practice with them, they'd ramp the zendo. I was furious. Couldn't they see that they were creating a catch-22? How could someone in wheelchair come to them if the place wasn't accessible in the first place? An inaccessible zendo sends out a message to the disabled community: You're not welcome here. And word gets around. Besides that, how would they feel if—back when they were first coming to the Zen Center—they'd been told that if they were really serious about Zen practice, the sangha would invest thousands of dollars to make it possible for them to be there? Talk about pressure.

They didn't get it.

But miraculously enough, someone showed up anyway. Judy Smith, a beautiful and talented dancer and artist who happens to be a quadriplegic rolled in at just that moment, fiercely determined to practice Zen and radiating warm, loving, irresistible vibes.

BZC eventually built a beautiful ramp and people changed their thinking over time. Judy became an active member of the *sangha*, was lay ordained this spring, and continues to practice there.

When I imagine myself as a Zen priest, which I sometimes do, there is at least one catch on the mundane level, namely, that it would be hell trying to manage those robes with one hand. It would probably be impossible for me to get the *okesa* [traditional ordination robes] fastened on the left shoulder without a right hand, an operation that a Zen priest has to frequently perform. It might also be impossible for me to eat oryoki meals with those big, flapping sleeves. They'd probably be unmanageable, and besides, my trick with oryoki has always been to wedge the bowls in under the rolled-up shirtsleeve of my right arm for support, so I can hold them while I eat, and that would no longer be possible.

Now of course I know that some Zen sewing angel would come up with brilliant variations on the usual robes; we'd work something out one way or another, a velcro *okesa* or a fastening on the right shoulder or whatever. I'd stop using oryoki bowls if necessary or not wear robes at all. Whatever. But still, you want to be like everyone else. That's the whole point of a uniform: uniformity.

The existence of disability in the human population raises some important questions for Zen practitioners. What is this Zen work really all about? Is it about sitting in a certain position, in a particular posture, eating soundlessly with chopsticks out of Japanese bowls? I don't think so.

Such a vision excludes a lot of people. My mother, for example. Her hands shake. They always have. She could never eat an oryoki meal without experiencing humiliation and failure.

Here at Springwater Center there is no emphasis at all placed on posture, endurance, or form. You can sit when you feel like it, in whatever position works best, in an armchair if you prefer. You can stay in bed. There is none of the athletic endurance quality so present in Zen practice, and none of the meticulous attention to ritualized detail.

I'm not opposed to rigorous, formal Zen practice, nor am I arguing that oryoki meals should be banned. Rigor and form are both potentially wonderful elements of Zen training, cultivating endurance, attention to detail, and a sense of the sacredness of the most ordinary tasks—or perhaps just providing a chance to thoroughly enjoy a completely absurd and beautiful choreography. What

I am questioning is a certain mentality that actually mistakes these rituals for the truth itself.

After being here at Springwater awhile, I experimented with sitting in a chair. It was amazing to see the stuff that came up when I hauled that chair into the sitting room. I can remember how, long ago at Berkeley Zen Center, when I'd see people who had to sit in chairs because of back problems, I'd think to myself that if I ever had to do that, I'd give up Zen. It wouldn't be real Zen if I sat in a chair! And now, here I was, in a chair. Layers of self-image revealed themselves and fell away; something opened and released.

Years ago, when I went through primal therapy, we had to spend three weeks in a room without doing anything at all. We weren't supposed to talk, read, write, take naps during the day, eat between meals, smoke, bite our nails, masturbate, do yoga, or exercise. And we weren't supposed to meditate either. To confront us totally with our discomfort, everything was removed that could possibly function as an escape valve from feeling our feelings, seeing our thoughts, and experiencing our actual bodily sensations.

It was an interesting three weeks, and being here at Springwater raises many similar questions. I can see that being in that ancient, sanctioned *zazen* position, doing something supposedly enlightening, can be a form of security seeking. I'm open to wondering about it. What is this practice, really?

And how does all this relate to disability? To people who are asymmetrical or unable to sit up straight or to walk or to wear robes and okesa and eat out of oryoki bowls? By our very nature we defy the compulsion to fit people into uniform patterns. Disabled people are a great corrective for a certain strain of Japanese Zen that emphasizes the details of form in such a way that correct technique becomes more important than the heart of the practice. What could be better than having a few visibly imperfect people around who twitch and drool and stumble and make noise and go the wrong way? Personally, I think it's been the saving grace of the Berkeley Zen Center to have people like Judy and me around, as well as a sangha member who has brain damage and frequently turns the wrong way, stands in the wrong place, and fluffs his cushion at the wrong time. His mistakes, my one-handed *gasshos* [traditional hand gestures], and the gentle humming of Judy's electric wheelchair have all become part of the morning service. Imperfection is a beautiful thing. It's the essence of being organic and alive.

I think this relates to the Buddhist wisdom of seeing what actually is instead of being caught up in what we think would be better. If someone has one hand or is paralyzed or has brain damage, can that simply be seen as how they are, without making it into a tragedy or an inspiration?

But if fear, revulsion, or pity are what we're feeling, then can we really see those feelings without trying to change them or do something about them? When there is real seeing, the organism corrects itself.

The next step is to get to know what you're afraid of, disgusted by, or pitying. If you actually look at a disabled body, or at a piece of unfamiliar equipment like a wheelchair, if you hang out with it and get to know it, you'll discover the horror was in your head.

I remember the first time I really looked at my arm. I was twenty-five years old, and sobering up from a nearly suicidal nose-dive into substance abuse. It was a terrifying moment. I was drenched in sweat, literally. But the arm I saw was not, after all, the loathsome, scary object I had imagined.

For years I avoided contact with other disabled people. I wanted to pass as normal. But after sobering up, I joined a group of disabled women on the advice of my therapist. They were strong, funny women who shared many of what I had always thought were my own private experiences.

Then, suddenly, disability became a political issue. In the late seventies I participated in a month-long occupation of the San Francisco Federal Building, demanding civil rights legislation for disabled people. It was the longest occupation of a federal building in U.S. history, and we won.

We were a diverse group in every respect. We had quadriplegics, paraplegics, blind and deaf people, developmentally disabled (popularly known as mentally retarded) people, and people with cerebral palsy and multiple sclerosis. We had blacks, Latinos, whites, gay people and straight people, Republicans, Democrats, communists, professionals, street people, young and old. Most of us were "crips," as we fondly called ourselves, but we had "abs" as well—able-bodied sign language interpreters, attendants, lovers, and friends who came along and stayed. The Black Panther Party brought in our meals.

We had strategy meetings, study groups, wheelchair races, church services, work committees. We created a miniature society in that building, in which you never had to worry about being discriminated against because you were disabled. No one was going to tell you that you couldn't do a job because you only had one hand or because you were in a wheelchair. This was an amazing experience. I never realized how big a factor such discrimination was, in the world around me and inside my own head as well, until it wasn't there anymore.

If anything, the more disabled you were, the more status you had. I found myself feeling envious of the quads because they were more disabled and got to use electric wheelchairs. Walkies, like me, were definitely a notch down in this reversed hierarchy.

After a lifetime of being isolated from other disabled people, it was an amazing relief to be completely surrounded by them. For the first time in my life, I was a normal, full-fledged person. It was a coming of age for me.

After that, I took up karate and broke boards with my short arm. And after that I sat a *sesshin* at Berkeley Zen Center and saw my one-armed shadow cast onto the white wall in front of me, and I realized that I was perfect just the way I was.

When I began doing massage as a livelihood, I was breaking another taboo. You aren't supposed to touch people with a supposedly "deformed" body part because it may be disgusting to them. That deep feeling of being disgusting is still alive in me, resurfacing every time I touch someone for the first time with my short arm. The healing occurs slowly, over a lifetime, and collectively over many generations. Buddhist practice plays a part in it, learning to simply be there with the thus-ness of life. Healing myself isn't about healing just myself; it's about healing all of us, our whole collective human body that feels disgusting, that can't accept our imperfections.

The worst thing for me about being disabled is not the physical or mechanical problems of the disability, although when other people imagine losing an arm, that's what springs to mind, of course.

That part of my disability is relatively easy to adjust to. What's hard is the attitudes you have to live with every day, not just in others, but internalized in yourself as well. Figuring out how to do one-handed karate was not such a big problem, but dealing with the fears in people's heads can be hell.

The other painful thing for me about disability is seeing all the obstacles to inclusion that could so easily be removed if people cared enough to do it, by creating wheelchair access to buildings, and so forth. Even though I don't personally need wheelchair access, it affects me because the attitudes that prevent making buildings wheelchair accessible speak to me as a disabled person, too. Every time people open their hearts around disability, it's healing for me, too, and every time they don't, it reopens those wounds. And also, of course, I have friends in wheelchairs, and when I'm with them, the lack of access does directly affect me. It would not be that hard to create a society where being disabled isn't such a big deal.

The solution to our collective fears of disability rests in non-judgmental seeing, and in sharing aloud our histories, our conditionings, and our true thoughts and feelings. We all need permission to be real, and we need accessibility so we can meet each other. Accessibility is only the beginning.

Sometimes I get tired of struggling for this stuff year after year, coming up against the same questions over and over, trying to be calm and loving each time. I'm working for accessibility here at Springwater right now. The building was designed with that possibility in mind, and it seems that everyone here is in support of making it happen, at least eventually. But the other day someone on staff was questioning it again, and I lost my temper completely and ended up calling this person, whom I love, an asshole. Then last night someone else told me that the first draft of this article sounded "bitter and accusatory." Heaven forbid! Well, sometimes I am bitter and angry, not at the fact of having one hand (which I'm mostly at peace with), but rather at the whole endless scenario of dealing with everyone else's reactions to it, which is an ongoing challenge. As another disabled person once said to me, "I hate being a fucking cripple!"

The other side of the coin is that being disabled is an inextricable part of who I am, a continuing source of insight, humor, and compassion, and a graphic lesson in Basic Buddhism. In a sense, disabled people embody the imperfection that everyone feels, and make visible our human vulnerability to death and change. Unlike Bodhidharma, I'm not about to cut off my other arm. Of course, no one wants to become disabled, and when it happens, it is a loss. But as Buddhists know, light and dark are hard to tell apart in the long run, and I honestly don't think I'd trade this life of mine for any other.

As we make the changes in our society that enable more people to participate fully in the common life, we'll find that our world expands in ways we never dreamed of. Disabled people have a piece of the human truth, a particular wisdom that I believe can, and will, contribute significantly to Buddhist practice. All we have to do is open the door.

(1990)

DEALING WITH THE ANGER CAUSED BY RACISM

Robin Hart

I need to find a way to deal with my anger at racism before it overwhelms me. I behave in a civilized manner. I don't scream at or beat or kill anyone, but anger festers within me, keeping me from being aware of my own potential.

Buddhism provides concrete methods to deal with anger, but it's difficult to practice the precepts while under constant attack. I think of the Zen Buddhist story about the traveling monks who were suddenly confronted by assailants. One monk chose to sit and meditate while the others ran off. His screams as he was murdered were heard a great distance away. This is my dilemma, too. In moments of crisis, how is Buddhism practiced?

I am an African American female, raised in a two-parent home by college-educated parents. I was always taught that education was primary and that my potential was unlimited if I achieved academic success. I went to the best schools, graduating from Mills College and Georgetown University Law Center. I worked as a congressional aide in Washington, D.C., and as an attorney at a San Francisco law firm. I am presently a student at the Pacific School of Religion, one of the top-rated theological schools in the nation.

I would say that at each successive level of my advancement, the racism I experienced became more intense. It started in high school when I left my all-black junior high school and went into a mainly white environment. It got worse at Mills College. Subsequently, I was shocked to find racism among the progressive whites in my radical African American congressman's office. Yet, all of my previous experience did not compare with the degradation I went through every single day at my law firm. I was the only African American out of approximately two hundred attorneys. Despite the fact that I made an extra effort to dress in a professional manner, always wearing quality suits, silk blouses, and gold jewelry, I was constantly mistaken for a secretary and treated rudely and with little respect. When I walked into a partner's office I was often asked with a scowl, "What do you want?" When I identified myself and the legal rationale for entering the office, an apology soon followed.

I recognize that general statements don't apply to every white person. However, I make such assertions consciously to enable the white reader to feel what black people always feel. We are judged as a whole by the actions of the worst of us, while the best of us are seen as exceptions.

After I left the law firm, I took time to heal myself. I exercised and meditated, read enjoyable books, and spent time with my family and friends. In the fall of last year, I entered theology school in good spirits. I was friendly, positive, and eager to start anew in what I thought would be an environment of spiritually minded people living in harmony with themselves, others, and the universe. But even here, racist comments were common from people who consider themselves to be nonracist. For example, a white woman in class talked about her relationship with a black man and called him all kinds of names. After class, she came to me and wanted to know if I had any problem with what she had said. I felt that she should have gone to the white people in the class and asked them if they had any problems. What I actually said to her was that she might look inside of herself to find the answer to her question. She got very upset and never spoke to me again. When white people believe themselves to be free of racism, it becomes impossible even to dialogue with them about racism because of their denial. Just to hint at the existence of racism brings anger down on the head of the one making the assertion.

As a result, during my second semester, I became increasingly withdrawn. I grew tired of explaining, educating, compromising, accommodating, being silent in the face of ignorance, smiling in public, and crying in private. There grew within me a feeling of hopelessness. Thus far, I have been around many different types of white people—those who think of themselves as progressive, conservative, corporate, and, now, spiritual. This broad exposure has caused me to finally acknowledge that racism is so prominent, even among those who mean to act otherwise, that I cannot imagine its demise. For me, this means that, despite my parents' best hopes and dreams for their educated daughter, I will never achieve the equality expected by all residents of the United States. That potential will always be threatened by people who view me first and foremost as someone who is less than, a liability, a threat, and somebody to hate and despise. The beautiful gift of my African American heritage is not a means to success in this society.

Yet, I know within the depths of my consciousness that I am limitless in my ability to create all that I need and desire. I know that I could not survive, and my people could not have survived the horrors inflicted upon us, but for some invincible power within each and every one of us that enables us to persevere. But I have allowed myself to believe that all of my power emanates from without. That is the source of my anger: they won't give me; they won't let me; they deny me opportunities; they are in control; I control nothing.

Buddhism teaches that anger is one of the Three Fires, also called the Three Poisons (desire, anger or aversion, and delusion). As long as I feel anger, I cannot experience *anatta*, or no-self. It's not possible for me to immediately eradicate my anger, but I can work to loosen its hold on me. It's important for me to realize that I do not have anger, anger has me, if it is affecting my life in such a way that I cannot think clearly and my aspirations are diminished.

Buddhism teaches that life is marked by impermanence. We go from state to state throughout the day and throughout our lives. I wake up in the morning refreshed from a good night's sleep. On the way to class I become annoyed because I smile and say "good morning!" to someone who looks directly at me and walks past without speaking. At the library, I am happy to find the book that is perfect for my research. In the afternoon, I simmer with anger because I walk into a store and am stopped for setting off the alarm while the two white people simultaneously going out of the store are ignored.

This is the Wheel upon which we go around and around every minute, every hour, every day, year after year.

The cause of our suffering is desire. We strive for what we think will make us happy or rich or free. Many African Americans believe that achieving a certain economic status will make us immune to racism. We work hard to assimilate into the dominant culture. Wanting to feel equal, we buy beautiful clothes, cars, and houses. We travel and interact with various people and cultures, always seeking to go beyond the limitations imposed by a society that refuses to acknowledge our worth and ignores our achievements. When, after all of this, we still do not receive the respect we deserve, we become angry, and this anger is only another aspect of desire. But for the thirst to be equal, to be free, to be respected, there would be no anger.

Yet how can I not desire decent housing, quality education, and the right to make a living based upon my skill and potential? How can I not be angry at a system of justice that puts my brothers in prison for life for selling a packet of crack, but ignores white corporate thieves, or releases incarcerated white child molesters again and again until they finally commit one murder too many? Every single day I am treated as though I have no intelligence, no feelings, as though my checks are automatically suspect, as though I am a thief, as though I am a nonentity, as though my opinions have no worth, as though I am not competent—I could fill this page, but I will stop. And I am an educated, trained attorney with over a decade's experience in the political arena of Washington, D.C. What must an uneducated or underemployed young black man experience? What must he feel?

Is it enough to tell us to meditate, to focus on our breath? It's one thing to meditate in a peaceful retreat or monastery somewhere, preaching love and compassion. It's quite another matter to talk the Buddhist talk while getting beaten over the head. Where can black people go to get away from the madness that engulfs us?

On an intellectual level, I tell myself that white people are suffering. If people are truly at peace, they do not have the inclination to cause pain to others. I know that some people are responding to their own insecurities when they put me down; they must assert a false superiority over me. At times, I can have the compassion that is the ideal of Buddhist practice, but never-ending rain will wear down even a stone.

I am tired of being angry. I am tired of hatred and bitterness. I am tired of living in pain. White people are on the Wheel, too. We are all propelling it. It doesn't matter why we are on it. We are on it, going around and around to nowhere.

Buddhism teaches that one should neither give in to anger nor deny it. Buddhist practice is to be aware of the anger itself. This is a very difficult concept. Most African Americans feel at ease when they are not in a racist environment, but even if racism did not exist, anger would still exist. And learning to work with our anger is constructive.

Viewing racism from this perspective allows African Americans to experience our struggles as mental and spiritual conditioning similar to the constructive pain that an Olympic athlete goes through to develop the kind of muscular, strong, efficient body capable of bringing home the gold. It is with the strength developed by practicing in adverse conditions and with scarce resources that black athletes are able to excel in sports.

In *Peace Is Every Step*, Thich Nhat Hanh writes,

> When we are angry, we are not usually inclined to return to ourselves. We want to think about the person who is making us angry, to think about his hateful aspects—his rudeness, dishonesty, cruelty, maliciousness, and so on. The more we think about him, listen to him, or look at him, the more our anger flares. His dishonesty and hatefulness may be real, imaginary, or exaggerated, but, in fact, the root of the problem is the anger itself, and we have to come back and look first of all inside ourselves. It is best if we do not listen to or look at the person whom we consider to be the cause of our anger. Like a fireman, we have to pour water on the blaze first and not waste time looking for the one who set the house on fire.

We must transform the energy of anger into an energy of empowerment and love.

Insight meditation is practiced to develop the ability to see without reacting to the whole process of our life experience. When one is able to see with balanced, clear observation, one develops insight and wisdom and is able to see things as they really are. Maybe we see that the people persecuting us have serious emotional problems or that their status in life is not as secure as we first thought. From a victim's viewpoint, sometimes we get so used to living in a cage that when the cage is removed we are still bound by the bars of our minds. Insight meditation helps us to see this.

For a long while I felt that I was not getting anything from meditation. Nothing was changing in my life. My mind was constantly wandering; I could rarely focus it on one object. One day while walking around Lake Merritt in Oakland, I noticed that I kept clenching my hand. Repeatedly, a fist would form unconsciously. I believe that I became aware of this movement because, through meditation, I had continuously focused on being aware of my body and, finally, the training took effect in this one small instance.

It took many months just to form this one awareness. This is why mindfulness is to be cultivated. There is no quick result. The harvest does not occur immediately after the seeds are planted. I now watch for the emergence of that tension and patiently track its origin. An alternative to *vipassana* [insight into the true nature of things] is to continue to be angry, anxious, and tense. I want to move away from these states of mind; thus, I am willing to pursue the path of insight meditation.

Mindfulness involves looking at life the way a scientist observes a specimen. When being mindful of the breath, one need not say, "I am breathing hard. I must relax." One merely observes the breath without making any judgment, just taking an interest in how it works. Learning to observe the breath in this way will enable a person, one day, to be similarly mindful about the people, circumstances, and conditions which seem to cause anger.

In examining anger, one must try to see clearly how it arises and what causes it. Watch to see how and when it disappears. Try not to have any subjective reaction. This is a discipline, just like lifting weights. At first, one can only lift two pounds. Later, one may be able to lift fifty. I practice this new discipline in minor, day-to-day situations. I don't yet have the ability to observe my anger when the racism is acutely painful, but this is all right; the seeds are planted.

In a process I call "tracing back," I notice my anger in a particular situation and keep asking myself, "Why did that upset you?" I answer myself, "Because she thinks I took the book." "Did you take the book?" "No." "Then why are you upset? Do you think she thinks you took it because you're black?" "Probably." "Are you sure that's the reason?" "No." "Even if it is, is that your problem or hers? How does her thought affect your life at this moment?" My self-conversation usually results in my feeling that the issue is not worth my time, and my anger subsides. For instance, I ponder whether it is more productive to take a few minutes to respond calmly to a false accusation than it is to enter into a major argument about how wrong the person is and then to be upset the rest of the day. By not reacting, sometimes I discover that the situation causing the anger is not about me at all. This is not to discount the people and the situations that indeed cause pain and oppression, but if I continue to match their angry energy, I remain bound to the Wheel of Change. I seek to grow beyond these conditions.

My anger many times has its roots in the past. If I had no memory of the history of my people or of white people, or of the oppression in the world, I probably would not have half the perceptions that make me angry. This leads to another very important aspect of mindfulness: being in the present. Venerable Ajahn Sumedho writes:

> Yesterday is a memory.
> Tomorrow is the unknown.
> Now is the knowing.

If I did not seek to be free, I would not be angry at those who put obstacles in my way. I would say, "This moment, I am free to walk and to see. I have a mind to think. Today, I have a roof over my head and enough food to eat."

I believe that, because of racism, I did not develop into the lawyer that I expected to become; but ten years from now I may say that, because of racism, I became the writer that I never thought I would be. Who knows? If it is the latter, then I have wasted a lot of time being angry. Insight meditation enables me to see the bigger picture. Right now, this minute, I am doing what I want to do.

Buddhism allows me to be where I am right this moment. I do not have to condemn or approve of my anger and pain. Neither do I have to deny these feelings. I can simply be with them, observing their rising and falling, their impact on me and others.

I can observe my anger at a safe distance from my "assailants." I may interact more closely with them when my strength develops to the point where I can be among them without pain. Right now, I see the worth of Buddhist practice, of being aware of my body, my breath, and my pain. This is where I start.

(1997)

MAKING PEACE WITH MYSELF

Jenna Jordison

My father, Roy Jordison, created flower gardens wherever we lived. He worked for a nursery before he became an ordained minister. After retiring from the United Church of Canada in 1978, he followed his heart's calling and joined a ministry on the flower-laden Caribbean island of Grenada. Four years into his posting, on a night in 1982, his home was invaded and he was suffocated to death. The motive was robbery. By the time I got the call, there had been a few arrests. After the funeral, after I left the island and returned to Canada, there were trials with convictions. The aftershocks still shake me. I miss my father. Tears come easily still.

Rose Whiteman worked hard with her hands all her life to earn a living for her six children. She saw her youngest child make unwise choices and get into trouble. For the last nineteen years she has only been able to visit him in prison. Now, at eighty-one, she has returned to Grenada from New York in order to visit him more regularly. I met her there when I went to meet her son, the man who killed my father. As a mother, I know that no matter what, we do what we can for our children.

Victor Whiteman lives in a prison without flower gardens. In adversity and supported by others, his own spiritual life is blossoming.

Today I can write that sentence calmly. In 1999, seventeen years after the murder, I received some letters that disturbed the calm. Until then, I had thought that the intruders had been convicted and hanged, in spite of the fact that my brother and I had written to the

Grenadian government to voice our opposition to capital punishment. I had been misinformed.

The letters were from one of the murderers, Victor Whiteman, age forty. A minister who had befriended Victor during pastoral care at the prison sent our family these letters in the hope that somehow we could help facilitate his release on parole. It seemed to me to be an inappropriate request. I thought that a desperate man might say anything to gain his freedom. I didn't owe him anything. Not wanting him to be hanged was very different from wanting him to be free.

When I looked at his handwriting I was terrified. How could the hands that wrote those well-formed words be the same hands that squeezed the life air out of my father? I couldn't face the feelings that arose in me. I couldn't face my grief. The letters went into a drawer.

Six months later, after a meditation retreat, when my mind was still and my heart was open, I took the letters out. I squirmed and wept as I wrote to Victor Whiteman. I spoke of my hope for reconciliation for myself and for him. I asked him personal questions. I introduced my children—Eva, seven, and James, twelve—and sent a photo of our family. I acknowledged my own courage and his, if he were to reply. Without bitterness, I stated that it was no business of mine whether or when he was released. My hand trembled as I mailed that letter.

Back on my cushion, some insights arose. Knowing them is easier than acting by their light, but knowing them helps:

Holding my heart tight in resentment hurts; releasing it is a compassionate act to myself.

I cannot remedy injustice by raging against it.

At times we all act out of greed, anger, and ignorance. We are mistreated and we mistreat others.

Forgiving ourselves and others is a commitment to life's continuation.

Forgiving is only optional if we don't need each other. Do we need each other?

Forgiving is a way of breaking the chain of retribution and suffering.

The most powerful act is setting the intention to forgive. Everything else follows from that.

And so I set my intention to learn to forgive.

My chest froze when his reply came. Holding the envelope felt like an unwished-for intimacy. His words turned my fear into amazement. I saw how much I had invested in holding him in a villainous light, and how I had not seen his humanity. This is what I found difficult in his letter: His handwriting was orderly and balanced. His vocabulary and grammar were good. His thoughts had integrity and depth of understanding. He expressed remorse for the mistake he made when he was "young, ignorant, and impulsive," acknowledging the past and future suffering that he had brought to my family and his own family.

Most difficult was his spiritual connection. He wrote, "This is a lesson of shame, pain, regrets, and a tremendous amount of humiliation for me, not so much in the sight of man, but in the sight of the Creator. . . . Through God's love and forgiving spirit I pray and hope one day I will be able to meet you face to face and ask your forgiveness. . . . My prayers are not so much for freedom per se but for eventual forgiveness. Because even though I were to obtain a Governmental pardon, without your pardon I would not be totally free." How could I reconcile the searing loss of my father with the man who wrote those words? Was he genuine?

Believing in the transforming power of art and knowing he liked to paint, I sent Victor art supplies and asked him to paint pictures for my children. I wanted to help free them, too, from the horror of their grandfather's murder. Three carefully brushed paintings arrived in the mail, one of a beach, one of a sailboat, and one of a town, all subjects Victor never sees close-up.

Gradually, as I learned about Victor's life, about his work in the carpentry shop, about his daily schedule, I started to associate him with more than just the crime. The paintings showed me directly that he could do something positive. Grace slid in between the cracks in my armor.

In October 2000, on Ambleside Beach in Vancouver, under the stars, my partner Mark, our children, and I held hands in a circle and spoke aloud our intention to take the five-thousand-mile journey to meet Victor. Against any doubts, we affirmed that people can change, even people who do despicable things. I didn't want to die regretting not having done what I could to heal myself. I was willing to face the demons, if necessary. And I took the word *forgiveness* off the agenda for myself and for our meetings: that overlay felt like pressure.

Deciding to go to Grenada was a huge leap of faith. I was confident that the details and arrangements, which were very complex, would work out. And one by one they did. The real difficulties were not practical—they were in my heart. I was going into uncharted territory. Was it wise to put myself voluntarily in such a vulnerable position?

Before the trip, out of need, I reached out to complete strangers and found support and inspiration. I met Roman Catholic and Salvation Army prison chaplains, Mennonites, Anglicans, Lutherans, Methodists, and Buddhists, all dedicated to healing for both victims and offenders. I met a group of prisoners who are committed to Restorative Justice. Some of them are serving terms for murder. Nothing prepared me better for my journey than sitting with them and sharing our stories. They told of strong bonds they still felt to their victims even after eighteen years, of pain and remorse still present, of fear of rejection if they were to communicate with the victims. The air was alive with our unspoken questions: What if she were my victim? What if he were my offender?

Those weeks before the trip, I became more aware of the depth of my own and all human suffering. In order to heal my wound I had to reopen it. I was tired and sensitive. There were many meals I could not cook. I asked friends to write messages of support that we could take with us on our journey. I was grateful to each person who offered encouragement. Many of them had previously known nothing of my father's end.

Two weeks before getting on the plane, I slipped and badly sprained my right wrist. Instead of being disheartened by this slowdown, my resolve to carry on grew stronger. I refocused my energy on healing on many levels. I was changing major habits by having to use my nondominant, left hand for everything. At the same time I was changing major habits of resentment.

Every person everywhere has been hurt. Not everyone has the chance to acknowledge it in a spirit of equanimity and to move on, but the conditions present for me were exceptionally fortunate. I was willing and able. My biggest shock the day I met Victor was how clear and free of any fear I felt. I was held in a caring web of good wishes from Canada, the United States and Grenada.

As the car climbed the winding, narrow road to Richmond Hill Prison, my work was only to be present and to trust in the unfolding. After a meeting with the warden and the senior officials, we walked to a small visiting room off the hot concrete courtyard. Those steps that I had so dreaded felt sure and safe. Inmates offered friendly greetings to my guide, Christine Brathwaite, who, as a member of the Prison Visiting Committee, had over months of e-mail arrangements become my beacon of hope. She was clearly theirs too.

We sat waiting. His head tilted in a shy bow, Victor stepped into the room, smiling radiantly. I stood and shook hands without hesitation. This civilized gesture overrode any misgivings. Something genuine had instantly happened—an assurance of nonaggression. As he introduced himself in a soft voice, I hurried to adjust my ears to his pattern of speech. In his second breath were the words "deeply regret the harm I have done to you." I observed his features carefully. He emanated a deep emotionality, closing his eyes and smiling from time to time as if to let the feelings sink in. I wondered: "How could it be you?" Others who have met him also ask themselves how this affable man could have killed Reverend Jordison.

Two days later, flanked by Mark and our mediator, Rev. Andrew Baker, I heard Victor's story. It took all of my listening skills. My wanting to know overshadowed my apprehension. When he came to the part about attacking my father, I reached into my pocket and held my touchstone, a palm-sized round stone I had found on a beach on Lasqueti Island. The words "I take refuge in the Dharma" came to me. I affirmed my trust that the truth would free me from bondage to the horror of that event. As the intensity mounted, I repeated the words to myself like a mantra.

At no time did I forget that Victor was not required to tell us anything. When he finished, the picture puzzle pieces were in place and we had heard the worst. I could handle it, but would need time to assimilate it. Now I was free from imagining something even more terrible, and so I felt a kind of relief. My supporters looked at me as if assessing a postoperative case. Had the surgery been successful?

Beside Mark in the car, I cried.

In the afternoon, when it was my turn to speak, Victor listened while I told of my memories of my father, and of my family's losses. I had decided and Victor had agreed that holding a memorial service for my father would be appropriate. There in the administrative wing of the prison, with the sounds of the inmates working outside, we began the service with the words "May the light of understanding illuminate our darkness. May the warmth of sharing bring us peace." While I was speaking through tears, eyes closed, to the memory of my father, I felt two hands reach across the table to rest on mine. Thick-fingered and brown, they were the same hands that had killed my father. Soon Mark's and Rev. Baker's hands joined them. Eight hands in a hub, our arms the spokes, we were a wheel of life turning.

How could I reconcile my grief with the offender's inherent worth and dignity? I couldn't do it in those weeks after returning home to Canada. Only in meditation, when I was able to allow both truths to coexist in the spaciousness of a bigger mind and heart, could I do it. My grief becomes just grief. The stretched heart hurts but can hold it all.

When I look into Victor's eyes I see that his deepest wish is to be free of July 23, 1982. Would I want to be defined for the rest of my life by my most despicable act, as he is? Victor had spent four years and four months on death row under severe and solitary conditions before his sentence was commuted to life in prison. When he joined the regular prison population, certain inmates encouraged him to continue his schooling. His success in correspondence courses combined with the hope and guidance from visiting clergy who have really cared about him have set him in a new and positive direction. There is a strong Christian presence among the prisoners at Richmond Hill. In this context, he feels sure about leaving drugs and alcohol behind. He tries to convince other inmates to change their ways and stay out of jail once they are released.

Even though I believed that Victor would not kill again, accountability was on my mind. I asked him whether, if he were ever released, he would care for the four palm trees planted in memory of my father on the grounds of his former church in Grenada. Without hesitation, he agreed.

At times I have regretted having started this process. Healing is painful. There are deeply entrenched patterns that get challenged. Nevertheless, I am now sure that it is possible for anything that torments the mind to settle into the heart peacefully. The facts of the injury do not change, but in peace there is no energy bound up in despising or dreading. I am no longer spooked by my father's murder monster. Even though I am not finished with this process, I am moving on in my life. Snapdragons and peonies fill my vase. Under the vase is an intricate doily crocheted for me by Rose Whiteman. Its presence brings some uneasiness. Still, my family and I will enjoy the flowers until they wilt. Then they will naturally decay in my compost box, and I will grow something new with the compost—perhaps delphiniums like my father grew.

(2001)

HEALING AND EMPOWERMENT

Sally Clay

I don't think I will ever recover from mental illness. The last time I got manic, five years ago, I holed up in my apartment, turned up my stereo as loud as it would go, and embarked on a psychedelic trip to nowhere. This was the same trip I have taken countless times, for nearly forty years. Although I have never used street drugs, my manic episodes are remarkably like LSD trips. They always start with intense visions of spiritual power and worldwide enlightenment. They always end in disaster.

During that last episode, I enjoyed the first part of the mania, listening to my favorite rock artists and gathering all of their messages about saving the world. Unfortunately, my stereo was directly below the bedroom of a young professional couple. When I get manic I do not sleep, and my loud rock music continued well into the night. Shortly after midnight my unfortunate neighbors began calling, begging me to turn down the music. I said "yes," and turned it down a little. But within ten minutes the urgent prophecies and visceral rhythms captured me again, and I turned the music up. Within the mania I could not permit anything or anyone to interrupt the imperatives of my delusions—not my neighbors, not my friends, not anybody.

Somewhere in the middle of the night of the second day, after several fruitless phone calls to me, my neighbors called the police. The police came to the door and warned me about the loud music, and I promised to turn it down. But soon I turned it right back up.

On the third night, the police were not so patient. They

arrested me, turned off the stereo, and took me to jail. I spent the rest of the night on a hard metal cot in a cell. In the morning I went home again to my stereo. I was dragged off to jail three times, each time returning to my apartment and my fantastic mental journey, which became progressively wilder. One night, I decided to get drunk, and I became even crazier than I already was. This time an ambulance came to get me, probably summoned by my desperate neighbors. I was taken to the local hospital where I slept off the alcohol in the emergency room. In the morning, I was assured that I was in the hospital on a voluntary basis. All I had to do was to have a brief interview with a psychologist and then I could leave.

If only I could have kept my mouth shut! I managed to have a fairly rational conversation with the psychologist until I blurted out, "Where is Dr. Kevorkian when you need him!" I meant this as a joke, but the psychologist did not laugh. She decided that because of that statement I was suicidal—and in two shakes of a shrink's tale, I was whisked away to the psychiatric ward on the top floor and involuntarily committed.

I spent a miserable week in the psych unit, forced to swallow medicine that I tried to refuse. When I was finally released, I found that I had lost my job, had been evicted from my apartment, and faced a stiff fine, possibly even a jail sentence, for disturbing the peace.

That is how I wound up moving from Massachusetts to Florida. As with past manic episodes, I had to pick up the pieces of my life and start again from scratch. It was not so easy this time because I was not as young and resilient as I once had been. After that brief time of mania, I had to cope with weeks of depression and despair. Nevertheless, within a few months I settled down in my new home and again resumed my career.

There are plenty of people who do recover from mental illness. Tipper Gore has recovered, and so has Mike Wallace. Yet most of us who identify as "mental health consumers" have not really recovered. A "final" state of recovery is no longer my goal, for I have learned that someone with serious mental illness does not have to fully recover to be successful. For the last twenty years I have worked as a peer advocate for people with psychiatric disabilities, started two drop-in centers, and helped to form a third. I have been hired as a consultant by a number of organizations, and I am on the steering committee of a major federal research project. This work has changed my life forever. I have not recovered, but I have healed from the wounds of stigma and shame. I have friends and a successful career. I have found my place in the world.

Becoming stabilized is not the same thing as recovering, but it is essential to gain some control over our own minds and not to live at the mercy of our delusions or hallucinations or depression. For some consumers, the medications taken while in crisis are sufficient, and once the emergency is over they can get off the meds and maintain stability. For others, it is necessary to find the right dose and continue taking it to maintain stability. For still others, meds and other forms of psychiatric treatment are not the answer, and tools for stable living are found in a spiritual context.

In my case, all of these tools apply. When I am in the midst of a manic episode, only psychotropic drugs will calm me down. After I am stabilized, I continue to take a low dose of lithium. Before my last episode I had tried, with the help of my psychiatrist, to discontinue the lithium—but clearly, that did not work. Now I am back on the lithium, despite its side effects.

But the greatest preventative for me has proved to be a spiritual practice. If I were to choose a watershed moment in my life, a time when I finally gained confidence that I was worthy to live alongside other people without the shame of being mentally ill, it would be when I first visited Karma Triyana Dharmachakra (KTD), the Tibetan Buddhist monastery in Woodstock, New York. In an interview with Khenpo Rinpoche, the abbot, I fervently described the fantastic journeys I had taken in my mind—all the times that I had visualized scenarios for changing the world and saving other people. As I described these psychotic episodes, I hung my head in embarrassment but admitted that I could not get it out of my head that there was truth in these visions and that was why I kept coming back to them. I begged him to give me a spiritual discipline that would protect me from these painful episodes and that would cure me from mental illness.

To my great surprise, Rinpoche smiled at me and said without hesitation that if I felt that I had learned something from my experiences, then I should take what I had learned back to the community and use it to help others. It was as simple as that. He did not even give me instructions in the esoteric spiritual practices that I had gone to him hoping to receive.

That was in the late 1970s. After my interview with Rinpoche, I returned to my home in Portland, Maine, and continued trying to hold down a job and live my life. I did not know what to do with the advice my teacher had given me. It was not until 1981, and another involuntary hospitalization, that I finally figured out what I had to do. I joined the Alliance for the Mentally Ill and later organized one of the first mental health consumer-operated programs in the country, the Portland Coalition for the Psychiatrically Labeled. I spent several years working for the coalition, all the while continuing to experience yearly manic episodes and hospitalizations.

In 1987, I finally returned to KTD for serious study and took up residence in Woodstock. Rinpoche gave me instructions in the Green Tara meditation, which I began to practice daily. By regularly following these spiritual disciplines, I trained my mind and finally found mental stability. The manic episode that I described earlier is the only one I have experienced since I started the spiritual discipline, now nearly fifteen years ago. As a result, I no longer have to live under the constant threat of psychosis and I am no longer helplessly dependent on the mental health system.

The currently fashionable view of mental illness is that we have a "broken brain." Under this view, the very defectiveness of our brains means that we cannot decide for ourselves. Especially, it means that we cannot be trusted to choose our own treatment or our own way of life.

Under the medical model, the definition of recovery is usually limited to the idea of stability. Adherents of the medical model usually believe that recovery means symptom management—and that if mental patients would only take their meds, everything would be fine. But as mental health consumers, we know that although medications can manage our symptoms, they cannot give us quality of life.

I, for one, reject the medical model. I am not simply a brain, an object that can be broken. My life is much richer and more complex than that. If I am not allowed to choose my own way of life and to work for my own empowerment, my mental stability will remain fragile and I will always regard myself as defective and hopeless.

Although recovery would be nice, the important thing is not whether we are "normal" but whether our lives are satisfying and meaningful. For me, recovering from mental illness would be like recovering from being human. The manic highs and depressive lows I have experienced for all these years are, for better or worse, part of who I am. If I were given a magic pill that would clear up my depression, I would not recognize my own mind. If I were given another magic pill that would put the reins on my flights of manic fantasies, I might be a lot more sensible than I am now, but I would no longer be "me."

My own definition of recovery is the same as what I believe it means to be fully human: to treat oneself and others with loving-kindness and respect, and to recognize the buddha-nature that is in everyone since birth. If I do not regard myself as a human being with buddha-nature, then I will be forever defined by my illness.

If I can live every day in my community alongside other people who have needs, desires, and problems, just as I do, then it really is not so important whether I still occasionally cope with my particular symptoms or foibles—whether they be called mental illness or not. I have learned several tools for maintaining my equilibrium, not the least of which is my daily *sadhana,* or spiritual practice. Still, I will always be vulnerable to the extreme highs and lows of bipolar disorder, and there is always the possibility that I will suffer another manic episode. I have to live with that, knowing that at least now I have the ability to get through such an episode and get back on my feet.

I know, too, that buddha-nature can never be lost or taken away. My own identity—who I am as a human being—is who I have been all along, and that is something good. That has never been broken.

(2002)

SHADOWS OF WAR AND CLASS

Annette Herskovits

As I kneel in my Berkeley kitchen, scrubbing the floor with a wet rag, I remember the maid who worked for my adoptive family when I was navigating a wretched adolescence. This was in Paris in the 1950s. I would spend non-school days in my bedroom, studying, lying on the bed with a book, or playing the piano. Sometimes, when I wandered into the kitchen looking for something to drink, the maid would be washing the floor on her knees, emanating wetness and bleach. She was in her fifties, but it would never have entered my mind to offer to help her. She had her role and I had mine. We were not particularly wealthy—a maid was then a normal appendage of middle-class life in France.

But there was a twist to our relationship. I was an adopted child, a war orphan. My parents had been killed in Auschwitz. Our family had been poor, living in a shabby, fifth-floor walk-up in a working-class neighborhood—five of us in three minuscule rooms, with "Turkish toilets" between floors for two families, a stairwell smelling of food and urine, and no place to bathe except the kitchen sink. My father and mother had immigrated to France from Romania in the early 1920s, with barely a cent in their pockets. My father, a self-taught man who spoke perfect French, had found work as a typesetter—quite a feat and a relatively well-paid job—but eventually, with three children, money was scarce.

My brother, sister, and I survived the war. My father sent the three of us to the countryside in early 1943, as the persecution of Jews escalated. He and my mother remained in Paris; he had to keep his job—money was needed to pay for the foster care of my sister, then twelve years old, and myself, just short of four. We were placed in the home of a forester, recommended to my parents by their downstairs neighbors, where several other foster children besides ourselves brought in desired income. My brother, who was then sixteen, lived and worked on a farm a few miles away. From that time until the end of the war, he was on his own, moving from farm to farm in search of work or to evade the Nazis and the French police, except for a brief period in Paris, where he found night work cleaning printing presses.

The forester sent my sister and me away shortly after my parents' arrest—no more money was coming for our keep and we were dangerous charges. The sequence of events from that moment until the end of the war remains blurred. We were shuffled, often separately but sometimes together, from foster home to foster home, to an orphanage, to a sanatorium, and so forth.

In 1945, after the war, my brother returned to Paris and quickly married. He survived on odd jobs, including a couple of years digging ditches for a salary that he, his wife, and their first child could barely live on. But then, by a stroke of luck, he was hired by a print shop and taught to do "photo retouching." He made a fair living—except when he was laid off for leading a strike: he was an active member of the Communist Party until the early 1960s. Yet, he and his wife continued to live in my parents' old apartment with their two daughters. He bought a small plot of land near Paris where they gardened passionately on weekends.

I was adopted right after the war, through a child welfare agency. My sister, a ward of the state, became a boarder in a high school. After graduating, she went to university erratically, supporting herself with secretarial jobs, and living in sixth-floor maid rooms, which I never visited.

What did I feel as I lay on my bed while the maid worked? I could not accept our role differences with the unquestioning ease of my adoptive mother, who stayed in bed with her morning cup of coffee until 9 A.M. or played bridge to fill her empty afternoons. I felt guilt then, and I feel shame now. (How could I have asked the maid to prepare a cup of tea for me?)

But I was immersed in a suffocating misery, never drawing an easy breath; all was guilt and confusion. Struggling with the legacy of my own war experience allowed me to focus on little more than surviving the next hour without being engulfed by fears I could not begin to tease apart and examine. In the process, internal guides to fair and kind action seemed lost.

My adoptive parents had shown an abysmal lack of insight into the mind of a six-year-old emerging from war. They treated me as a blank slate and never mentioned my birth parents or asked about my war experience. So I was left on my own to try to make sense of what had happened—why my parents had died, why we had been the target of hatred and murder.

My adoptive mother's primary concern was "discipline"—training me to be quiet, obedient, clean, orderly, and hard-working. When I was fifteen and objected when she hit a two-year-old grandnephew who would not eat, she said: "Children are like animals; they have to be trained." Her "principles"—children were not to talk unless spoken to first, children must never express a personal opinion, children must never question their parents—were standard for her generation and class, but she applied them with a thoroughness and cruelty, the motives for which remain a mystery to me. She died when I turned eighteen, before I could still my rage enough to ask.

My adoptive parents did not sever my relationship with my brother and sister. They dutifully—if reluctantly—sent me to my brother's about once a month, and they received my sister in their home for an occasional lunch. But I could hear, loud and clear, their disdain—which extended naturally to include my brother and sister—for the secretaries and salesgirls in the neighborhood streets with clothes and hairdos in "vulgar" taste; for the "low-class" speech of the working men who came to do repairs in their home; for the maid, who had to climb up and down the five flights of a back stairway with the heavy garbage can while we always used the elevator in the front. My brother, his wife, and my sister spoke, dressed, and lived much like these people.

My adoptive parents established distance in more direct ways too. My brother was treated with a mix of trite approval and condescension: he was a good boy, a hard worker, he did not drink, did not mix with hoodlums. When, very rarely, they invited him to their home, I could sense his discomfort at the dining room table as the maid served him and the strained conversation chugged along. His table manners were like those my adoptive mother scolded me harshly about—he kept his hands under the table and slurped his soup. When I once asked my mother about the slurping, she said it was through no fault of his—he had not had the luck of being "well brought up."

My sister was the object of searing contempt. As they saw her, she was a ne'er-do-well, an airhead with ambitions beyond her reach because of her laziness. But there was something worse, something wrong about her character that was always discussed in impenetrable language. I soon figured out they were alluding to her relations with men.

My adoptive parents believed unquestioningly that their manners, tastes, pastimes, and, most importantly, their morals, placed them squarely above my birth family. "Morals" connoted a combination of order, cleanliness, and self-discipline, which my own family had somehow lacked. In our home, teasing and bantering had flown freely between parents and children; my parents never forced us to eat something we hated; my brother and sister played in the streets, wandered as they pleased, and came home when they were hungry; the apartment was untidy.

In my mind, my adoptive mother's idea of moral virtue—which I was never able to satisfy—became associated with survival. Those who had it survived; those who did not had been killed—the messy ones, who spoke with an accent and often too loudly, who did not know the rules of polite behavior. In fact, this had an element of truth: the Jews most likely to survive the war in France were those from moneyed, old French stock.

Yet I felt at ease at my brother's, where laughter came freely, everyone talked out of turn, and no mishandling of the fork or improper way of speaking would attract wrath. Never, of course, did my adoptive parents set foot in his home.

When I was fifteen, my sister gave birth to a child out of wedlock. My mother hid the pregnancy from me, finally telling me about the child a month or so after it was born. She explained that, had the child died, there would have been no need to tell me—being an unmarried mother was a great shame and she worried about the influence my sister's misconduct could have on me. But I was starting to show some independence in more than thought, and I visited my sister and the child often to assert solidarity. Somehow my mother knew not to interfere.

After my adoptive mother died, the maid took over the full care of the household with quiet dignity and kind patience. When I turned twenty-two, she fell ill—some mysterious heart ailment that doctors could not diagnose—and spent months in the hospital. I visited her twice, and then lost track of her. When I evoke her image now, I feel love for her and helpless sorrow. I know she loved me, whom she had seen grow up. But I could not then embrace that love wholeheartedly.

My sister married a soldier from a U.S. base near the provincial town where she was living, and eventually left with him and her four-year-old daughter for Topeka, Kansas. My father objected to my going to the wedding—again, to protect me from my sister's influence. He did not know I had slept with several men even before my mother's death.

I was drawn to Buddhism from the age of fifteen, reading any books I could find in secret—such absorption would have seemed bizarre to everyone around me. Eventually, I wrote to Hubert Benoit, French author of *Zen and the Psychology of Transformation*, and started to see him in "therapy" sessions. It was odd therapy. Dr. Benoit did almost all the talking, discoursing about the metaphysical distress of "meeting the not-self," the illusory nature of ego, the intuition of a true Self beyond time and phenomena, the illumination of selfless love, and surrender to the nature of things. "'Yes' is the ultimate word of wisdom," he once told me. The question of what precisely I had to say "yes" to—the cruelty and death of the concentration camps—was never broached. In fact, I never talked about the past after our first session. His teaching went mostly over my head, but something rang true and I absorbed it hungrily.

Yet, the urgency of constructing a self the world would consider worthy—the world that had tried to kill me as a child—engaged all my energy. One measure of success I sought was acceptance in the city's bohemian milieu. I hung out in the right cafés and fantasized a self that would be a blend of an enlightened Zen master and a French intellectual, but I remained only a very quiet, very shy, and very awkward young woman who attempted to alleviate existential distress mainly through sexual seduction.

At about that time—the early 1960s—I took on the task of steering my brother's eldest daughter toward higher education and cultural pursuits. She was bright and eager. My brother must have had mixed feelings about our increasingly close relationship. His daughter expressed her adolescent rebellion through open contempt for her parents' "lack of culture" and "bad taste." It must have hurt, but he did not take it too hard. And he was not going to stand in the way of her ambitions.

No doubt my brother saw clearly that I believed, though I did not express it, that my cultural hankerings must confer on me some ineffable worth he lacked. Yet, the sense of superiority I was able to draw from the fact that he did not read Faulkner, did not appreciate Picasso, and knew nothing of Buddhism, felt insubstantial.

I came to the United States in 1967, at age twenty-eight, ostensibly to study, but really to flee a country where every encounter touched off pain. I made a trip to France every year or so. Each time, I would spend a day with my brother and his wife. I admired their garden, we went for a walk in the nearby woods, but he and I did not talk about the questions that most deeply troubled us—our murdered parents, our life during the war, his conflict with his eldest daughter, or the social distance that separated us.

I talked with my sister regularly, but during the few visits I made to Aurora, Illinois, where she was then living, I experienced embarrassment and shame. Her husband, who had become a railroad conductor after leaving the military, had abused her and the children—there were now three. She was divorced and a fortuneteller by profession. Her clients were mostly "white trash," she said, but she talked about them with affection and concern. She saw herself as part psychotherapist and part medical doctor, as she offered a sympathetic ear and advice about diet and vitamins. Her home was overrun with clothes and beauty products that she and her two daughters bought in almost daily trips to the mall. The television was on day and night.

Buddhism remained at the center of my thoughts. When I moved from Boston to San Francisco in 1970, I began sitting at the Zen Center. The ethos of the place, as I saw it, held that to dwell on one's personal history was only attachment to ego. But what I needed most was to pay close attention to that personal history, to investigate the rage and grief it deposited in every thought and feeling.

In the 1990s, I turned to *vipassana* (insight) and *metta* (loving-kindness) practice, which gave me a gentle nudge toward self-acceptance and opening to others. The permission to say with a whole heart, "May I be happy," brought a deep release. And "May all beings be happy" opened my mind to the possibilities of forgiveness—and I had a lot to forgive, both in others and in myself. The words of the *Metta Sutta*: "Let no one despise any being in any state," brought out tears of yearning and grief—yearning for reconciliation, for unobstructed love; grief for the contempt received and the contempt inflicted.

Over the years, some healing has come—a growing trust in my own innocence, in letting whatever arose in my mind be, and in the reality of compassion in others. While Buddhist teachings and practice certainly played a role, I feel the healing mostly as a gift from two people, a wonderful life companion and a wonderful psychiatrist. But looking back, I also see an extended network of relationships, going back to my own parents' love, the maid's affection, and even my adoptive parents' closed-minded but not loveless protection of me, and including meeting with a couple of Buddhist teachers who listened with full attention and true compassion. Every word of kindness and acceptance was like a drink of magic, cool water.

On a trip to France in 1992, I had lunch with my brother and his wife at their eldest daughter's home, where I was staying. Next to my bed I had left a book on the Holocaust, one of a great many I had read. The next day, I found in it a note to me from my brother: "I am sure it is not necessary to continue researching all details of the sufferings of the Jews during the war. It is something that keeps happening, to many people and many races, even in 1992, and it goes back to the beginnings of man's life on earth. One must know how to learn enough of the truth, but one must also know how not to suffer. With love, Aimé." Yes, my brother had something to teach me.

Last year, I invited my brother and sister to spend three weeks in my home in California. This was the first time we had been together under the same roof for more than a few hours since 1942, and the first time my brother and sister had seen each other in twenty-five years. We did the usual tourist things, but along the way we talked of life before the war, of how each of us had lived through it, and of our parents' struggle to escape the Nazi noose and their eventual capture and death.

I was discovering who my brother was: his humor, his keen eye for ironies and pretensions, his kindness and compassion for others' pains and difficulties. He would poke gentle fun at my sister's fortune-telling and her preoccupation with dreams. But he was always the one next to her, helping her without the least impatience, as she, hampered by her weight, tried to keep up with the rest of us. He was a man at peace with himself, with no regrets about occasions missed, curious about others and about this country he was visiting for the first time. He even talked of his declining strength and not too distant death with equanimity, my brother the Buddhist, who knows nothing about Buddhism, and may, for all I know, still think that "religion is the opiate of the people."

He told stories of how he had survived the war and how he had saved my life: shortly after our parents' capture, I was dispatched to him in Paris where he was hiding in a hotel. He decided against entrusting me to the official Jewish Social Services organization. He understood that the Germans had full information about the children's homes run by the organization, and saw clearly they had no intention of sparing the children. And in fact, the homes were eventually raided and all the children deported to the east and murdered.

After a few weeks of trying to care for me and earn a living, he found someone he felt he could trust, who knew of a clandestine child rescue organization. My brother took me to a contact person and the organization took over, assuming the rescue of my sister as well.

In fact, there was hardly anything new to me in that story. I remembered some of it and had heard most of the rest from his daughter. But something, perhaps residues of the old prejudices, had prevented me from formulating it in simple, clear terms: my brother had saved my life through a mix of courage, good judgment of people, and clear understanding of a situation tragically misunderstood by the adults in charge.

My sister basked in the glow of family restored—she who had brought up three children alone in the harsh, alien environment of the poorest quarter of a Chicago suburb. But as she rushed from store to store, buying T-shirts with pictures of cable cars for each child and grandchild, key rings, toys, postcards, and so on, and as she told stories which jarred my sense of plausibility, I felt the old acrid taste of contempt rising in my throat. I know she is easygoing and good-hearted; she has taken care of her children with steadfastness and generosity; she even adopted and raised her son's daughter after his wife bolted; and she has never held my occasional harsh remarks against me. I also know that the losses and terrors of the war wrought unfathomable injuries on her adolescent self, and that after the war she found only loneliness and contempt as she went from boarding school to callous weekend caretakers. So why is it so difficult for me to utter simple words of appreciation?

At times, however, all walls disappear. As my brother pokes around the house fixing things or works in the garden, and my sister sits at the kitchen table talking away about her grandchildren and her clients, a flow of happiness runs over me. At least for now, the world seems to have gone back to some original order, with love at its center.

(2000)

DEAD MAN'S COAT

Jarvis Jay Masters

It was so cold that morning we were all plastered against the high brick wall that provided the only shield from the chilling winds. We stood in the prison exercise yard, listening to the chattering sound of each other's dismay.

"Man, man!" said Freddie, shivering. "If I had known it was this damn cold I be damn if I had came out here, in all this shitty-ass weather!"

"Me, too," said Troy. "This cold is whippin' my ass, my hands, my feet, my ears.... Everything is freezin', you know?"

Only a few of us had opted to leave the confinement of our cells to brave the cold. The dread of being cooped up in the stench inside, waiting seventy-two more hours before being allowed out of our cells again, was why we stood almost paralyzed against the high gray wall, dressed in our dingy state-issued clothing, trying to make the best of it.

"Hey," said Skip, "what if we all just tell the guard we want off the yard, to take us all back in?"

"That ain't goin' to happen," I said, as I stomped my feet to stay warm. "'Cause they ain't goin' to stop the program inside just to come and escort us back in. Plus, how many of y'all righteously believe they actually goin' to come out here in this cold to get us?"

"They goin' to have to," said Leo, "at some point—right? So why not now instead of one o'clock?"

"They ain't comin' now," said Freddie, his teeth chattering, "'cause they like seein' us freezin' our asses off! Think about it! If they didn't, they would have given us better coats. They know how cold it is."

"Yeah," said Skip, "it's not the cold weather, it's this shit they got us wearin'. One pair of socks, state jeans, our sweatshirts, and these thin-ass cotton jackets. Man, this is the real problem!"

"Why you think nobody else is out here?" said Freddie, rubbing his bare hands together like two sticks to get fire. "Look around....We're the only fools, just the five of us out of fifty or so who could be out here wit' us. They had the sense to know. But us—like jackasses! Next time I'm keepin' my bad ass indoors."

A few minutes passed.

"Say, Jarvis," said Troy, with a quick glance down at my coat, "how long you been wearin' that coat?"

"Why?" I asked, looking down.

"Man, look at it! It looks older than Methuselah! Man, they don't even make state coats like that no mo'." The other guys started laughing.

I looked down at my coat again. There were a few holes in it. "I haven't had it that long," I said. "A year or two."

"He's right," said Skip, "'cause I remember Pitchfork havin' that same coat whenever I seen him."

"Hell, ol' Pitch got killed," said Freddie. "Remember? He got killed over there on the north block yard."

"Nah, that wasn't him," said Skip. "The last I heard he got out, paroled."

"Man, I'm tellin' y'all," said Freddie. "That was Pitch who got shot and killed. A dude I know workin' in the hospital tol' me. He seen Pitchfork stretched out dead!"

"Is that right?" we all hummed, each of us having his own memories of Pitchfork.

"And I tell you somethin' else," Freddie went on. "I'm willin' to bet those holes you got in your coat are holes from the bullets that killed Pitchfork."

I glanced down at the nickel-sized holes in my coat. There was one on the shoulder, and two more around the collar. "You crazy, Freddie! These ain't no bullet holes, dude!"

"They might jus' be," said Troy. "Watch—I can put my finger

right in one like this." He stuck his index finger inside the hole in the shoulder.

"Man, Troy," I said, "leave my damn coat alone. It ain't messin' wit' you."

"Let me see," said Freddie, inching close, "if my finger fits this other hole."

"Hey! Are you guys losin' your minds?" I said. I jumped away from their inspection of my coat. "Getcha paws off me! I know what's really goin' on," I joked. "Y'all is so cold, you tryin' to find somethin' to do, and my poor coat is it."

"That's not it," Skip said, laughing. "Man, Jarvis. Jus' trip off this: Here we are, stuck like Chuck in this cold-ass weather. And jus' when we think it can't get no worser, lo and behold," he said, bending over laughing, "we see you wearin'—and I don't mean no disrespect to ol' Pitchfork—a dead man's coat! Man, San Quentin ain't right. They got you wearin' a dead man's coat, bullet holes and all! Yo, Freddie," he said. "Tell Jarvis what he got on."

"Shoot! A dead man's coat."

"Troy, Leo. Tell the man," said Skip, still laughing, "what he got on."

"Shit! A dead man's coat."

"A dead man's coat," they all chimed in.

"It ain't no way around it, bro," said Skip. "The proof is in the holes." And they *all* burst into laughter. The joking made me feel as if we'd been brought in out of the icy cold.

"Well, in that case," I said, "this means—and y'all can tell me if I'm right or wrong—we're all wearin' a dead man's coat."

"No, you wrong about that," Troy said. "My coat was new when I got it. It's worn out now, no doubt," he said, glancing down at it, "but I tell you this—it was brand new when I got it."

"Ours, too," said Leo. "Look at 'em, Jarvis. They don't got no bullet holes. No damn holes in front or back. So I guess you deader wrong than that ol' raggedy coat of yours." And the four of them started laughing again.

"Wait a second," I said. "I still think we're all wearin' a dead man's coat. 'Cause the way I see it. . ."

"Is what?" Skip laughed.

"The way I see it, Skip: We're all on death row."

"Yeah, but. . ."

"Man," I said. "These are all dead men's coats we have. We're all wearin' a dead man's coat!"

They looked down at their coats. No one said a word.

And in less than a second, it became freezing cold again.

(2001)

THE BREAKFAST CLUB

Michael Acutt

Is there a sense of community among people living on the street? Absolutely. I used to belong to a group of outsiders called the Breakfast Club. We'd meet at the grill in Ohlone Park around 6:30 every morning, then we would ritualistically empty our pockets and pool our change on the picnic table. We'd buy beer or wine and try to get everybody "well." Then, after reading the paper and kibitzing and passing the latest street news—who just got out of jail, who got arrested last night—we'd split up into parties and go to work.

Begging is a form of work—I want to make that clear. A lot of people think the homeless are shiftless bums who wouldn't do an honest day's work if you paid them. It's true there are folks out there like that, and I have mixed feelings about it. But the fact is, much of the available work in twentieth-century America is so demeaning that begging seems like a viable alternative.

The "homeless" people I know and was one of (and they don't call themselves homeless) sometimes sit around the park reading the paper and smoking a cigarette and having *satsang* [spiritual fellowship] or whatever, and a sort of magic moment arrives when there are no more libations, or somebody's hungry, so they decide to have a cookout. Someone will say, "Well, I'll take McDonald's, how about if you guys do the benches next to the French Hotel, and we'll meet back here at three." And somebody else will say, "Okay, let's not get too scattered. What are we going for? We'll get sausages, eggs, bread, and beer, and we'll meet back here." It can be quite organized.

Some people on the outside are in the tradition of the mendicant monk. I know a man called Coach, a former professor in his early sixties who has lived outside for many years. He's a father figure for many folks on the street—a peacemaker, mediator, and general cooler-outer of difficult situations. He's one of the beer-sipping kind of alcoholics. He's always clean and well-presented, well read, and up to the minute on external reality; he's one of the most compassionate men I've ever met, and a very articulate and interesting man. He came of age in the 1950s, and was imbued with that Beat, Kerouac-type spirit and just never bothered to reenter the mainstream.

Coach has been deemed mentally disturbed by the State and receives a social security check, so he could be living inside somewhere. But he chooses to live outside. He likes sleeping under the trees and stars, and doesn't like rules and regulations or small, confined spaces. He likes his family—who are the "outsiders." Coach always has Band-Aids, aspirin, vitamins, ointment for a cut, and first-aid advice for the kinds of things that occur on the street. He's very welcoming, and deeply sad about the condition of humanity, which he sees quite clearly.

Some interesting things happen on the street. One night around last Thanksgiving, I was standing on Vine Street early in the evening, with my bedroll under my arm. I remember I had nine cents in my pocket. I was just standing there, deciding whether to go panhandle and get a cup of coffee, or go lie down somewhere. A man walked by me, I'd say roughly my age, forty-ish, expensive clothes and briefcase, perhaps a musician or radical lawyer. He got about ten feet past me, turned, and said, "Are you homeless?"

I had to think for a second, because I always disidentify, out of denial, but I said "yes." So he stepped up to me and handed me a bill. I said, "Well, thank you," and he walked away.

I held it up to the streetlight just so I could see what it was, and by that time he was about thirty feet away. He turned around and said, "It's real"—he could see me examining it—"be careful where you spend it." I saw that it was a hundred-dollar bill, and a jolt of electricity rushed through me and all these doors of opportunity opened.

I ran around the corner to this café (where I've been known for many years in previous incarnations as a well-dressed, inside person) to cash it, because I was worried about whether it was real or not, and I was worried about having a hundred-dollar bill on the street. I ordered a caffe latte and got ninety-eight dollars and a few cents change, which I stuffed in my pocket, and stood outside, throbbing with adrenaline. I immediately wanted to share my good fortune with one of my compadres, and the first person I bumped into a few minutes later was a former lead guitarist of several rock bands, a guy called Berkeley Red—one of the people on the street who doesn't drink, used to take a lot of amphetamines, but doesn't use anything now. I said, "Hey, Red, let's have dinner."

He said, "Yeah, in the park?"

"No, let's have a real dinner," I said, "There's this great Chinese restaurant, Veggie Foods, right here."

He said, "Inside? I haven't been inside a restaurant in about ten years!" Once we were inside the restaurant, he kept saying, "What'll I do? What'll I do?"

I said, "Just copy me."

And he would pick up the fork and say, "Is this right? Are they all watching me?" Of course, the people in the restaurant were, like most people everywhere, totally self-absorbed in their own private worlds. Nobody gives a rat's ass about your divorce or whatever. The staff in the restaurant was very kind. We had hot and sour soup, and then after we had another dish, we both began to get the sweats and the shakes. He was getting the sweats from the soup and I needed a drink. So we left.

Three times I went cold turkey on the street. To replace the "next-fix-focus," I'd examine my immediate needs, make a shopping list, and beg for the list. My feet were often pretty wounded with cuts and sores, so I'd get ointment and bandages. Then I'd buy scissors, a razor, shampoo, deodorant, and all those little things that make me feel human. I can only beg for so long. I guess it's partly about self-esteem. Self-esteem is reinforced by others, and what you get from others when you're begging is negative esteem. You're esteemed as an asshole and a blight on society.

Within days of getting sober, I'd find myself working again; it's simply easier than begging. I'd sleep in the park and start saving to get inside. One more time!

Now that I'm formally practicing meditation again on a daily basis, and I'm living in a *sangha* [spiritual community] inside that has at its heart active compassion, I feel less nervous about being with my former compadres than I did when my sangha was primarily AA. I owe my very life to my friends in AA, but I feel supported in a different way by a Buddhist sangha. My Buddhist friends don't think it's weird that I keep friendships with the poor and oppressed.

When I was on the outside, I felt my situation was temporary, but I tried not to think about it. I tried to stay in a particular state of consciousness that was very much in the present, and eliminated the past and future. I needed a certain level of alcohol in the blood to maintain this consciousness. It was painful to think soberly about what had brought me to the street, what was keeping me there, and what I was not doing about the rest of my life.

In my case, I felt it was my responsibility that I was on the outside. But I also knew folks who were so badly damaged as children that it was almost inevitable that they end up outside the system. Damaged by their parents and schooling—not necessarily poverty, but emotional and spiritual deprivation. By the time folks become outsiders, if they're substance abusers, they frequently descend from more interesting drugs to alcohol. A big part of it is its social availability—it's cheap, and ever present at mom-and-pop stores. You can get it at 6 A.M. You can beg a few pennies for a bottle of wine; you don't have to steal a car radio or pull some other nonsense and involve yourself in breaking the law.

There are many folks on the street who don't use alcohol or drugs. Others are on hospital drugs, which frequently makes it difficult for them to be employed. In some cases, the drugs and their side effects make it even more difficult for them to function in society than if they were just dealing with their hallucinations and voices. It's hard to dig a ditch when you're doing the Thorazine shuffle! (I worked as a counselor for schizophrenics in London for several years, so this isn't a flip observation.)

Now that I'm inside again, I know that this too is impermanent. Having a room of one's own, a warm place to sleep, and a place to take a shower is an extraordinary luxury, a wonderful gift that on a daily basis I reflect is not shared by millions of souls all over this planet. Folks on the outside in this country are in the minority, but they share the reality of most people on this planet—which is that life is dangerous and difficult, everything is in short supply, and you never know how long you're going to live.

And it's also a matter of attitude. I remember sitting on the sidewalk a few years ago, begging, on a dreary, drizzling day, and suddenly realizing that I was existing in the realm of the hungry ghosts, where beings endlessly suffer the torment of hunger because their bellies are immense but their mouths are as tiny as the eye of a needle. Somehow, so many of us find ourselves at the banquet table, going hungry because we are unable to take in life's readily available sustenance.

Since Buddha is the "awakened one," I always translate Buddhism, if asked, as "wake-uppery." My experiences of deprivation and dirt, rejection and compassion, beauty and ugliness, have indeed served as a vehicle for awakening. For that I'm grateful. I express that gratitude quietly, acting as a bridge for street people I know personally, and who are ready to "come inside." Stay warm!

(1992)

PART TWO

Taking the Practice into the World

INTRODUCTION TO PART TWO

In Part One we heard from people working with the suffering in their hearts. In Part Two we hear from people working with suffering outside the door. Some of them travel thousands of miles; some of them walk down the block. These are not stories about boy scouts helping old ladies across the street (or girl scouts helping old men across, either), although that's all very well in its way. The thing is, old ladies aren't usually waiting at the street corner just making themselves available to folks who want to do their good deed for the day. And besides, the traffic keeps getting worse, and what are we going to do about *that*?

It takes some effort to find our way to the activist work we want to do. It takes courage to step forward. *What if I make a fool of myself?* But if we're not stepping forward, we're hanging back. Sometimes hanging back is what we need to do, but not all the time, not most of the time. Life doesn't hang back, time doesn't hang back, opportunities for us to meet each other—as sandal meets footpath—aren't hanging back. It's all flowing along.

So it's helpful to hear from ordinary human beings who did step forward, willing to make mistakes. Who asked, as Thich Nhat Hanh suggests we ask the people around us, "Sweetheart, how can I help you?" We can ask this question of everyone on the planet.

The suffering in the world is so vast and the abuse of power is so great that the thought naturally arises: "Hey, I'm just one person! You expect *me* to stop the multinationals from destroying sustainable agriculture?!?" Here are the voices of people who didn't let such thoughts stop them. These voices remind me: Sometimes you aren't really sure whether you're helping very much at all—you just keep on doing the work anyway. It's what you do. And you don't have to do this work alone—you *can't* do it alone.

It takes courage to do this work, this work of going out on a limb for the sake of peace and justice, and it takes another kind of courage to write about it. I'm grateful to the people here, who share themselves with others twice, first by making a peace walk in Cambodia or working against the death penalty in California, and who share themselves all over again by telling about it.

—S.M.

SEEKING EVIL,
FINDING ONLY GOOD

Melody Ermachild Chavis

Hefting box after box, I recently moved all of my old death penalty case files, some of them nearly collapsed into shapeless heaps of cardboard. I felt the weight of all the investigation reports I have written for trials and appeals over twenty years, since capital punishment was brought back to California by popular vote. Heaving it all into my new storage space, I had the depressing thought, "This is my life. From age thirty-five to fifty-five, this room-sized tower of paper is what I have done."

Now, there are 512 people sentenced to die in California, ten of them women. The men are all in San Quentin; the women are kept separately at Chowchilla prison in southern California. The prison bus brings another man to death row at San Quentin about every two weeks. There isn't enough space anymore in the visiting room for all the families. Every hour and a half the guards make everyone leave, and then they bring in a new group.

Many people suggest that the answer to the crowding on death row is to speed the executions. And they will come faster now, as appeals have been limited by Congress and the courts, but even if one person were killed every day, it would still take eighteen months to kill them all, even if nobody new were sentenced.

Each of my dozens of boxes has on it the name of a person who was a defendant in a capital case. Many of them were sentenced to prison terms, but not to death; a few were acquitted and went home; and several dozen are living on death row.

The system is so capricious that if someone were to read all of my murder case files and try to guess which ones got the death sentences, they could never do it based on the facts.

As far as I know, every former client of mine is still alive. The execution of one of them is a bridge I have not yet crossed, and I have no more idea of how I will react when it happens than I know how I will meet my own death—with some kind of composure, I hope. I always wonder if the execution of someone I know well will be what finally causes me to quit my job.

I've come close a few times. Death verdicts at the end of long trials so devastated me that I was hardly able to work for weeks afterward—so bitterly flattened have I felt by such defeats, and so worried about the young man I'd gotten to know well, sent up to live among the condemned.

It was the fifth execution in California since the resumption of the death penalty in 1978, the death of Thomas Thompson in the spring of 1998, which has so far been the hardest for me. He was convicted of raping and killing a woman, but many questions emerged about the case: whether the sex had been consensual, whether in fact the woman's former boyfriend could have killed her. I've worked on trials where less reasonable doubt than this resulted in acquittal. Even a number of prosecutors asked that Thomas Thompson be given a hearing. He wasn't my client—I didn't even know him, but each time I went to the prison, I saw him, spending his last visits with his wife, sister, and nieces and nephews, and I'll always remember him that way.

San Quentin memories for me are associated with the smell of the place: the disinfectant inmates futilely swab onto the broken linoleum, and the odor of stale vending machine popcorn laced with rancid fake butter. After twenty years, a breath of San Quentin can still get me down, wear me out, and give me a headache.

In the end, the push to execute Thomas Thompson gained so much momentum that the court refused a stay because of some procedural errors that had been made during the appeals process.

No one had yet been executed in California with the case against him in such disarray. It hit everyone on death row hard, and made the reassurances of legal workers like me sound hollow.

I was so low that evening that for the first time, I couldn't go to

San Quentin to join the demonstrators singing and praying at the gate. I couldn't face the television lights, the caterwauls of the pro-death crowd. One attorney who is a good friend told me he felt the same. He left his office to go to the prison that night and found himself driving home instead, too heartsick to stand at the gate waiting for the midnight hour. I had vowed to go and vigil at every execution, and I hadn't expected ever to break that promise, but instead I arranged to baby-sit my grandchildren, bathing them and reading them stories to comfort myself.

People don't realize how hard it is to win appeals. New trials are hardly ever granted, no matter how poorly the original trial was conducted. When Thomas Thompson died, I couldn't imagine how my work could possibly save the life of any of my clients, when even his life couldn't be saved. I felt useless, like I was wasting my time, and my life.

At such times, I ask myself, "What is it I'm trying to do anyway?" I pick up the newspaper and read that a hurricane killed thousands in the Caribbean—yet I work with teams of other legal workers to save one person who may have taken life himself. What is the sense of all my effort? Wouldn't it be better to simply feed children or send medicines where they are needed?

The next time I went to the Zen Center, there on the altar was a white card with Thomas Thompson's name on it, next to the cards of others who had died and were being remembered. I was surprised to see it, and I thought, "Here is a place where people care about this person's life." No one said anything about it to me, but just the knowledge that the card was there changed something for me. It gave me back some confidence, and I began to give myself a talking-to, as I have done so many times over the years, about why I do this work.

Comparisons don't help, I tell myself. It's good to send medicine and it's good to fight the death penalty. My colleagues and I don't work to raise up one life over another; we work against a law that empowers our government, in all its folly, to murder a human being. The small white card on the altar says it best: one life is worth honoring.

A person has to honor her own life to keep going in any hard struggle. I have to try to treat myself gently when I see that my courage isn't steady. I watch my spirits die down and flare up like a campfire on a rainy night. One moment I feel frightened by the hatred aimed at my clients and all of us who defend them. The next, my heart burns bright again for this job.

In the summer after Thomas Thompson died, I was able to prove that many of the crimes one of my clients had been convicted of were actually done by another man, something no one had suspected. Pleased with myself, I noticed how satisfying it was to bring to light the sloppy work of a bunch of gung-ho deputy sheriffs. I wish I could say that what I found out will guarantee my client a new trial, but I can't. All his lawyers can do is submit my proof to the court and hope they think it matters. Amazingly, they could easily call it "harmless error," and if they do, I'll once again have to face the frustration of doing my best and losing anyway.

At such times, I go back to my inner pep talks: It's good to choose a thing and do it for a long time, I lecture myself. A cause needs people loyal to it, to build it steadfastly over years. Just do it, like meditation. Like sitting down in the middle of everything without asking why. Think of a woman who sits in a tree, fighting for a forest. When it's cut down, she doesn't give up. She goes on and fights for the next stand of trees.

Over and over, I have the same experience: I get a new case, and start by reading a stack of police reports and news reports about the crime and arrest of my client. I am shaken, even horrified and frightened. "How will I meet this man?" I think. "How will I establish any connection with such a person?"

When I started out in this job, at my first meeting with a new client, I used to wonder, "Is he guilty?" I thought I should work harder for people who weren't guilty. As I learned more about the U.S. Constitution and the body of living law that has grown up around it, I became more committed to the justice of every person having the best possible defense team, and I saw how my personal integrity depended on my doing my own best job for everyone. Our adversarial legal system mandates that we legal workers find defenses for our clients whether or not they've committed crimes, and I do my best to contribute to at least showing mitigating circumstances. In the end, I've come to feel that all death row defendants are wrongfully sentenced, because I've been able to witness first-hand how wrong the system is. The kind of help I give doesn't change, whether my client denies everything, confesses, or is innocent. In fact, I've realized that innocent people don't need my personal support as much as "guilty" ones, because when a person has really done something very bad, he or she needs help the most.

At first, my new client might seem guilty of something terrible. But that first impression gets complicated as the story of his life unfolds. I go out to interview witnesses, and in the listening, I become a witness. I find some more people who are "guilty," too—perhaps parents whose love failed.

As I work, the guilt in my client that seemed so solid begins to come apart in my hands. All I can find in the end are causes and conditions in an endlessly tangled web. Investigating any life, one sees how currents coming from very far away can meet within a person: echoes of a long-ago massacre, hurts barely spoken, then a dark street, a shout, a bullet—a lethal moment.

Does this mean that responsibility lies nowhere? No. We are each responsible for what we set into motion. Yet we can never isolate one current of karma from the ocean of creation.

I think our idea of "deterrence" as the answer to aggression is a legacy of war. For fifty years, our minds have been trained in this way of thinking, a kind of infrastructure of dualistic thought that has not yet been disarmed.

Now we have identified "criminals," who are really our own nation's children, as our enemy, and we are impoverishing ourselves to build prisons instead of schools and universities. A powerful financial and industrial complex is rising up around prisons that will be as difficult to dismantle as the missile systems are.

If I have learned anything, it's that people must be treated with exquisite individuality. The more we classify people and warehouse them in groups—"prisoners," "mentally ill," "condemned"—the less we can see who they are and be of help.

I keep a quote from Suzuki Roshi taped onto my computer: "To realize that things are one is a very sympathetic understanding. But how to treat things one by one, each in a different way, with full care, that, I think, is your practice."

"Full care" might sound utopian. But in the lives of my clients, those lost moments when even a little care might have gone a long way leap at me off the pages of school records, juvenile hall files, and medical reports.

New understandings are being reached about human behavior, yet so little of this new knowledge informs our judicial system. We know much more now about what children need and how they grow than we knew when I began this work. And every day we find out more about the things that can go wrong. I could make a long list: the neurological damage done to a fetus by exposure to alcohol and other drugs and a host of substances such as lead; brain damage and chemical imbalance and genetic defects of all kinds; drug-induced psychosis; learning disabilities; and above all, the effects of trauma. These are the kinds of deficits from which nearly all of my clients suffer. Many have not one, but multiple diagnoses such as these.

Yet it's as if the world of behavioral sciences and psychology and the world of jurisprudence and corrections exist on separate continents, drifting apart on a sea of ignorance.

I'm interested, when I meet a new client, in the question, "How did this human being come to be sitting before me in this cell?"

At the end of the investigation, I still have questions: "What can be done to help him now? How can he live out the remainder of his life in the most safety, doing the least harm? How can he still serve his life purpose? Can he perhaps do some good?" These are questions our society wants to answer with a needle of poison.

The most disturbing idea abroad now is that the executions are done for the satisfaction of the family members of murder victims. We hear politicians crying for speedier executions, saying, "This victim's family has waited too long for justice." This is vengeance, pure and simple. This is not the rule of law, as we understand it, even in our flawed democracy. The law is supposed to mete out justice, not retribution. If the government kills a man to assuage the pain of a victim's loved ones, why not let the victim's family kill him themselves? Why not kill him by torture? Such an idea leads to hands chopped off for theft, and the like, as is done in some countries.

The voices of those families who do not want their loved one's killer to die are drowned out. And there are those families. I've met a woman who regularly visits her son's killer on death row. Somehow they began to correspond, and she realized he is not so different from her own son, so that now she has taken him in as one of her own.

How does grief heal? I wouldn't presume to know how murder victims' families feel. But I know that their grief is not always lessened by an execution. Sometimes the real mourning begins afterwards, when the execution, sadly, has not brought back the one they lost. Perhaps some people's minds are eased because one part of the story has come to an end, but we cannot, as a society, go down the path of vengeance.

Many death penalty proponents believe that evil infects people like my clients, who must therefore be extinguished.

This view is reinforced by the opinions of some forensic "experts" who come to court as prosecution witnesses with mechanistic check lists by which they "diagnose" people as "sociopaths"—as if children who wet the bed, harm animals, or set fires are somehow "born" to be killers, without asking why the circumstances of his life might bring a child to do such things. These "experts" talk about sociopaths while they ignore the pathology of society.

All during my childhood, my mother and I were at war. When she lost control of herself, as she often did, she screamed at me that I was evil. And so I thought it must be the evil in me that caused my mother to slap and kick me, pound my head against the floor, slash at my face with a knife. As I grew, I came to believe in return that my mother was evil, because I couldn't imagine anything that could cause her to do such things except the devil.

It's been clear to me for some time that I've undertaken my long investigation of evil because of the violence in my background, violence I know I share with so many others.

For twenty years I have searched for evil, and nowhere have I found it. I find causes and conditions aplenty, and I have found something I wasn't looking for: inexhaustible quantities of love.

Suddenly, in every case—and it always comes as a surprise—I find someone giving love against all odds, someone reaching out where it seems nothing but hatred prevails, someone finding it in themselves to forgive against storms of bitter anger. These are often unexpected people, unsung heroes and heroines who want no thanks: a man's long-ago juvenile hall counselor who comes to testify; a former special education teacher, retired with a bad heart, who flies on three airplanes to get to the trial to ask jurors to spare her former student's life.

Love, I have seen, is a force alive in the world.

By the time I scattered my mother's ashes gently into the Pacific, I had learned something about causes and conditions, forgiveness and love.

People ask me how being a student of Buddhist teachings helps me in my work. Practicing meditation has opened me more to my clients. Sitting, I've had to sit with the violence inside of myself, so that I no longer feel myself so separate from people in prison. My self-image has loosened a lot, and I'm not so attached to who I think I am as I pass through the prison gate. I go in less as a do-gooder, more as an ordinary, suffering human being.

The fact is, my work and the teachings are in a constant dialogue; Buddhist practice helps my work, and my work helps my Buddhist practice because it wakes me up to my life.

I've taken the risk of caring about my clients, and as I do so, I see the world through their eyes. I long to share with them what they can never have in a prison: time with children, time with trees. Time under the open sky. Because I go into prisons, I'm grateful for those simple, priceless things in my life.

I began this work filled with a sense of drama about death, hyper-aware that my clients were going to die. Over the years, a number of the attorneys I worked closely with have died, leaving our clients living on death row, and that has changed my perspective. When I say good-bye at the end of a prison visit, I am aware that although my client is condemned, and the prison is a very dangerous place, with high rates of murder and suicide, I could easily be the one to die first. I've realized that both I and the man I'm visiting need to wake up to our deaths, regardless of which side of the bars we are sitting on.

Whenever I chant, "Dharma gates are boundless, I vow to enter them," I picture San Quentin's gate.

Before I was a Buddhist student, San Quentin got me down, and I didn't like going there. Now I try to make each trip to death row a pilgrimage—sad, but spirit-opening.

As I drive over the Richmond Bridge, I see Mount Tamalpais, the mountain many call the Sleeping Lady, at rest over the prison, her green, brown, purple, blue clothes changing moment to moment with the light. Morning and night, she wraps herself in a white shawl of fog. The men inside the prison can't see that they live at the edge of water on the skirt of a sleeping mountain.

Beside the parking lot at San Quentin is a little cove on the bay, a crescent between the western foot of the gray steel bridge and the prison. Wood scraps and bits of trash drift in and out on the gentle slap of the water against a beach of algae-covered rocks. Neither the birds nor the tides that swoop into that cove and swirl out alter their rhythms because of anything that goes on inside the prison walls above, not even an execution.

As I sit on a log, breathing out the prison, I remember the last midnight vigil I attended at San Quentin's gate. As the lethal injection was done, we drew our little crowd close. In silence, each of us reached out to those around us. Through my coat, I felt the press of a comforting hand on my back between my shoulder blades. My fingers found the warmth of a stranger's hand. The pastor who ministers inside the prison began a prayer: for the executed man and his family, for the victims and their families, and for the prison staff who had to carry out this act. Then she added a prayer for the legal workers. "This is not about winning or losing," she said. "This is about doing our very best, every day."

Sometimes I forget that my life in this struggle is not mine alone; we who oppose the death penalty are connected, as if we stood close enough to touch all the time. My life in this job is not a dusty box of papers after all. It's my life, shared with others.

I've renewed my vow to go to the gate for every execution.

(1999)

BEING ARRESTED

Maylie Scott

JANUARY 10, 1990

The eight o'clock morning traffic along Port Chicago Highway just outside of Concord, California, is brisk. A trumpet from the Naval Weapons Base across the street from our peace camp, which we call the Nuremberg Action Site, blows a crisp reveille, which is followed by a loud, blurred recording of the "Star Spangled Banner." The air is chilly and the wind bears a faint chemical bitterness. A heron flies overhead, toward what used to be marshlands and is now increasingly industrial sites. Many smokestacks are already streaming their white or gray plumes toward the sky. Mount Diablo presides to the southeast. Blackbirds, enjoying the daily offering of seeds put out for them, make a bright, musical background for the sounds of traffic.

The peace camp is lodged in a thin, triangular wedge between the Navy road to Port Chicago on one side and Port Chicago Highway on the other. A blue tarp makes a roof over the living area, which consists of two cots, an armchair, and a table with leaflets and files. A few white plastic chairs are scattered about, waiting for the day's business. Beyond them are six full-length black cardboard coffins, commemorating the deaths of the Jesuits killed in El Salvador. Beyond the coffins, Tibetan prayer flags hanging from a post make a roadside altar. An outhouse—a small green rectangle with a yellow crescent moon painted on the center of the door—marks the end of the site. The area is intermittently bordered by large logs and good-sized rocks, in the hope that they might have a protective effect should a vehicle swerve in from the road. White wooden crosses inscribed with names of victims of U.S.-supplied wars lean wherever it is convenient. The vulnerability of the site, where people have been living by day and sleeping by night since Brian Willson was maimed in September 1987, testifies to vulnerability everywhere.

For two years the Nuremberg Action Site has been my educator. I have come once a week, most weeks, for a few hours—to "hang out," or to walk up and down with a cross as cars drive by, some yelling insults, some encouragements, or to participate in the Thursday morning "Nonviolent Workshops" led by inveterate peaceworker David Hartsough, or to meditate with the Buddhist Peace Fellowship group on the third Sunday of the month, or to get arrested.

Lately, the group of five or so constant site residents has been thinning out and I have been spending one night a week there. So far, at night there have always been at least two people on site. Last night was enlivened by a couple of teenagers who ran past and threw rocks at Greg. He ran after them but couldn't catch them. Some time after that, I was awakened by a slight weight on my legs. I sat up and a rat and I looked at each other. We were equally startled; she left as I said, "Go." Living here, even on a very part-time basis, pushes at one's middle-class insulation.

This morning there are three "full-timers": Greg, Steve, and Diane. Greg, combing his tangled hair with his fingers, sits on a plastic chair, listening intently to the KPFA morning news. Steve, who is skinny, is clapping his hands and sides to recover from the cold. We have just had bread (food is sometimes donated but there always seems to be a supply of bread) and hot drinks, from water heated on the propane stove in the "kitchen" on the back of a truck parked across the street. Diane, in her usual costume of maroon head scarf, purple sweatshirt, orange, tie-dyed long skirt, and Tibetan boots, is writing the routine morning note to the Base, advising them of our intention to block any weapons train. She straightens and focuses a pair of binoculars on the Base. She reports a build-up of sheriffs' cars that suggests a train may be about to come.

We begin to rearrange the site, so that none of the property will be confiscated. The limits of where protective rocks, posters, and other property may be in the event of a train passage have been worked out with the Navy by trial and error over a period of months. It is one aspect of a network of agreements constituting a code of behaviors that both protestors and authorities are fairly protective of. We carry the increasingly flabby coffins across the street, move some of the rocks, and generally consolidate other effects. As I help, I remember that it has been several months since my last arrest, and that my day is relatively free; a good day to block. The other three won't mind skipping a jail day. So I volunteer and sit cross-legged on the tracks at about the place that Brian Willson was hit—this seems respectful—and watch the group of Navy brass, men and women, who begin to saunter out from the base. Behind them, twenty-odd sailors, also of both sexes, as well as different colors, jog out, in step, toward us. They are dressed in camouflage fatigues and carry riot sticks at their belts. We are outnumbered by almost ten to one. It is quite complimentary to be taken seriously. Unexpectedly, Diane sits down next to me, saying, "I realize I'd like to spend the day with you." I am very touched. Diane is a mainstay of the encampment; her energy, dedication, and ability to articulate her intention have drawn my admiration for a long time.

The arrest process is the basic ritual of the site. It varies according to the group of protesters present, to their emotional level as well as to their dramatic ability. Diane and I sit, circled by our friends. A sheriff, not bothering to use his bullhorn, tells us that anyone who does not go to the other side of the highway within sixty seconds will be arrested. Our friends, in not too much of a hurry, do cross the street, all except for Greg, who remains on a prearranged spot, with the site video camera. The presence of the camera has stopped any rough handling of arrestees. Diane and I are asked if we will "cooperate." Diane says, matter-of-factly, that she will not move so long as U.S. weapons are illegally killing innocents abroad. We are asked to stand, and we both do. (Some "go limp" at this point and are laid in rubber nets and placed in the back of a truck.) The sheriffs are gentle and help us stand. Diane is cuffed. A sheriff warns me that the car is hot and I will be warm in my down jacket. He helps me take it off before handcuffing me. We are escorted to the car, and are reminded to lower our heads as we awkwardly climb in. The heater is going. It is warm.

Diane immediately resumes a conversation we'd begun earlier. An arrest is hardly a noticeable event for her. She is beginning to feel that the time is coming for her to leave the site; she has lived there for most of the last two years, except for a four-month jail stint and a three-month trip to China and Tibet. She is not sure whether this changing sense of direction is due more to the stress of the tracks or to a new calling. The shape of the new adventure is not yet clear but something new is arising. The trip to China, as well as an encounter in a convent in Tibet, renewed her interest in Buddhism. She has been sitting more. She has emerged from a prolonged despair. In the last week, the urgent injunction she had felt to somehow change the disastrous course of events in the world has fallen off; all she needs to do is find the best way that she can live. She feels light and hopeful.

Traffic has halted and the weapons train is moving toward us as we sit in the police car. The tall yellow engine, with the heads of the two drivers way up in the cabin, like eyes, hauls a procession of white boxcars, each marked with a cautionary sign. We are silent. The first cars are labeled "inert." Nerve gas? Then comes a long line of cars, "Explosive A," "Explosive B." Each label has a little picture of an explosion, just in case the words are insufficient warning. It is difficult to keep attention wholly on the train; I am surprised by the irrelevant and trivial thoughts that arise. I keep returning to the exact fit of the metal wheels on the metal track. A long train. When it passes, cars that have been stopped in both directions are allowed to proceed. Meanwhile another train, coming toward the base from the direction of the port, has arrived and is waiting to cross.

Diane continues in her positive vein. She describes how the protesters "won" a struggle with the county; pain holds have been barred, due to the suit won by the three men whose arms were broken during arrest. Local law enforcement officials are generally friendly and protective. This year the site has been allowed to keep a tarp up over the cots. Sheriffs respond quickly and supportively to threats and harassments. Indeed, today, Dave, our arresting officer, and Diane are on familiar and friendly terms. Dave simply copies all of her identifying information from her arrest sheet of last week to this week's. He gives her some tips as to how she may be allowed to keep her scarf while in jail. Later, as she is describing to me how she thinks this country has "lost its ideals," he interrupts and asks her when she thinks this happened. He listens responsively to her careful historical analysis and then is quiet. Diane has a large classroom.

We arrive at the Martinez County Jail and pull up at the closed door of the garage. Dave makes a bantering identification into his microphone, a heavy door rises, and we drive in. A man in an orange prison suit, whose ankles are chained, is hobbling over to a van parked ahead of us. A heavy woman is jumping up and down, yelling something at a sheriff. She is handcuffed. She runs over to the far side of a parked car. A loudspeaker voice says, "Toilet call." We get out and stand by while our property is catalogued and put into plastic bags. Another round of identification questioning. "Born 3/29/35. Five foot nine. 130 pounds." Is my hair brown or gray? I say, "both." Employed? "Yes. Priest at the Berkeley Zen Center." I have lived in California for twenty-seven years, in the same house for twenty-five. I'm not sure how many times I've been arrested—perhaps six. Never convicted. Not on probation or parole. I say no to a long list of medical ailments. The little chips of one's identity are fed into a powerful invisible machine. We are charged with the usual misdemeanor, "637c," blocking a public thoroughfare. We are ushered through two locked doors into the holding unit. Our bodies are patted by a female deputy. We sit and take off our socks and turn them inside out for inspection. We stand, back against wall, for our "mug-shots." The camera whines as the shutter closes.

Despite Dave's coaching Diane is not allowed to keep her scarf. The women's section of the holding unit is quite empty. Four women are half-watching the TV that is fixed high up on the wall.

Diane and I get back to our conversation. We are interrupted briefly for fingerprinting and then, at last, are undisturbed. A year ago I spent three months in a practice period at Tassajara Zen Mountain Center while Diane spent four months in jail (in Richmond) on an accumulation of charges. We speculate on the similarities of jail and monastic experience. Diane would just as soon spend time in jail as out. She finds it centers and focuses her; it does away with the pressure of "extra" possibilities.

She described an effective substance abuse program, DUCE, which is offered to inmates at Richmond. She put the program's lesson plans onto the jail's Macintosh, thereby gaining access to the Mac herself. (In her previous life, she worked as a computer programmer.) She wrote and desktop-published a book, which she sold when she got out. The sales helped finance the summer trip to China and Tibet. Jail gave her support; she found her moodiness was stabilized. She observed, with some humor, a rise in her anxiety level in the week before she was to be released. This is a common phenomenon, known to detainees as "short-end shit."

I had wanted to go to Tassajara for many years, and I wasn't disappointed. It was not, however, the complete "fit" that I had thought it might be. While appreciating the clarifying effect of the austere schedule, the long silences, and the natural beauty of life on the floor of a coastal mountain canyon, I was uncomfortable with what I perceived to be a protective insularity that eclipsed but did not address the problems of the outside world.

How, we wonder, do we find the "right fit"? I say I experience the Nuremberg Action site as a powerful monastic presence: a monastery with no walls, a place, in the midst of the noise of the highway and the smells of the nearby factories, where the long hours of silence and the inevitable rising of discomforts are the strict and true tests of commitment. Diane agrees. Nothing really "happens" on the site; it is primarily a place of being. The potency of its being manifests in its tolerance—all kinds of lifestyles, ages, religious beliefs, and political views are included. Even violence is included, although not permitted. People come and go and return, and the site, in its formless way, endures. Healing occurs; people who have lived scattered lives, on margins, find purpose and appreciation. I recall that some time ago Diane had remarked that "just being" on the site, responding to its various demands to the best of her ability, was as challenging as any job she had ever had. (And she is not without a résumé of demanding, skilled, and lucrative work experience.) Diane observes that the site's monastic conditions of no property, no devotion to comfort, and sustained vulnerability very successfully weed out people who should not be included. Nonetheless, Diane longs for a community based on a shared, religious life.

How might such a community begin? We start to imagine a group committed to voluntary homelessness. A group that would avoid the "missionary" aspect of returning to a safe place after the job is done. A group that knows that the only way to heal ourselves is by living an inclusive life, a group that would share a Buddhist practice of meditation and ritual. There would be no property, nothing to protect. In this way it would be as "pure" as the site. The vision grew in vivid intensity—shaved heads, robes, shopping carts? Celibacy? A minimum of seven? We are interrupted by a sheriff summoning the men to lunch: "Please, gentlemen, come out and line up." I recall that I have been hungry for some time.

The men, perhaps twenty, line up. They are mostly casually dressed, with a couple of strikingly middle-class exceptions. Diane points to a T-shirt worn by a hefty sort with a beard and longish hair. The front in large letters says "DAMN." The back says "Drunks against MADD mothers." Lunch is served to the women. We are each handed two sandwiches, one with a thin slice of cheese, another with a thin slice of bologna, a small package of mayonnaise and another of mustard, and a half pint of low-fat milk. Everyone is hungry and Diane and I easily find takers for our meat sandwiches. The TV has been on continuously, tuned mostly to the soaps, although no one seems to watch it enough to follow the plots. Nor do we need to; the plots are ours—addiction, craving, disappointment—the actors are rich and beautiful, costuming the familiar suffering.

I am short on sleep and become drowsy and unfocused. Napping is not easy because the TV is loud and the chair uncomfortable. I would like to continue our conversation but can think of nothing to say. I am aware of all the impediments, internal and external, that distance me from the reality of our visionary talk. And yet, some energy, some clarity persists. All the other women are called to the sheriff's desk and sent on their ways. We turn off the TV. I fall into a sleepy *zazen* and time passes quickly. By the time another woman comes in and requests that the TV be turned on, it is nearly 5:00. We watch the news, are served a supper identical to our lunch, and are called to be released. Our property is returned, from a window just outside of the holding unit. Looking out onto the parking lot, I see the sun setting.

We telephone the site beeper, and, in a few minutes, Greg returns the call. He will come to get us. We walk up and down in the fresh air of the parking lot. The interior foggy paralysis lifts. The twenty-minute drive back is fresh, as the world is after *sesshin* [a meditation retreat]. The enormous Chevron plant, illuminated by hundreds of different-colored lights swirling in patches of white smoke, is like the body of a mysterious dragon kingdom. Greg says the air has been especially bad. The nearly full moon, not yet risen, lights the clouds over the peaceful dark hills. "Home again," Diane says as we pull up at the site. It is cold. We hug. I get into my car, looking forward to a hot bath and supper, as she moves back into the site. Our separateness is painful. I start the car.

(1994)

LANDMINES OF THE HEART

Bob Maat

When asked by someone who comes into the Dhammayietra Center, "Besides peace walks, do you people do anything else?" I answer frankly, "No, that's about all I do. But I walk a lot!" Venerable Maha Ghosananda, the spiritual patron of the Center, preaches that the Dhammayietra (dhamma peace walk) is not a once-a-year event but indeed a daily, step-by-step process. "Our journey for peace begins today and every day. Each step is a prayer, each step is a meditation, each step will build a bridge." I do walk a lot.

A recent pilgrimage took me to a western province along the Thai-Cambodian border. Several international Dhammayietras have traversed this countryside, where the people have yet to taste the fruit of the Paris Peace Accords of October 1991. It's a province of contested territories, of violent skirmishes and sporadic shelling, of ground continuously seeded with more landmines than there are feet to walk upon them, of a people displaced so often it seems normal.

Inspired by Maha Ghosananda's teaching to find the courage to leave our temples and enter the temples of human experience, temples that are filled with suffering, I set off. My striped plastic sack, identified as a smuggler's bag by the border region's local people, was filled to the brim with stories of last year's Dhammayietra, as well as copies of a recent talk given by Maha Ghosananda on International Peace Day. In that homily he stresses the need to remove the "landmines of the heart."

"A crazy foreigner has come, Mom," a young child called out, announcing my arrival to the whole village as she hid behind her mother's sarong. Unable to dispute the diagnosis, I smiled at the woman, who had another babe at the breast.

A young boy, encouraged by his grandmother, came forward with palms held together and respectfully begged for a little money. The elderly woman with betel-nut teeth whispered loudly to her grandson, and he promptly upped his request to five hundred riels (twenty U.S. cents). "We have no food," the old woman explained.

"Nowadays we are eating *babah*," another volunteered. Babah is a kind of soup that serves as a "rice stretcher." I noticed a number of children with yellow streaks in their hair—a sign of malnutrition.

"Why are you walking to Bang Tha Kuon?" asked the woman with the baby.

"I work with the Dhammayietra and Samdech Song Maha Ghosananda. I walk and pass out stories from the Dhammayietra." I pulled out ten flyers and distributed them to the small crowd that had gathered.

"I don't know French," the mother exclaimed.

"It's in Khmer," said a teenage boy, eager to show off his reading ability. "The suffering of Cambodia has been deep," he read. "From this suffering comes great compassion. . . ."

"Tell Samdech we waited and waited for the Dhammayietra to come here last year, but it never came," said a new voice. "We have never had peace. They say even the Dhammayietra was afraid to come here. Tell Samdech we're still waiting."

"I will," I answered humbly. Indeed, at the last minute, in a moment of fear, Dhammayietra III had rerouted itself away from these people's suffering. I bid adieu, while the voice of our teenage preacher read on, ". . . a peaceful country makes a peaceful world. . ." and I continued westward.

"Chop! Chop! Barang! Barang Chop!" An unseen voice screamed at me to stop as I started to walk around a closed checkpoint. "Come here! Where are you going? What's in your bag?" the young soldier demanded, approaching me with his AK-47. This was one of the multiple illegal checkpoints set up near road bridges.

("The soldiers are supposed to guard the bridges," an old woman had once taught me. "But they're really here to 'guard' our money!" She winked.) "Okay, where's the money?" the soldier asked, rifling through my bag. He was young enough to be my son.

I told him I was a monk who walked with the Dhammayietra.

"If you're really a monk, then why do you have hair?"

"I'm a Christian monk. Jesus had hair."

The soldier offered me a bowl of water to drink, and I learned of his hard life story. No family, no salary in months, knowing only war since he was born. He asked me if I really believed Cambodia would ever have peace. "That's why I walk," I answered. He asked me to wait and ran into his hut. He slipped four baht into my hand, and wished me good luck as I walked away.

Friendly country banter went on all day:

"Why don't you ride?"

"'Cause if I were riding, I wouldn't have this opportunity to meet you!"

"What's this paper?"

"A gift from the Dhammayietra."

"That's all, eh? How about a dollar?"

"Are you the younger brother of Bob Maat, who used to work in Site Two?"

"Yes, much younger. Only kidding—it's me, Bob."

"Instead of walking, why don't you fix this road?"

"When will we have peace?"

"Samdech Song says peace will come, step by step."

"Yes, but how many more steps?"

"Are you afraid of the Khmer Rouge?"

"Samdech Song says if we are fearful, we will never have peace. Fear is death itself."

Old men on oxcarts, young children on bicycles, middle-aged women waiting along the road in front of their huts, all took flyers. Drivers of motorcycle taxis stopped to pick up a flyer. A young man in a wheelchair, a recent double amputee from a landmine, propelling himself with two poles like a dry-season, cross-country skier, stopped to ask if the Red Cross in Battambang still offered free prostheses, and took two flyers. Walking past a slow-moving oxcart, I heard a young father reading to his son beside him, "Peace-making begins with us," as the water buffaloes moseyed along on automatic pilot.

The shadows of the day were growing long. Nearly out of flyers, I arrived at the outskirts of a border town at dusk. Both sides of the road were marked with red skull-and-crossbones danger signs, evidence of a de-mining team's surveillance. I could hear the sounds of a market village coming to the end of another day, and see the smoke of the evening meals' fires curling. Suddenly the horizon erupted with tracer bullets flying in all directions, followed by a series of loud explosions.

Afraid of running into a minefield, I squatted in the road. Women and children screamed in the distance. Three men came running in my direction. "Can I go with you?" I called to the lead man.

"Are you a journalist?" he asked.

"No, no. I'm with the Dhammayietra."

"Come! The Khmer Rouge are attacking." Indeed, just a week before, a village fifteen kilometers south had been attacked by the Khmer Rouge. The villagers had been evacuated to Thailand, only to be repatriated by the Thai military a few days ago.

Running in a crouch, our leader took us eastward. The whistling sound of a shell overhead encouraged a "closer-to-the-earth" position. He jumped into a shallow ditch alongside the road; the rest of us followed suit. He said, "I don't think it's the Khmer Rouge. I don't hear any B40 rockets. It sounds like the Thais."

"That would be better," his friend responded. "At least they won't overrun us."

While the two were assessing the situation, the fellow next to me asked, "You wouldn't happen to have any more of those flyers I saw you passing out on the road earlier today, would you?" I handed him a torn copy of Maha Ghosananda's Peace Day talk.

As the four of us lay on our backs in the ditch, this man read out loud: "To make peace we must remove the landmines from our hearts which keep us from making peace: greed, hatred, and delusion." Oblivious of the red streaks zipping overhead, he carried on a running commentary with the text. "This is true. This is really very good." Meanwhile, we could hear the sounds of women and children in flight. The fighting increased in intensity before burning out thirty minutes later.

I got directions from my ditch companions and joined the procession of people, many pushing bicycles loaded down with all their portable possessions, moving toward the temple. It was on the eastern edge of the village and was considered a "safe area," geographically if not spiritually. The widespread rumor was that this latest peace violation wasn't initiated by the Khmer Rouge after all, but by a failed business deal. "They were trying to get a stolen vehicle across the border." People were told to stay put as the transaction would be attempted again that night. The man who had read to us in the ditch reminded us that one of the landmines of the heart that needs to be removed before peace comes is greed. "Do you really think Cambodia will ever have peace?" the boy soldier had asked earlier that day. As I talked with villagers late into the night, the question was repeated.

Dhammayietra are never easy. Sore feet, blistered lips, sunburned face, constipation (or worse), the uncertainty of where one will lay one's head at night, drunken soldiers (and sometimes sober ones) can be a challenge. The danger of landmines (in the heart as well as in the earth) is a constant reality on these country roads.

At the same time it is pure privilege to walk among these folks. Once they realize that you are one who walks with the Dhammayietra, they open up their hearts as well as their huts, and the gospel of the Dhammayietra comes alive on the back roads of Cambodia. We talked about everything from Buddha to Jesus to Mohammed, from landmines to AIDS to birth control, about poor rice harvests due to floods caused by deforestation, about the deep desire for peace while preparing for another season of war. On this solo Dhammayietra, the main realities people told me about were war and lack of food. Their vision of a better world is nearly blinded by the immediate needs of today. It is hard to dream the dream when one sleeps in fear and hunger.

(1996)

JOURNEY OF A BROKEN HEART

Marianne Dresser

It is cold, damp, and gray in central Poland in November, and the most notorious Nazi death camp seems an unlikely place for a pilgrimage. Here I will find no glorious cathedral or sublime sacred images, no miraculous fountain or boon-bestowing guru. Just a carefully preserved monument to humanity's darkest potential: Auschwitz-Birkenau.

A hundred and fifty or so North Americans and Europeans have gathered here for the third annual Bearing Witness retreat organized by Roshi Bernie Glassman and the Zen Peacemaker Order. We will spend five days here, living among the echoes of its history of immense cruelty and immense suffering, taking it "into our very marrow." We have journeyed to a place of great spiritual presence.

The first morning is given over to a tour of Auschwitz I, the original camp. We break into small groups and pass through the infamous iron gate with its cynical message: *Arbeit Macht Frei,* "Work makes us free." I express surprise at how small the gate seems, compared to its mythic dimensions in my mind, and at the intimate scale of the camp itself, which resembles a tidy European hamlet with handsome brick buildings laid out in a neat grid. "Big enough," Peter remarks. He's been here before and knows what lies ahead. Our group's guide, a stylish, well-informed young Polish woman, leads us efficiently through several of the buildings, which house various exhibits. Entire rooms full of suitcases, shoes, household goods, hairbrushes and combs, and women's hair, which was to be used for stuffing mattresses. A massive accumulation of ordinary human objects that represents only a small fraction of the remnants of a million lives. This is our initiation into the physical reality, the true scale and scope, of Auschwitz.

The entire group reconvenes at the killing wall, an execution ground between two buildings with boarded-up windows. The ground in front of the wall is covered with bouquets and candles. We say Kaddish, the Jewish prayer for the dead, in the original Aramaic and in several translations. As we pray here, strong emotions break through the shock brought on by immersion in the atrocity exhibitions. Many weep openly. Others stand with heads bowed. We have gotten in touch with the task before us.

The rest of the retreat follows a simple schedule: after breakfast and small group discussions, we walk the two kilometers from our lodgings in Oswiecim, where Auschwitz I is located, to Birkenau, the larger of the two camps, a huge, efficient factory of death. We follow the railway tracks that bisect the grounds and that lead, ultimately, to the crematoria at the far end. We form a large circle at the former selection site along the tracks and sit in meditation all morning. People at four points along the circle take turns reading names, taken from Nazi archives, of individuals—and whole families—who were killed here. The voices sometimes catch on unfamiliar Eastern European names or break into weeping. The unusual cadence settles over us with the ground-hugging mist.

We break into smaller groups for prayer services—Jewish, Christian, Buddhist, and Sufi—then follow the haunting sound of the *shofar* (ram's horn) to the ruins of one of the crematoria where we again chant Kaddish. The group disperses and slowly walks back the length of the camp to the main gate for the midday meal. Bread and a bowl of hot soup, served and eaten with no spoon—the way prisoners ate. Here, possession of a utensil ranked you among the very fortunate.

After lunch, we follow the tracks back into Birkenau. More sitting, more names. The heavy mist turns to a cold rain, so we crowd into one of the drafty barracks, which offers marginal protection. Candles are placed along the concrete latrine that runs down the center of the room. We sit on the packed earth floor and sing Kaddish. Then a Rom woman begins a plaintive song from the Gypsies who were brought here. She falters, and her husband quietly takes up the song. The rough wooden walls absorb the sound like parched earth soaking up rainwater.

One afternoon, as the group gathers to sit, a few people drift off toward the neat rows of buildings and the birch forest that lent Birkenau its name. I am among them. I walk for hours, pausing only occasionally to read one of the information panels placed around the camp. I pass the former site of Mengele's "laboratory." And a clearing in the woods where trainloads of new arrivals were forced to wait their turn, in sight of the crematoria operating at full capacity, smoke billowing from the chimneys.

Walking is a pilgrim's practice, but in Birkenau it feels like an escape attempt, as if by staying in motion I might outpace the anguish that permeates the very ground. I want to take the measure of this place: perhaps by walking its vastness I may be able to grasp its enormity in my mind. But understanding eludes me, and grief soon overtakes me.

All pilgrimages involve a degree of risk and sacrifice. Yet whatever discomfort I might experience pales in comparison to what hundreds of thousands endured in this place. It is hubris to think that I can truly imagine what it would have been like to have been imprisoned here. I am not Jewish, nor a member of one of the other European populations the Nazis deemed inferior and expendable.

The one characteristic I share with those "lives not worthy of being lived," in the twisted Nazi ideology, is my homosexuality. Zen teacher Pat Enkyo O'Hara asked me to bear witness when I came here to "the latest incarnation of this kind of hatred in the world." I honor her request and invoke the name of Matthew Shepard when it is my turn to read. But the difficulty of collapsing the wall between victim and perpetrator remains. It is far easier to identify with the oppressed than with the oppressor, especially here. The deepest challenge of Auschwitz-Birkenau is to recognize the human totality of this place, in all its guises and faces.

During an evening discussion, Roshi Bernie Glassman remarks that, for him, "The place is the teacher." We are encouraged to "become intimate" with Auschwitz-Birkenau. On my solitary walk I notice the unnerving formal beauty of the camp, the evidence of

Bauhaus-era design in the stanchions and watchtowers. I see semaphores in the shapes of twisted barbed wire; I take in the pastel hues of the stones lining the tracks, the delicate layer of moss on the caved-in roof of a crematorium, the reflection of stately birches on the glassy surface of a pond where the ashes of thousands were dumped. A friend tells me of Elie Wiesel's comment, on returning to Auschwitz for a memorial ceremony: "I didn't know it would be so beautiful."

And I see too that the rigorous symmetry of the electric fences, the intersecting lines of tracks, the grid of the barracks, the precisely placed guard towers, all support a specific function. The structure of the camp—physical and psychological—enforced separation of people: from their families and possessions; from their community, culture, religion, and language; from their dignity and integrity; from solidarity with others; and ultimately from their very lives. Genocidal programs, now as then, are based on the principle of radical separation, designed to cleave certain human beings from the body of humanity itself.

Reflecting on this, I grow to appreciate what our group—a diverse mix of personalities, ethnicities, nationalities, cultural and religious traditions, including Holocaust survivors, the relatives of survivors, and the relatives of former Nazis—represents. Our pilgrimage here is a corrective response, a stance of resistance, to the deadly separation between people that feeds divisiveness, conflict, and violence throughout the world.

Over the course of the days here I also come to a deeper appreciation of the Zen Peacemaker Order's tenets that frame the retreat: Not Knowing, Bearing Witness, Healing. Never before has the classic Zen injunction to abide in "not knowing," with all its layers of meaning, felt so intensely palpable. I do not know, cannot fully know, the suffering held by this place. I cannot really even fathom it, yet I can bear witness to its lingering traces. Bearing witness calls me to complete presence, asks me to open, again and again, to the entire range of responses evoked by this place—disbelief, numbness, rage, guilt, despair, sorrow, gratitude, compassion, even joy.

Healing turns out to be the most difficult and subtle tenet of the three. For some, coming to terms with their own histories of denial, separation, and suffering brings a sense of wholeness; for others, whose lives have never been free of the shadow of the Holocaust, healing remains elusive—especially if it demands forgiveness. But just as with bodily disease, being healed does not necessarily equal being cured. Healing the spirit may not require forgiving all wrongs and wrongdoers—an impossible task for some—but fully acknowledging suffering and its roots in hatred and delusion.

Healing, in whatever form it may take, is a divine blessing. Perhaps it is the hidden boon received by some from this uneasy place of pilgrimage. For me, the gift of Auschwitz is instead a new wound: a wider heart, stretched beyond what I believed was its capacity—a broken-open heart.

(1999)

IMPOSSIBLE CHOICES

Maia Duerr

I used to live in a state mental hospital, the kind you see in the movies: a red brick building sitting on a lone hill, screams emanating from the barred windows, people wandering around the well-manicured grounds talking to themselves.

I wasn't there as a patient—I doubt that I would feel comfortable disclosing this honestly to you right now if I had been. My job as a music therapist brought me inside those walls every day, and for a while, I lived in the hospital dormitory with other staff. My first day there, I was petrified and wondered if I would be hacked to death by someone in a psychotic rage—a fear no doubt greatly influenced by headlines like one that actually appeared in 1999 in the *New York Daily News*: "Get the Violent Crazies off Our Streets." My fears gradually dissipated as I came to know the patients as people rather than diagnoses. After three years of working at the hospital, I felt safer there than on many city streets. But it always pulled at my conscience that I locked up patients in the wards behind me as I went home each day.

Over the next ten years, I worked in a number of other positions in the mental health system. Eventually, I became burned out, but not for the reasons you might think. It wasn't the people I worked with who frustrated me—it was the system within which we all had to navigate. I witnessed the revolving door of patients going out of the hospital and into the community only to be readmitted a short time later. It seemed to me that we were missing an essential piece. My work required me to come up with treatment plans for the "rehabilitation" of my clients, but I kept wondering how being avoided, feared, pitied, locked up, and medicated to the point of oblivion affected a person's mental health, beyond any psychiatric challenge he or she faced.

I reached a low point one day when I was working as an outreach counselor in Oregon. I was scheduled to see my favorite client, Joe. Joe and I couldn't have been more different—he was a large man in his forties, with a nose ring, homemade tattoos, and a diagnosis of paranoid schizophrenia. I was in my early thirties, trying to be an upwardly mobile professional. He'd spent most of his life in the Oregon mental health system, a good part of it hospitalized for psychotic episodes that were worsened by his use of marijuana and harder street drugs. I had lived a fairly conventional, privileged life, and my knowledge of drugs was limited to a few puffs on a joint (I did inhale). And yet, after three years of working together and getting to know each other, Joe and I had developed a strong bond. I knew the things he loved best—going fishing and drinking coffee—and I was lucky enough to work for an agency that realized the therapeutic value of developing genuine, trusting relationships with our clients. So Joe and I did plenty of fishing and coffee drinking in between more mundane tasks like finding him a safe place to live and straightening out his Social Security benefits.

On this bright spring day, I drove to his house in the ancient, rattling agency car and caught a glimpse of snow on the MacKenzie Mountains in the distance. I wondered what I would encounter when I saw him: reports from coworkers were that he had been acting "crazy" lately.

When I got to the house, I noticed that the hallway light bulb had been painted red, giving the room an eerie glow. I found Joe in the backyard burning a pile of magazines. In the friendliest voice I could muster, I told him that he needed to stop because the city fire code prohibited burning and the neighbors might call the fire department. Though he usually gave me a warm greeting, this time he glared at me and growled, "I have to do this. And don't call me Joe. That's not me. That's some other sorry son-of-a-bitch who was locked up in the hospital. Why are you calling me that?"

I got a glimpse of his hands; the skin was peeling off and it looked like he had burned or poured some chemical on them. I sighed heavily. "Here we go again," I thought to myself. I walked around to the side of the yard and saw a can of gasoline.

"Joe, have you been sniffing gas?" (This was something he did when he began to, in the professional jargon, "decompensate.")

He became angrier. "I told you not to call me that! Why do you accuse me of doing these things? Why can't I get any peace around here?"

His voice was hoarse. It was obvious that he had been yelling at other people besides me. His housemates, who looked like they'd had just about enough of Joe, moved around discreetly behind us and left the house. I found out from them that he had been up all night flushing large objects down the toilet and keeping his housemates awake. He told me there was nothing wrong, then he told me that he was Johnny Cash.

I lectured him about taking his meds, and I told him that I was concerned for his safety. Joe replied that all he needed was a pat on the back and a cup of coffee, but it seemed to me that we were beyond that point. My presence was only agitating him more, so I returned to the office and worked out a plan with my coworkers to get him into the hospital. There was a deep pit in my stomach. He would not go to the hospital willingly; I knew this from experience. If I called the police, they would handcuff him and load him into the squad car like a criminal, in full view of all the neighbors. In the hospital (which was located in the same building as the county jail), he would be stripped of his clothing and possessions, locked in a small "cell," and tied down and forcibly injected with Haldol, an antipsychotic drug notorious for its wretched side effects. I knew this routine from experience, too. If I didn't call the police, he might end up, as he had in the past, standing in the middle of a highway and daring people to run him over. (Though he looked intimidating, Joe never hurt anyone; his angst was always turned on himself.) What could I do?

I ended up calling the police, and the scenario played out much as I expected. But after a week of hospitalization, Joe was discharged and back to his friendly self. He was even grateful to me for getting him there, though he retained horrible memories of the "incarceration" itself. He had a few more "good" months before the same cycle repeated itself, as it had many previous times in his life.

I no longer work in the mental health system, and it's been a long time since I've had to choose between calling the police to commit someone to the hospital or letting them self-destruct. Still, as I walk through downtown San Francisco and pass a young man talking to himself in tortured tones, I know that some other mental health worker is faced with these same impossible choices. The questions and moral choices I faced during those years continued to haunt me. Eventually, I found that subsequent training as a cultural anthropologist and my Buddhist practice helped me to understand those experiences from another point of view.

The issue of how to treat people with mental illness brings up many ethical questions: What do we do when a person clearly needs some kind of psychiatric help yet refuses it? To what extent do we let self-determination rule over societal safety? At what point does freedom of expression cross the line into harassment or endangerment?

But maybe there is another way to look at things. As socially engaged Buddhists, we can reframe these questions to encompass a larger perspective. How is our view of mental illness grounded in a dualistic viewpoint? How can we heal the separation that comes from dividing people into "mentally ill" and "normal"? How can we create treatment approaches that operate from an assumption of healing, not coercion? How can we cultivate a society that has more openness to different ways of being in the world?

A Buddhist perspective calls for us to apply our understanding of interconnectedness to this issue. Mental illness is no longer an individual matter, a case of one person's psyche gone awry, but rather it sits in the context of our society and culture. Emotional suffering and mental distress may be a universal experience, but the ways they manifest are unique from place to place. By way of illustration, a 1980 study by the World Health Organization found that the incidence of the bundle of symptoms known as schizophrenia was about the same in nine different countries, but people in developing countries without formal mental health services recovered more quickly than people in areas that had hospitals and medications.

In working with Joe, I noticed that there was a distinct difference between his "normal" craziness and the kind that got him into trouble. He could often keep a handle on things until faced with the Kafkaesque maze of social service systems that he had to navigate to get his disability benefits. I also saw him go into spirals of psychosis when he felt socially isolated and not seen by others. In contrast, I saw him blossom when someone thanked him for his efforts to clean up the town. (He saw it as his job to keep the streets clean and spent hours picking up trash in the most squalid neighborhoods.) It was a gift to see his face light up in a coffee shop when a waitress was kind to him rather than dismissive because of his admittedly strange appearance, and several "good," lucid days would usually follow. It was clear to me that it wasn't simply the whims of his psychiatric condition that dictated his mental state.

The biomedical system, the predominant approach to illness in the West, has done an excellent job of making us believe that the most effective (and often the only) way to treat mental illness is with medications. But you don't often hear about the horrific side effects of these medications, sometimes worse than the symptoms they are intended to treat, and the fact that drug prescribing is still essentially a guessing game. You don't hear about the conflict of interest in having psychotropic drug research funded by pharmaceutical companies with a huge financial incentive to generate certain findings. The biomedical model, with its focus on biological causes, also tends to cut off dialogue on other conditions that can affect mental health. A number of ex-patients whom I interviewed found that medications were beneficial to them at some points in their life, but felt that there should be awareness that it may obscure the deeper, social dimensions of the problem.

A socially engaged Buddhist perspective will lead us to inquire about our obligation to treat not only the person but also the environment that has contributed to the conditions that create suffering. Thich Nhat Hanh wrote about this eloquently in *The Path of Compassion*:

> Restoring mental health does not mean simply adjusting individuals to the modern world of rapid economic growth. The world is ill, and adapting to an ill environment cannot bring real mental health. . . . Psychiatric treatment requires environmental

change and psychiatrists must participate in efforts to change the environment, but that is only half the task. The other half is to help individuals be themselves, not by helping them adapt to an ill environment, but by providing them with the strength to change it. To tranquilize them is not the Way. The explosion of bombs, the burning of napalm, the violent death of our neighbors and relatives, the pressure of time, noise, and pollution, the lonely crowds—these have all been created by the disruptive course of our economic growth. They are all sources of mental illness, and they must be ended.

Wonderful words—but still, what do you do when you see someone in immense mental suffering and on the verge of either harming themselves or someone else, and they refuse help? Maybe we need to rethink our definition of "help."

It may seem that the choices are limited, as I experienced during my time working in the field. Since then, I have learned about other kinds of treatment approaches, some of them even rooted in Buddhist practice. Windhorse, for example, is a treatment community in Northampton, Massachusetts, that places the cultivation of attention to body, mind, and environment and the development of compassion at the center of its philosophy of healing. The first Windhorse center was established in 1981 through the Naropa Institute in Boulder, Colorado, by Jeff and Molly Fortuna and Dr. Edward Podvoll, who drew on their background in both Eastern and Western psychology to develop a holistic treatment approach. Medication may or may not be a part of treatment, but when used, it is within the context of other health-enhancing practices such as nutrition, stress reduction, rest, and exercise.

Another key to deepening our understanding is to listen to the people who are really the experts on this subject: those who have received services from the mental health system. A growing number of these people identify themselves as "consumers" and "survivors." Collectively, they make up a movement similar to other social movements that address issues of institutionalized oppression. This movement challenges us to think outside of the medical definition of "mental illness," and to consider human rights concerns and how economic and political realities affect people living with a psychiatric disability.

There are no easy answers to the ethical dilemmas inherent in taking care of those who are emotionally troubled or who operate outside the social norms. At one time or another we all have been or will be in those categories. It's easy to get tangled up in debates about the "myth of mental illness," to use Thomas Szasz's phrase. But this is more than a philosophical debate—it's about the level of compassion we have for those of us in dire straits. Perhaps the best contribution we can make as Buddhists is to ask the questions differently and to offer our understanding of the endless web of conditions, biological and otherwise, that are part of the joy and suffering in each of our lives.

(2002)

NOWHERE TO RUN: PORTRAITS OF LIFE ON THE STREET

Tony Patchell

Tony Patchell is a psychotherapist who works with the Homeless Program at the Tom Waddell Clinic in San Francisco. The clinic, part of the Department of Public Health, serves people who live on the margins of society: homeless, drug users, alcoholics, poor people with AIDS. As a case manager, Tony serves his clients in many ways: from obtaining housing and health care, to buying shoes and bus tickets, to summoning the coroner, if it comes to that.

The accounts that follow are excerpts from the personal/work journal Tony has kept since 1992. The names of Tony's clients have been changed.

WEDNESDAY, JANUARY 22

It's very, very cold outside. Homeless folks are wet, miserable, all problems intensified by the bad weather. The temporary shelter in the old KGO building is bedlam. The women's low-ceilinged room is jammed full. Lots of young, loud, black people are teasing an old white lady who finally screams and picks up a metal folding chair and slings it like a frisbee across the room. It slams against the wall with a loud crash. The young folks laugh and jump up and down and clap their hands. Those who were asleep wake up with a start, eyes tired and wide. They look around and roll back up in their blankets on the floor along the walls, trying to escape the confusion. Four black queens are camping it up at a table in the middle of the room, whirling about, dancing, talking dirty, shoving their faux tits at the men along one wall who are in line waiting for medical services, and generally enjoying themselves.

Mary Mays shows me her exam room. It's down a short narrow hall. She has to shove the door open with her shoulder. The room is actually a closet, maybe six by eight feet. Mary uses a plank set across two metal chairs for an exam table, to do pelvics, etc. She works out of her backpack. The line out the door is one long train of coughs and sniffles. I see Priscilla in the line. She is depressed, using crack. She smells like old piss, which means she is not taking care of her diabetes, as usual.

WEDNESDAY, JANUARY 29

Woke up this A.M. with the unwanted thought that Anita has killed herself or managed to get herself murdered. I feel light-bodied and irritated. I sit and stare at the walls, take an hour to get up the nerve to go to Anita's hotel. I finally get up and go to the Tenderloin. Anita answers her door all cheerful. So much for my fabled intuition. More like burnout, I guess. Anita will forever be a problem for someone. She's pushing forty and is a third-generation prostitute. She grew up on the Lower East Side, NYC. When she was three years old, her mother set her on fire. Child Protective Services later returned her to her mom.

Once when Anita was six years old, social workers stopped by to check up on things and found her locked in a small bathroom, sitting on the floor playing with a doll. There was a dead junkie crammed into the bathtub and another corpse sitting on the toilet with a spike still stuck in his arm. When eleven years old, Anita was sold into prostitution. Five years later she was rescued by a sixteen-year-old boy, and they ran off and got married. A few months later, in the middle of the night while they were asleep, a bunch of Colombians broke into their room, held her husband down, and castrated him before stabbing him to death. They held Anita down and made her watch, and then they stabbed her thirteen times and left her for dead. This was retribution for a perceived dope rip-off.

Went with Marian to San Jose to a locked psych facility to visit Barbara Anderson. We first met Barbara at the temporary shelter last November. The other women called her "Stinky" and cleared a path wherever she went. Barbara is a forty-two-year-old white woman. When we found her she was so dirty she looked like a coal miner. Dirt, black and shiny, covered her face and arms. She went around barefoot with a rag hanging off her. When she had her period, she just let the blood run. It would mix with the street dirt on her legs and feet, and cake up into sticky black patches that would flake and peel and give off the odor of rotten meat. She did this on purpose to keep the predators away. Every isolated home-less woman is at any moment vulnerable to assault, rape, homicide, whatever. Barbara's mode of self-defense was to be so filthy that even the most depraved creeps and pigs would go out of their way to avoid her. At one time she had been a successful writer and had been married to a big-time attorney in Arizona. Out of nowhere she had some sort of psychotic break and it's been downhill ever since. Now she is locked up, probably for the rest of her life. It could happen to anybody. Blindsided and betrayed by your own brain, down, down, and out you go into the street, easy pickings for the vultures.

Barbara spends most of her time in her room with the door open. Staff and other patients like her. She is no trouble, shares her roll-your-own cigarettes, and remains preoccupied with her inter-nal world, which, she tells me, is full of "darkness, blood-screams, slivers of glass piercing my eyeballs, apocalypse fire, bodies in the street, rumbling from deep in the earth." Barbara has an East Coast private school accent. Every syllable is clearly enunciated while she keeps her teeth clenched together, like Sigourney Weaver or Jane Fonda. Her eyes are pale gray and she looks right through you when she's talking. I keep thinking that in some other time and place, Bar-bara would have been a poet, a saint, a magic woman.

Start my week, as usual, at the Ambassador Hotel. My first chore is to break up a lover's quarrel between Linda Kerrigan and Daniel Sanchez. I can hear them screaming at one another as I climb the stairs. I bang on their door and walk right in. Linda is backed up in a corner with a kitchen knife extended out. Daniel is trying to hit her with a can of peas. Linda has a big bump on her head, a swollen wrist, and deep-purple, finger-sized contusions around her throat. Daniel has one black eye swollen shut and fingernail gouges down his left cheek. The room smells like dirty socks and garbage. They have been drinking vodka and smoking crack all weekend. I begin my sophisticated couples' counseling by screaming, "What the fuck are you doing? Put that goddamn stuff down. Empty your hands."

They both do so with obvious relief and then each accuses the other of starting it all. Daniel is a full-blooded Apache. He has killed at least five men. He says, "I never killed a white woman before, but there's always a goddamn first time." Daniel is shirtless and covered with jailhouse tattoos. He has a full-size Colt .45 automatic tattooed under his left arm. Daniel has a hernia. The muscle wall below his navel is ripped and a grapefruit-sized lump of intestines protrudes out, held intact only by his skin. He tells me angrily that Linda had kicked him in that precise spot. I pick up the knife and the can of peas and put them on the windowsill. I sit Linda and Daniel down on their bed and get them to swear on the graves of their respective mothers not to harm each other until we find another place for Linda to stay.

TUESDAY, JUNE 9

Thomas Stillman, the Radio Man, comes into the clinic with his own peculiar brand of unpleasantness. The implanted radios are going full blast, sending him constant messages about the conspiracies against him. He's an old hippie-looking dude with an easy-going, country smile. I find out that he did seven years in the pen in Washington State for fucking his seven-year-old daughter, the numbers being a sort of coincidental quid pro quo. I think they should have locked up the poor, crazy motherfucker for life. "She really wanted it," he tells me, "I know she did." I find out later that he once hit another child so hard upside the head that he killed her, and did little or no time for it. Today he is making sure I know that he is closely associated with Jesse James. I tend to believe it. I cannot help but imagine the hell he lives in and, even worse, the suffering he has put on others. It does not surprise me, however, that he is running around loose. Your parking meter runs out of time—count on swift reprisal by the government in the form of at least a ticket. Rape and kill a child, do some time, plead crazy, which you certainly are, and you're eligible for free legal assistance, disability benefits, and state-subsidized health care. Am I bitter and confused? Am I moving to the right? The idea of just not thinking things through is, at times, very, very attractive. Thomas will, I know, get his benefits. His desire is to move to the desert to get away from the radio waves.

WEDNESDAY, NOVEMBER 4

Paul W's paranoia is on the loose again. He pages me at 10 A.M. Negative command hallucinations, a chorus of loud, raucous, derogatory voices urging him to kill. After a certain point in the process, the voices seem to come directly from innocent passers-by on the street. They start calling him names and then dare him to do something about it. He becomes more confused, more frightened, and loses the distinction between inner and outer worlds. Many years ago he killed a man at the urging of the voices and did seventeen years in the joint for it. He is terrified that this will happen again and he does his very best to prevent it. I have never known anyone to work so hard at staying sane. I can't help but think of him as some sort of unique saint, one with integrity and the clearest intention, for he knows that by staying sane he will not kill people or cause suffering.

THURSDAY, DECEMBER 3

The work day starts with Ozmo, Richard, Christine, and I having a cup of coffee upstairs at Pastel's, the coffee shop at the juncture of Polk, Fell, and Market. While discussing our cases we look out the window on the Fell Street side and watch a thin white woman in her late thirties, blond, in a tan beret, a darkly stained light blue turtleneck sweater, Levis, and a black knee-length coat wander through the three lanes of fast-moving traffic. As she gets closer and meanders under our window, we see that she is covered with blood. Christine and I go downstairs and out into the street to see what's up. Her name, she tells us, is "Marianne DeRoulat." She spells it out in a flat, nasty tone. I think of her as Blanche DuBois with a mean streak. She is a mess; someone gave her a thorough beating. Her nose is obviously broken, mashed flat, bloody, and sideways into her face. There is a wide, crusty laceration across the bridge. Her lower lip is split open and there is a tennis-ball-sized lump on the hinge of her right jaw. She has been crying and her mascara has run down her face in smeared, black lines. She is holding a soggy wad of paper towels in one hand and a half-eaten burrito in the other. Frijoles are dripping out one end onto her sweater and the tortilla is also soaked with blood. A half pint of vodka is sticking out of her coat pocket. Her speech is slurred but easy to understand.

"This is out of character for me," she says. "I will not go to the Ivy Street Clinic. I will not go to the hospital. I will not go to detox." She wanders away. I and a few other bystanders follow her and try to convince her to get treatment.

We pass an office building where a number of people are standing around smoking cigarettes. Two yuppies, white guys, are leaning against the wall. She pulls a butt out of the standing ashtray by the door and saunters up to them, all the while leaving a small trail of blood splatters, and asks them politely for a light. The two men, astoundingly, go on with their conversation as if she were not there. She, a thin, bloody wraith, moves closer to them, right into their faces. She waves her bloody burrito around and asks, once again, for a light. This time the men respond. One guy shrinks, presses himself against the wall. He cringes, arms crossed against his chest, hands flapping from his wrists. His eyes are wide and his mouth is tight and downturned. He is clearly in a panic and I am surprised to find that his pain touches me almost as much as hers. The other guy gets it together and quickly lights her cigarette, to which she replies softly and with great sarcasm, "Thank you very much."

WEDNESDAY, SEPTEMBER 1

At Sixth and Market, a shaggy young white guy weaves and staggers down the sidewalk. He opens a can of beer, takes one long gulp, and showing good form all the while, takes a pitcher's stance, winds up, and hurls the can like a fastball straight at the windshield of a parked pickup truck. The can ricochets off the glass with a loud cracking sound. It shoots a good twenty feet straight up and whirls round and round in the air, sending long, loopy streams of golden foam pinwheeling into the sunlight where they dissolve, float, and drift on down the street. The drunk lets out a loud warwhoop of success.

THURSDAY, NOVEMBER 4

HIV meeting. Ten or twelve clients have died during the last two weeks, so, as we often do, we give the meeting over to paying our respects, remembering, telling stories and anecdotes. We allow room for our collective sense of humor that is usually quite sick and morbid. When the door is closed, we can say what we goddamn please, and this helps both the quick and the dead move on. Doug, one of our MDs, tells us that he and Basil took Alvah Hamilton to a baseball game at Candlestick last summer. The Braves were in town and they tend to draw a crowd. Their seats were in one of the upper decks. Alvah, his O2 tank rolling and bumping behind him, plastic tubes shoved up his nose and taped to his face, patiently made the trip to their seats without complaint. He was happy to be out in the air and sunshine. I wonder how many physicians in this town, in this country, would, on their own time, accompany a slow-moving, hypoxic, homeless, and dying patient to a baseball game.

I walk home up Market from Sixth. Pale horizontal sunlight shoots down the street from the west. Shambling people, noisy vehicles, scrubby little piss-poisoned trees, all in black and white. Thick streamers of fog roll over Twin Peaks and a cold wind whips the trash around in little circles. The homeward bound and the homeless alike hunch up their shoulders and walk faster.

MONDAY, JULY 26

Monday morning, bright and sunny. I start the week off, as usual, by walking down Market to the Ambassador. Cissy, one of my most favorite clients and a success story in that she is off drugs, is going to school, has a job, and is not in jail, walks with me. We strategize about getting her kids out of foster care and back with her. Every man and half the women on the street check her out. She's wearing wraparound sunglasses, a tight, yellow tank top and white Levis. She strides like a man, long straight-legged steps, and her biceps and pectorals move with her walk. Her skin is brown and shiny and she has a don't-fuck-with-me attitude that works like a charm on the streets.

TUESDAY, SEPTEMBER 7

An easy day for a change. Bright and sunny with a slow, cool ocean breeze. Around noon, I walk to Civic Center Park and join a moderate-sized crowd of spectators who are watching the police fight crime directly across the street from City Hall. The criminals in this case being the "Food Not Bombs" people, the crime being their giving out free food to an obviously hungry crowd of forty or fifty homeless men and women.

I watch the food servers pull four large plastic buckets of vegetable soup from the back of a van. The cops walk over, take the buckets, carry them to the curb, and empty them into the gutter. The food people leave and come back within ten minutes with more soup and two large grocery bags full of bagels. The cops also take this soup and dump it. One cop turns the two grocery bags upside down and dozens of bagels hit the sidewalk. Tourists, both foreign and domestic, are watching with curious, confused, and disbelieving looks. Office workers from nearby buildings and the homeless are also watching, but they've seen it many times before.

The third van load of soup shows up, and with it two young people with video cameras. So this time the cops take the buckets of soup and place them in the trunks of their black and whites. Their shiny boots crunch and flatten the donated bagels as they go about their work. They close the trunk lids and take off to dump the food somewhere else. That's it, no more soup.

Spectators drift away back to work or back to being tourists. The homeless go back to the park benches and the patches of grass. A few yards away nickel/dime crack deals, which had never stopped, continue into the afternoon.

(1996)

THERE WAS A GUN
IN THE HOUSE

Lynn Dix *interviewed by* Susan Moon

I talked with Lynn Dix in January, 1998. We have a lot in common: we are both Buddhists, both the middle-aged Berkeley mothers of two sons. But both of my sons are alive. Lynn's son Kenzo was killed four years ago in a gun accident.

We don't need to be persuaded that handguns can cause terrible tragedies. But we may need to be reminded that the possibility of such tragedy is not so far away, and that we are not separate from the ones whose children die. The victims of gun violence are everywhere among us. We must give up the notion that it's the job of the parents, and the parents alone, to keep their children safe from guns. That's not enough. It's the job of all of us to make the world safe for all of our children.

Kenzo was a student at Berkeley High School when he died. There's a mural of him on the handball court there.

In the interview that follows, Lynn shares the circumstances of her son's death, how her Buddhist practice helped her to cope with the tragedy, and her work to prevent the loss of other innocent lives to gun violence. —

—Susan Moon

I got a call from Kenzo on a Sunday afternoon. He was at a friend's house and wanted to stay for dinner.

Later that afternoon, there was a knock at our door. Two people from Social Services said something had happened on the street where Kenzo's friend lived, and that we needed to go immediately to Children's Hospital. That's all they could say.

So my husband and I went to Children's Hospital, and waited. Finally they told us that Kenzo had been accidentally shot to death by his friend. They had done everything to try to save him, but he died. Our world shattered at that point.

The detective who had interviewed the other boy explained to us that Kenzo wasn't shot in anger. One thing came to me clearly, then. I felt I had to tell the boy that we knew he didn't do it on purpose.

The way it happened was that the boy got his father's gun, which was kept loaded in a camera case next to the bed. He wanted to show it to Kenzo. He was quite proud that he had been taught to use a gun at a shooting range. He knew the semiautomatic was loaded, and so he removed the clip and inserted a blank. Then he ran up the stairs and got into a shooting stance, pointing it at my son, you know, as a joke. He called to him, released the safety, and pulled the trigger. It went off. He'd forgotten to remove the one bullet that's in the chamber.

I had no idea they had guns in the house. You can't rely on the kids to tell you, or gun owners to keep their guns stored safely. The gun manufacturers say that the way to handle it is to educate the kids—the famous "Eddie Eagle" program. Teach every kid the dangers of guns. But the fact is, that's not a reliable way to protect our kids, any more than telling your kids to stay away from medicine bottles is. You put safety caps on; it's much more effective.

My son was fifteen and the other boy was fourteen. Especially at that age, kids are fascinated by guns. Due to the entertainment industry, a gun has a certain aura; it gives you a feeling of power. When you have a gun around, you want to see it, and you want to see what it feels like to pull the trigger. There's a natural curiosity about it. But the gun actually puts everyone in the house in much more danger than if you didn't have one. The idea is to protect your family, but statistics show that someone in the house is three times more likely to die from a gun if you have one. People don't realize that the leading cause of death for children in California is guns.

I never imagined that anybody I knew would have a gun in the house, especially if their kids were there. You see shooting on television, but it's just not real. You don't feel the impact of it; you don't see what guns can really do to our bodies and our families.

It turns out that 50 percent of American homes have guns. And people don't tell you, of course. Had I known, I would have told the kids to come to my house to play instead.

A friend of mine in San Diego was talking about what happened to me and to Kenzo to a group of her friends. She's a professor and they were all professional people. She asked, "Do you guys have guns?" and some did. We can't say it's only people who live in dangerous parts of town. People who live in nice neighborhoods have guns, too. They think someone's going to break into their houses and take their computers. She said, "But how can you do that? You have kids." You never know, just as I didn't know.

Different things made it possible for me to keep going. Meditation helped a lot, to stop the spinning in the head. Not that it ever really stops, and not that I'm a very good meditator. But it helped. And friends and family really helped a lot. And the neighbors. We didn't know each other that well at first, but this really pulled us together.

The day after, two neighbors came over and asked if they could do anything. I couldn't think of anything I needed except fresh air, and I said, "If you want to go for a walk with me, let's go at three." I looked out the window at three and there must have been fifty or sixty neighbors, from a ninety-year-old woman to little children. And we all walked together.

I didn't go back to work for a long time, and I just took time to be with the pain. I took some comfort from the Buddhist teaching not to turn away from suffering. Not avoiding the pain was important, not carrying on as usual. I mean, you can't carry on as usual—there's no way. So I just felt the pain, even though it was scary.

It helped me to connect with other parents who had lost a child. Nobody can really understand unless they've gone through it. It's just beyond anything you can imagine. I talked to survivors of the 101 California Street shooting [a law office in San Francisco where eight people were shot to death by an irate businessman in 1993]. But everybody's at different stages, and sometimes it wasn't helpful to talk to them. Sometimes people were consumed by anger, even years later. I didn't want to become bitter. What good would that do?

Also, I didn't want Kenzo's life just to be here and then forgotten the next day. There had to be some heritage, something done in his memory. I wanted to do something to make sure that other children didn't die the way he died. And so I started to do work for gun control, though it was hard.

I've given interviews on television, on Oprah Winfrey, for example. And to newspapers and NPR. I testified before the California State Legislature on gun bills. One bill has to do with effective load indicators, so people know that the gun is loaded, because with most guns, you can't even tell that they are loaded. Also, Kenzo's father and I are bringing a product-safety lawsuit against the gun manufacturer.

Kenzo's life was positive, and I hope something positive will come from his death, to make the world safer for other kids—not just kids, but other people. That's why I do the interviews. It's hard to talk about your child's death, you know. But I do it because I hope it has some impact. Otherwise I wouldn't do it.

I know my speaking out has made a difference, because friends tell me that they've told my story to people they know, and as a result, families have gotten rid of their guns. You can't know what lives this may have saved.

I've also worked with Californians for Responsible Gun Laws, which is a very good organization. I've testified at different city council hearings on banning cheaply made guns called "Saturday Night Specials," and that's been very successful. Some thirty-four communities—cities and counties—in California have banned the sale and manufacture of Saturday Night Specials.

After Kenzo died, I only spoke a little to the father of the boy who shot him. What was there to say? He apologized. I asked him why he had a gun at his house and he said it was for protection. And that was basically it. People said to me, "Don't you want to go to his house and just scream and yell at him?" Of course there was anger, but even greater was the tremendous, heavy sadness in my heart, and that was the biggest thing. The sadness of not having my son anymore. There's his room, his clothing, but he's not at the dinner table to talk to us.

As for the other boy, he was charged with involuntary manslaughter because he was fourteen, and according to California law, the child is responsible if he's fourteen or older. In this kind of situation, the court wants to know what the parents of the victim want to see done. Buddhism helps you put yourself in other people's shoes. We said we wanted to make sure there was no gun in the house anymore. When we heard the options—sending him to a boot camp, or juvenile hall—we didn't think it would do him any good. It would have been totally counterproductive to put him in that kind of environment. He was already feeling terrible about himself and he would have come out worse. So I wrote a letter to the court saying that we hoped he would grow up to be a responsible citizen, and that the best way that that would be served would be for him to remain in the custody of his parents, but not have any guns in the house. So that's what happened. It's not enforceable, by the way. Nobody's going to go check the house.

Buddhism helps, because you try to see things as they really are. I work for nonviolent solutions, but I try to understand why people would want guns. I try to take their perspective. What if the only people who had guns were the government? Depending on the government, that wouldn't be very good. Being in the Buddhist Peace Fellowship, I hope to talk to other people who are thinking about this. I think about the Indians in Chiapas who had no guns and were slaughtered. And I think: if they had guns, would they have been safer from attack? Or would they have lost the sympathy and attention of the international community?

The tendency is to demonize gun manufacturers and gun owners. I think about the Dalai Lama and how he doesn't want to alienate the Chinese. He says we should continue to communicate with them; they're people, too. It's important for me to understand that people who have a gun in their house may really believe they need it. So we should treat them respectfully, and not just call them "bad guys" and "gun nuts."

There's a better chance of reconciliation if we understand where they're coming from and see what solution we can come to together.

If you're concerned about guns, there are things you can do. First of all, keep informed, and contact legislators on bills that are coming up, because that has had an impact. A phone call or a fax at the right time makes a difference.

Although designed to kill, guns were excluded from the Consumer Product Safety Act in 1972, because legislators gave in to political pressure from the NRA. In a country where almost forty thousand people are killed by guns every year, guns need to be regulated. If any kind of product should have safety standards, it's guns.

Also, and I know this seems strange, just ask people if there are guns in the house. Especially if you have children, before you send your children there, ask if there are guns in the house and how they're stored. If you're hesitant to ask, just tell them that you heard a woman speak about how she lost her son, and you were moved by her story. If you need an excuse to ask, I'll be the excuse, because it happened to me. And I didn't think to ask.

(1998)

JUST TRUST YOURSELF

Wendy Egyoku Nakao

I fell into Zen practice quite by accident. It was the summer of 1975. My husband and I had just bought a house in Seattle and were in the middle of remodeling it. I was attending a summer program at the University of Washington, and the teacher announced that there would be a Zen *sesshin*—a meditation retreat—for seven days on Vashon Island, a small island in Puget Sound. I thought, "Gee, that sounds interesting."

I went up to the teacher and said, "I want to do this retreat." And he said simply, "Okay." No questions like, "Have you ever meditated? Do you know what you're getting into?" I told him many years later that it must have been because I have an Asian face that he assumed I knew all about meditation, but I knew nothing.

When I returned home, I told my husband and a friend who was visiting, "A Zen retreat is going to happen on an island in Puget Sound—you sit still and are quiet for seven days." Our friend said to me, "I'll bet you fifty bucks you can't do that." And I said, "Okay, I'm doing it!" My husband was not at all thrilled about this, but he went along with my little plan.

I took a ferry to Vashon Island with a group of people I had never met. There were about fifteen of us. We sat in an old Baptist retreat center for seven days, and it was absolutely grueling. The retreat was led by a Soto Zen priest who spoke no English. We sat for fifty-minute periods. Then the priest would ring a bell, we'd unfold our legs, and then he'd ring the bell again and we'd fold our legs back up and sit for another fifty minutes. I'd never been in a situation like that.

We did walking meditation for about twenty minutes after lunch, and the rest of the time we were put through this difficult regimen. I had no idea what was happening to me. Every so often the priest would quote Dogen Zenji, whom I had never heard of, and I'd think, "What in the world?!"

I don't know why, but it never occurred to me to leave that retreat. Perhaps because it was hard to get off the island. And besides, I was totally mesmerized. When the retreat ended, I went directly home, walked into the house, and said to my husband, "I'm leaving you." Just like that. "I don't know how to tell you this," I said, "but I haven't the foggiest notion who I am." When I think about it today, it sounds so trite! I said, "All I know is that I need to get out of here."

And that was the beginning of my Zen journey. Everyone who knew me then thought I was crazy.

When my mother called my husband, asking for me, he said, "She left."

"What do you mean, she left?" she asked.

He replied, "She doesn't know who she is."

Well, it's been a great journey, this journey of not knowing who "I" am. I've learned to trust the unfolding of life. If there's one message I have for all of us today, it's trust yourself. Students come to me wanting to know: Should they do this or should they do that?

And I say, "Trust yourself. Just trust yourself as the buddha-dharma. Is that so difficult?" Yes, it is.

One day during my early years at the Zen Center of Los Angeles, my teacher, Maezumi Roshi, asked me, very quietly, "Egyoku, what does it mean to be a woman?" I was in my early thirties, and I'd never thought about it! What does it mean to be a woman? He was asking me not for my answer, but so that I could turn the question over and over and over. It's a question I still come back to. At times I've hated this question, and thought it was a big pain in the ass, to put it bluntly. At times I've wondered why none of my dharma sisters were asking this question. And at times I've wondered why my dharma sisters *were* asking this question. And today, I come back to this question.

In the summer of 1996, I was preparing for dharma transmission with Roshi Bernie Tetsugen Glassman in Yonkers, New York, and part of the preparation was to do a solitary retreat and study our lineage. Roshi Glassman was about to remodel a convent that had been owned by a group of cloistered nuns for about seventy years. Their order had shrunk to the point where they had to sell the building.

So we decided that I would do my week of practice in this enormous three-story convent, and I moved in with an attendant. The nuns had left, and the remodeling had not quite started. I thought it would be scary but it was the most peaceful space. I could feel the spirit of the women who had lived there, keeping their round-the-clock vigils for all those years.

My retreat was mainly about the lineage—a long list of Patriarchs, from start to finish. There I was, at least three times a day, bowing to all these guys. And once a day, Roshi Glassman would come and ask, "How are you doing?"

I would reply, "Where are all the women? We need written documents about the transmission of women."

And he said, "You write it."

That was my beginning point in consciously acknowledging and supporting women in Buddhist practice. From a long, long time ago, and even longer ago than that, there were women, like you and me, practicing. Women have always accomplished the Way. But I hadn't been aware of that for most of the years of my training. We have practiced, we have manifested, we have realized, we have accomplished. There's no question about it. And it was important for me to acknowledge the obvious and say, "Hey, that's the way it is. That's the way it's always been." So I wrote down these thoughts: "The spiritual attainment and practice of women has flowed in a continuous yet sometimes hidden stream down to the present time. You and I are entrusted with this lineage. Please cherish it forever." Isn't it the most wonderful thing?

In the *Lotus Sutra*, Shakyamuni Buddha proclaimed the attainment of buddhahood for women—for the nun Prajapati, for the nun Yasodhara, for the six thousand female disciples present. And yet we've had to struggle, haven't we? We've had to rediscover, reconnect, reclaim, and rejoice. I love all those words; each one reveals some aspect of our journey.

After Maezumi Roshi died, I moved to Yonkers, New York. I returned to the Zen Center of Los Angeles several times to help sort through his belongings. It was a long and sad process. During one of my trips, a dharma brother of mine was leading a *sesshin*. He said to me, "By the way, I told everyone that you're going to give the talk tomorrow."

And I said, "Did you happen to mention what I am going to talk about?

"Yes," he said, "I told them you're going to talk about women. There are a lot of young women new to practice here, and all they have is an old geezer like me. Why don't you say something about being a woman in practice?"

"Okay, I'll say something."

I went to the zendo the next day and began to talk about the trials and tribulations of being a woman in Zen practice—this very masculine, male-dominated, Japanese, hierarchical form. And as I talked, a young woman in the back row began to cry. She cried and she cried. I wondered to myself: Did she lose a child? Her partner? Does she have an illness? But it would have been intrusive to ask her, so I just kept talking, and looking out of the corner of my eye at this beautiful woman just sobbing her heart out.

Days later, at the end of the *sesshin*, my dharma brother told me, "She's still crying."

"Why is she crying?" I asked, "I would like to know why she's crying."

He said, "When she came to see me this morning, I asked her as gently as I could why she was crying. And she said, 'I'm crying because I didn't know that a Buddha could be a woman.'"

She's a religious studies major now and writing a paper on women in Buddhism. Recently she interviewed me. I said, "I'll never forget the way you were sobbing in that zendo." My eyes teared up just recalling that moment, and I asked, "What was it?"

She said, "I felt this energy in me, and it was unstoppable. I felt something move in me that I hadn't even known was there. They were tears of discovery." It's amazing how such an obvious thing has been so hidden, so hidden from ourselves.

Maezumi Roshi was a strong proponent of women's practice, in spite of the system he came out of. Before any of us even thought of asking the question about women in the practice, he raised it. He ordained several women, including married women and women with young children. This really goes against the grain of Japanese Zen. He would always say to me, "I can plant a seed, but you have to make it grow. In your own time and place, you must nurture it and make it grow. Have confidence that you can do it, and you will do it. Because nobody can do it for you."

After Maezumi Roshi's death, Zen Center of Los Angeles was run by one of my dharma brothers, and within a year, the center was embroiled in a scandal involving student-teacher relationships.

When I first heard of the scandal, my whole body went into spasms. I had this sinking feeling that I might be asked to go back. I didn't want to. I liked my life in Yonkers. But when the situation worsened, Roshi Glassman did ask me to return. Reluctantly. He said, "How about if you go back for just three months and work on healing the Zen Center?"

I'd been through so many scandals in my life in Zen, and I just didn't have it in me to go through another one. But I knew the people there, and the dharma is my life. So I decided I'd return for this period of healing, but on my own terms. I said, "If I return for this work, I want to be paid for it. I want to have my time off. I want to be free to experiment with the changes I think we need. And I want to go back with the understanding that I'm going to do what I can, and if it doesn't work, I'm out of there."

Roshi Glassman agreed. He said, "You can go back on those terms, and we'll work together." I felt I would be supported, and I especially appreciated his capacity to let go and see what arises in any situation.

Returning to ZCLA was very difficult. What made it possible was that there are terrific practitioners there and I loved them; but what was difficult was the invisible hold the forms had on us—the patriarchal forms, the male-dominated forms, the dominator forms, the Japanese monastic forms. It was an invisible system, but you could feel it everywhere.

Fortunately for me, the Center was in chaos. There were some very old-timers there who were used to the established forms, and there were new people, who were eagerly taking in new forms.

The first thing I said was, "I'm not holding any private interviews for an indefinite period of time." At ZCLA, this was challenging a sacred cow. The one thing we don't give up is our private interviews with the teacher. So people asked me how I was going to teach, and I said, "Is that what teaching is to you? Going into a little room, saying your blah-blah, listening to me say my blah-blah, and then going happily on your way?"

I didn't know what I was going to do, but I wasn't going to hide in the hierarchy. This caused tremendous discomfort for the community. It wasn't uncomfortable for me—it was great—but for the community it was very disconcerting, particularly since they were already in so much chaos. But I didn't want a hundred people coming to me privately and telling me what was wrong with everything. I wanted them to talk to each other and learn from each other.

Several years before he died, Maezumi Roshi began to emphasize strongly the Sangha Treasure, this jewel of all of us working together. When he first started to talk about it, I resisted. I would say to him, "I live with these people, work with these people, and sit with these people. Now you want me to *love* these people. Give me a break!" But he was unrelenting. And when he died, this was the teaching that really stuck in my mind and my heart and my body—the teaching of *sangha*, this jewel of harmony. It's not the kind of harmony where everything's smooth and undifferentiated, but the kind of harmony that is alive, pulsating with our differences.

Our *sangha* relationships were very weak, partly because everyone was fixated on the teacher. We didn't truly communicate about our issues until there was a scandal, and then it was too late. And yet, over and over, Maezumi Roshi had said to us, "Learn to work together." The Sangha Treasure heals. Embracing our oneness and our diversity—this is where our practice can rest. We did not know how to meet together. We had spent years sitting *sesshin* silently, side by side, never having to say anything. We didn't know how to talk to each other. What were we going to do about that?

So I sat the *sangha* down in circles and councils: circles for this, and councils for that. I sat in the circles, too, like everyone else. At first that was confusing to people, and when they spoke, they'd look at me, as if I were the authority in the room. But we've all learned together, and now they don't pay any special attention to me. It's wonderful for me, because I can have a practice, too, and people can see that.

When we sit in a circle, there's a flattening of the hierarchy. Everyone gets heard, and everyone realizes the tremendous wisdom and compassion that is inherent in every single person, not just the teacher. We have learned that our diversity is not a problem, it's our strength.

I grew up in a Japanese-Portuguese family, and my *koan* was: How can I be both? My Portuguese friends talked a lot and laughed a lot. My Japanese friends were much quieter. Where did I belong? I agonized over this true-life *koan* of mine. I was still agonizing over it when I was in my twenties, and one day a friend said to me, "You're so lucky to have all of that!" Then I realized the obvious. I am all of it. The diversity is me.

So the question comes: How can I include all of it, truly realize our all-inclusive nature? Can I be that open? Can I include all of these people, all these lights and shadows? And the answer of course is, "Yes!" This is, after all, what we are.

So the circle and council practices have challenged us to trust ourselves, to trust that the teachings of the buddha-dharma are active in our life, and that our lives, as we are living them now, are manifestations of the teachings. That's a big leap.

What are the forms that we as women will create? What practice structures will come out of our own lives? What skillful means will we bring forth out of our being? People say, "Don't throw the baby out with the bath water." And I say, "What's the baby? What's the bath water? Throw it all out and let's see what arises from the vast unknowing."

Of course, form and practice are inseparable. However we practice is our form. But what if we throw out the belief that we have to do things in one particular way? Just be willing to step over the edge. You know the Zen *koan*: How do I step off the top of a hundred-foot pole? This is where we have to trust ourselves, our understanding, our realization, our practice. When we go deeply inside, the voice we hear may tell us some surprising things. Listen carefully!

Open the practice up in the context of your life as it is; experiment with forms and let them teach you. Be open to so-called new forms that may naturally arise to bring the teachings to life.

Have the courage to let go of all you know. Trust yourself. We are the buddha-dharma itself. Isn't it wonderful?

(1999)

BECOMING THE LANDSCAPE

Nanao Sakaki *interviewed by* Trevor Carolan

The life of Japanese writer, environmental activist, and wanderer Nanao Sakaki is the stuff of legend. As a radarman in the Japanese Imperial Navy during World War II, he tracked America's B-29 bombers on their fateful mission to Nagasaki. His wartime experiences, including visiting bombsites where human beings had been vaporized to shadows on concrete, led him to denounce militarism and abandon mainstream society. He cofounded the Bum Academy, a renegade group of artists influential in Japan's postwar counterculture. In the early 1960s, Sakaki befriended American writers Gary Snyder and Allen Ginsberg, who were then living in Tokyo, and the three became lifelong friends. Snyder joined Sakaki in building an ecologically attuned agricultural community on a volcanic island in the East China Sea, the "Banyan Ashram" chronicled in Snyder's influential book Earth House Hold.

For five decades Sakaki has led a vagabond life in the tradition of Japan's wandering Zen poet-storytellers, walking the length and breadth of the Japanese islands, writing poems, and speaking out against nuclear technology and industrial degradation of the environment. He is equally at home in the deserts, western mountains, and coastal regions of North America. His crazy wisdom poetry, published in Break the Mirror, Let's Eat Stars, *and* Real Play, *calls to mind Charlie Chaplin, Basho, and the anonymous Asian masters immortalized in Paul Reps and Ngoyen Senzaki's* Zen Flesh, Zen Bones.

The following is adapted from conversations during a visit Nanao Sakaki made to British Columbia.

—Trevor Carolan

Many people think that the new millennium is very important for human beings. But that's all wrong. We must think another way about history—not just two thousand or five thousand years back, but millions of years back, to amoeba time, to the place we come from. Why? This is our home, our family, so we must take better care of them.

The Hopi people believe you shouldn't make an important decision unless you think through its effects for seven generations. This means we have to imagine how we, and the consequences of our actions, fit into the scale of things. Think of trees—they usually live longer than humans. Harvesting a tree can be like destroying your own great-grandfather. So, rightly, we should think, "What's the appropriate thing to do here?"

My love for the wild began after I read Sir Laurens Van der Post's *The Lost World of the Kalahari*. I was so excited after reading it that I couldn't sleep for almost three days. It was so new, so different. Here's this hostile desert environment of lions and poisonous snakes. But Van der Post wants to understand the Bushmen so much he finally comes to comprehend their philosophy, which is: "There is a dream that is dreaming us." That's very interesting to me! It's similar to the Taoist master Chuang Tzu's "Am I a man dreaming of a butterfly, or is the butterfly dreaming me?" So, as a young man, I began to think about what's real. I understand that we must go with the dream; there is no other choice.

The wild is a good place to think about history and the future. The far north has many wild places, glaciers, bears, foxes. Not so much human culture. San Francisco, Tokyo, New York—terrible places! Everyone has to move fast; there is so much noise and confusion. After the war, I worked for a big publisher in Tokyo. I met many famous writers and artists. But I had to leave. Too many people. So much activity, like living in a beehive! There are no mosquitoes there. No wild places. Not even flies! It's a miserable feeling.

I don't want to go to such places now. Instead, I walk the mountains, in the north. I love glaciers and the desert. No civilization. You can think clearly—who we are, where we are going. So, get away sometime. All your personal history—good-bye! You get a much wider perspective. And life is much simpler. You must carry your own things, your own rucksack. It's a good way. Everybody wants to live a long time, but in India, for centuries, at fifty years old people went to the forest to die. They lived quietly, in meditation; they ate a little, begged food from the village, took water, then died peacefully. Look at me: already I'm seventy-seven. I'm ready!

In the twenty-first century our job is to reverse the big construction projects—dams, energy projects—that have wiped out the fish runs in our rivers and polluted our soil and air and water. Why does the Japanese government build another dam? To keep construction companies busy! China is building the Three Gorges Dam on the Yangtze, creating lots of environmental problems: deforestation, pollution. So many fish and animals die; wetlands for birds are disappearing. Who will be left? Only people. Very unnatural. It's time to reverse this. Already in Japan we are seeing legal cases where representatives of endangered species are suing the government. Japan still has many rich, wild spaces and two thousand black and grizzly bears, where in other island's ecologies, like Britain's, they have disappeared.

It's very important to speak out. Speak out! For instance, in Japan, the government wants to dam the Yoshino River. So in the spring we organize "Walk the River," in which a group of us spends about ten days walking, camping, and reading poetry along the river for 220 kilometers. In Japan, people don't often openly criticize government policy. But we must. I wrote a poem, "Don't Cry, Yoshino River." It's so important that we speak out.

One answer may be no more big cities. Why does everybody want to live in a big city anyway? Perhaps we can have smaller cities for people to live in, in a more environmentally healthy scale—everybody has a small place, small gardens, some wild land close by. I say to young people in Japan: Go to the mountain farm areas. Since the war, many people went to the cities, so now many villages are abandoned. But you can live in a rural village for almost no rent. It's possible to grow your own food and live quietly. You can pick plants for medicine.

I study botany because I like to know the names of the plants I meet. Sometimes I find the same plants in Alaska and in New Mexico, and I feel as if I'm seeing an old friend. Like kinnikinnick: "Oh, I haven't seen you for so long a time!" It's the same with stars, birds, mammals—always I'm happy to meet bear, caribou, coyote, eagle. It's a good feeling.

In my work and travels I have come in contact with Aboriginal people from Australia and Tasmania, and with Navajo people from the American Southwest, who live in timeless landscapes. That's good for me, you see, because I'm crazy for wild landscapes; always I wish to see the desert or volcanoes—big spaces, pure like the empty mind of Buddha.

I never call myself a *Zen Buddhist*, or a *beatnik*, or a *hippie*—anything. Most Japanese Zen is uninteresting to me. It's too linked to the samurai tradition—to militarism. The samurai class that many have associated with Zen was in fact deeply Confucian; it was concerned with power. The Zen I'm interested in is that of the great teachers of China's Tang dynasty, such as Linji. This was a nonintellectual Zen. It came from farmers—so simple. Someone became enlightened, others talked to him, learned, and were told, "Now you go and teach." When Japan tried to adopt this tradition it was hopeless. The emperor sent scholars [to China] but with their high-flown language and ideas, they couldn't understand.

Today many young people have lost their way. They're looking for salvation. They read Zen anecdotes, see Zen pictures—it seems perfect! Then they think about achieving enlightenment, but it's not so easy. I always say, "Just forget about enlightenment. Everybody's already enlightened: people work at their jobs, the traffic moves along, so things are okay." A mother looks after her children; she makes their lunch, does her job well—that's enlightenment, just doing a good job.

Some aspects of Zen practice may be good for Westerners—monastery life, for example. So little food, maybe only 1,500 calories per day, and lots of walking. Near Taos I lived in a cave—just like ancient times, very cold in winter! And almost fasting: just some brown rice to eat and a little water. Just enough. Western people eat so much. At dinner last night, so much food was left over. What happens to it? In Southeast Asia many people have only a little food to eat. So maybe the West can give some extra food to other people.

Once, while hitchhiking in southern Japan, I met my cousin who told me my father was very sick. We went to the hospital to see him. He was surprised to see me. I said, "So you are going to become Buddha!" In the Amida sect of my family [Jodo Shinshu], we say that when you die you're becoming Buddha. My father sort of half-smiled. His face brightened, and he said, "Yes, I'm going to become Buddha, looks like!" That's it. When it's time to sleep, just sleep; when you're sick, just be sick; when you're going to die, just die! Enlightenment!

Real compassion goes beyond human society—it extends to animal life, trees, water, stones. If we think this way it becomes easy to relate to the environmental movement. Buddhism says we are all the same; the West, I think, is missing this. Indian sutras discuss the perfect wholeness of all things and how they are joined.

The way to compassion is to slow down. Slow down the metabolism. Compassion is like a shadow—like the Hopi thinking seven generations on. After all, how we work out our difficulties is a social question, not spiritual or mental. If we have no vision as a society, all we're left with is bureaucratic process. That's too sad! Artists and poets have a responsibility to the landscape, to wild nature. As a poet I feel my poems are also sutras; a painter's work is also a kind of visual dharma. And as listeners, if we meet a good poem—or discover a new landscape—we must have a good response. In the end it becomes spontaneous. It's like hearing good music; it calls to me, I start humming, moving—I find I'm dancing! That's Zen—not thinking, not stopping halfway, not copying the landscape but finally *becoming* the landscape.

(2002)

PART THREE

Food for Thought

INTRODUCTION TO PART THREE

In Part Three we hear about the ideas behind the actions. We are invited into a conversation with people who have been thinking about the dharma and social change for a long time, including many well-known dharma teachers. When we consider our particular actions in the larger context of socially engaged Buddhism, we can see them more clearly; it's like matting and framing a photograph.

This conversation includes history, theory, analysis, and imagination. We need to start where we are, with some understanding of how we got here, and describe to ourselves what we see in front of us, and then we need to consider where we are going and how to get there. We need rigorous thinking, a willingness not to turn away from seeing what Suzuki Roshi called "things as it is," and we need imagination, to open our minds as well as our hearts to new possibilities. The dharma asks us to "see things as they are"; sometimes the language used is "to accept things as they are." According to the practitioners who speak in this section, this doesn't mean things shouldn't be changed. It means we need to accept that they are as they are before we can change them. We need to know where we are on the map before we can use it for navigation. Then we can consider where we want to go together and what tools we need for the journey.

We are given many tools here: tools for dealing with our discouragement, for raising our children with hope, for forgiving ourselves and others, for finding connection and courage.

—S.M.

THE PRACTICE OF PEACE

Thich Nhat Hanh

The following is adapted from a talk given by Thich Nhat Hanh at the Berkeley Community Theater in Berkeley, California, on April 16, 1991.

> Breathing in, I feel myself as a flower,
> Breathing out, I feel fresh.
> Breathing in, I feel myself as a mountain,
> Breathing out, I feel solid.
> Breathing in, I feel myself as a still pond,
> Breathing out, I reflect things as they are.
> Breathing in, I feel space within and without,
> Breathing out, I feel free.

What happened in Los Angeles the night that Rodney King was beaten was seen by people around the world. I saw it too. My first reaction was that it was I who was beaten. Tomorrow, or the day after, it could be me. It could be all of us. In fact, I was the person who was beaten by the five policemen. I suffered from violence and hatred and fear.

But as I continued looking deeply, I saw myself as one of the five policemen. Because the society is filled with violence and hatred and fear. If I were a young man entering into the police training academy, I might easily become one of the five. At first, you want to serve the society; you want to enforce law and order. But when you study to be a policeman, you are told by your trainers that there is a lot of violence on the streets, and you must take care of yourself. You could be killed by anyone—a poor person or a rich person, someone driving a motorcycle or someone driving a Cadillac. This is the training in the police academy: you have to be careful, you might be killed. And each morning when the policeman begins his job, he might practice something like, "Breathing in, I am aware that I might be killed. Breathing out, I must be quick to shoot first, before I am shot." This is the practice of fear. And when a policeman or policewoman is killed, the entire force comes to the funeral to demonstrate their fear, their anger. I feel that I understand that; I could become one of the five.

In the *Majjima Nikaya,* the Buddha said, "This is like this, because that is like that." Our society is like this; therefore the policemen are like that. We are coresponsible. If you fire the police chief or put the policemen in jail, you don't solve the problem. You have to solve the problem on the level of the basement, not of the living room.

Let us meditate on the Iraq war. Let us visualize the 500,000 soldiers who were stationed in Saudi Arabia ready for a land offensive. On TV in France, I saw an American soldier holding his bayonet jump up and down and scream like a beast. Then he plunged the bayonet into a sandbag that represented an Iraqi soldier. The allied soldiers had to practice in that way every day, because they knew the land offensive was near. They knew they had to kill in order to be able to go home. Their mothers were waiting for them at home—and their wives and their children. But how can you thrust a bayonet into the belly of a human being if you are a human being yourself? You have to train yourself to become a beast, jumping and screaming. This is the practice of hatred. Many soldiers practiced like that for six months, not only during the day, but during the night, in their nightmares. "I want to go home to my family, so I have to learn to kill." On the other side, one million Iraqi soldiers were practicing the same.

All of us were practicing violence, hatred, and fear, collectively, as a *sangha*. And many in the United States supported that kind of practice—I heard that 80 percent supported the war. The people of the U.S. did not see deeply enough into the soul of the soldier, into the basement. They may have thought that the war was clean, the war was moral, the war was quick, that there was not much damage, were not many casualties. On TV one only saw the bridges and a number of houses destroyed.

Few practiced looking deeply in order to see the real casualties that the 500,000 brought home with them. Can one practice the way the soldiers did and remain oneself? No—you get deeply wounded in your store consciousness. The returning soldier cries because he is alive. His mother, his wife, his children cry for joy. But what will happen after one or two weeks? The war will slowly come up from the basement, from the store consciousness. And who will have to endure that? The soldier's family and the whole society.

I have led retreats for Vietnam veterans in the United States, and I know the tremendous amount of suffering that American veterans had to endure. One veteran told me that for twelve years he could not bear being in the same room with children. Every time there was a child in the room, he had to run out, because in Vietnam he had killed children. He told me that several friends in his unit had been killed in an ambush. Hatred and anger overwhelmed him, and he set up a small ambush in a village. He hid and watched as five children came out to play and were killed by his ambush. That image was stored in his consciousness, and after he went back to America, he could not bear to be around children. It took him more than twelve years to come to a meditation retreat and to practice breathing, walking, looking, and transforming the seeds of suffering. It is very difficult; it takes time to transform. But it is not difficult to get the seeds of suffering into your store consciousness.

A medical doctor who went with the American Army to the Gulf told me that he was deeply wounded in his soul. He didn't fight, but what he heard and what he saw wounded him deeply. He had the role of transporting the wounded soldiers back. He said that when a soldier holds his automatic rifle and begins to fire, he is overwhelmed by fear, and once he has pulled the trigger, he just cannot stop. He has to continue firing until he runs out of ammunition because he is afraid that if he stops, he will be fired upon. The doctor told me that in the old days, when someone killed someone else with a sword or a bayonet, the vibration would come back to him and he would know that he was killing a person. But in dropping bombs or firing automatic weapons, you don't get that kind of feedback. When the soldier is firing his automatic weapon, he can't hear anything, including orders from his superior. He hears only his own fear. That is the heritage of war. The War in Vietnam still has a lot of mental formations, a lot of seeds of suffering in the American soul, and now you've had to suffer from the Gulf.

We must practice in such a way that we can see clearly. If you are a psychologist, if you are a playwright, if you are a novelist, a composer, a filmmaker, a peacemaker, or an environmentalist, please look deeply into the soul of the soldier who has just returned, in order to see the amount of suffering that the war has caused, not only to that person, but to everyone on the earth. Then you will be able to project that image onto a huge screen for the whole nation to see and to learn. If you are able to see the truth concerning the Iraq war, I don't think you are going to start another war like that in the future. How can you talk about a victory? A victory for whom?

The night President Bush gave the order to attack Iraq, I could not sleep. I was angry. I was overwhelmed. It was too much for me. I was in a winter retreat at Plum Village in France, and I was teaching the *Avatamsaka Sutra*. The next morning, in the middle of the lecture—I could not stop it, it just came up from deep in my store consciousness—I said to the class, "My friends, I don't think that I'm going to go to North America this spring. I just cannot. I don't have any desire now to go there and lead retreats and give talks." Then I realized that I had interrupted the lecture, and I resumed it.

Afterward, we had walking meditation, and then a silent meal. At three o'clock we had a tea meditation, and during the tea meditation an American student who was living at Plum Village told me, "Thây, I think you have to go to America. Many friends have worked so hard to arrange these retreats and talks, and I think that you should go there and tell us how you feel." I did not say anything; I was not sure of anything at the time. But I practiced breathing in and out, and walking, and sitting; and a few days after that I decided to come. I saw that you and I, we are the same person. I saw that I was one with the American people, I was one with President Bush, I was one with

Saddam Hussein. I did not see him as an enemy. I had been angry with President Bush, of course, but after having practiced breathing in and out, I saw myself as President Bush. I deserve President Bush. I deserve Saddam Hussein.

The war has to do with our happiness. Because we are not happy enough, we had a war. When we are not happy, we take refuge in many things, like alcohol, drugs, action, and war. I have worked with young people a lot. I have led many retreats for young people in many countries, and they've told me this: the most precious gift that parents can give to their children is their own happiness. If parents know how to make themselves happy, children will receive a lot of seeds of happiness in their store consciousness, and when they grow up, they will know how to be happy and to make other people happy. When they get married, they will know how to make their partner happy. I think that statement made by the young people is very important. Every time parents fight and make each other suffer, they sow seeds of suffering in the hearts of their children. With that kind of heritage, children will grow up unhappy, and that is the root of war. If they are unhappy, they will look for other things that are very much like war. Alcohol is war. Drugs are war. Television is war.

We know that if we don't eat properly, we get sick. To heal our body, we have to follow a diet. We have to avoid ingesting more poisons into our body. If we know how to breathe in and out deeply, to bring in more oxygen, then we improve the quality of our blood, and our blood will be able to eliminate the toxins in our body. If we practice massage, we'll be able to bring the blood into the painful zones of our body in order for the blood to wash away the toxins that are there and to transform the pain. We have to be careful about eating, practicing breathing in and out deeply, and practicing massage. The circulation of the blood is very important for our health.

From the point of view of our psyche, we also need good circulation. We ingest a lot of poisons into our consciousness. We consume a lot of "cultural products," which put poison in our consciousness. The practice of peace is to follow a diet, to refrain from ingesting more toxic products. We must learn to do this as individuals, and we must teach our children, our community, our town, our city and our nation to do so. If you are a playwright, a novelist, a filmmaker, or an educator, please practice so that we all can follow a diet that will help us transform our consciousness. Because transforming our collective consciousness is the only way to make peace and to prevent war.

After a day of work, we feel tired, and yet when we go home we don't know how to relax, to recover ourselves. So we turn on the television; we want to consume more and more, because there is a vacuum inside. That is the product of our civilization; we always feel we lack something, and we want to fill it with whatever is available. A woman who came to Plum Village said to me, "Thây, every time fear and agitation come up, I just open my refrigerator and eat." A lot of these cultural items make you feel hungry after you eat them, and you want to eat even more. The kind of civilization in which we find ourselves makes us feel alienated from ourselves. We don't want to go back and face our true self because we are afraid. There is so much anger, hatred, and fear in us, and we want to suppress it. And in order to suppress these things, we fill ourselves with poisons. Even though the television is very noisy, and all the screaming, the shooting, the fear, and the strong emotions make us tired, we do not have the courage to turn it off because we are afraid of going back to ourselves. And that is the root of the war.

How can we transform our consciousness, and the collective consciousness of our society, if we practice filling every moment with TV and other cultural products? That is why we must be in touch with what is healing, refreshing, and joyful. This is very important. When we practice walking meditation, we get in touch with the earth, our mother, with the air, with the trees, and with ourselves, and we water the seeds of peace and joy, as individuals, and as a community.

Buddhism is made of non-Buddhist elements, a flower is made of non-flower elements, and President Bush is made of non-Bush elements—that's you and me. If we take care of the non-Bush elements, we take care of Bush. You may think that if there were another person in the White House, the situation would be different. But the nature of the society is like this, and therefore its government must be like that. It cannot be very different from what it is now, and therefore we have to change at the base, and the base is the store consciousness.

We have to understand in order to be of help. We all have pain, but we tend to suppress it, because we don't want it to come from the basement up to our living room. The most important thing is that we need to be understood. We need someone to be able to listen to us and to understand us. Then we will suffer less. But everyone is suffering, and no one wants to listen. We don't know how to express ourselves so that people can understand. Because we suffer so much, the way we express our pain hurts other people, and they don't want to listen.

Listening is a very deep practice. Avalokiteshvara Bodhisattva has a very deep talent for listening. The name means "listening to the cries of the world." You have to empty yourself. You have to leave space in order to listen. A person suffers so much that he might die, he might explode like a bomb, and he needs us to listen. "Darling, I know that you have suffered a great deal. I know that. I know that I have contributed to your suffering, and I feel sorry, responsible. So please give me a chance, tell me of your suffering, I want to hear." If you can begin to say things like that, the other person will begin to suffer less. We have to listen in our family. And then we have to listen in our community, and to everyone, especially to the people we think are our enemies—the ones we believe are making the situation worse. Our government also. When you have shown your capacity for listening and understanding, the other person will begin to listen to you, and you have a chance to tell him or her of your pain, and it's your turn to get healed. This is the practice of peace.

Peace and joy are available in each moment, to some extent, and you can help yourself to them. Breathe in and out, and touch the beautiful sky. Know that you are alive, that your eyes are there, that your heart is functioning well, that you can practice walking and sitting, that your loved one is still there, that the flower is still fresh and the mountain is still solid. Each second of our daily lives is a diamond, containing the earth, the sky, the cloud, the wind, rain, birds, trees. You can be very happy just by breathing mindfully. Then every look, every smile, every gesture you make is a diamond that can make other people happy. If you are peaceful, if you are happy, whatever you do will be an offering for the people around you.

(1991)

WELLSPRINGS OF
ENGAGED BUDDHISM

Kenneth Kraft

Have you seen the T-shirt with the guy wringing his hands and saying, "Nuclear war?! Oh no! There goes my career!"? In the early days
of many American Buddhist communities, the caption might have
been: "Nuclear war?! Oh no! There goes my practice!"

Things are changing. Now there are Western Buddhists who are
working to halt the nuclear arms race. Other practitioners have become
concerned about an array of issues ranging from political oppression to
environmental pollution. A new term, "engaged Buddhism," desig-
nates this involvement of Buddhists in social, political, and economic
affairs. Engaged Buddhists are attempting to develop the means to ac-
tualize Buddhism's traditional ideals of wisdom and compassion in
today's world.

Like the fledgling movement to which it refers, the term "engaged Buddhism" is currently in the process of definition. Let's
begin by examining engaged Buddhism's theoretical underpinnings,
synthesizing material from a variety of sources. Step one is a re-
assessment of the Buddhist tradition—its past performance as a historical institution, its inherent resources, and its future potential.

Engaged Buddhists concede that traditional Buddhism in the
Asian cultural context has generally been politically passive. Its
strengths were in the realms of the individual and the universal,
not the social. On the specific issue of peace, the record is mixed.
Buddhists did not fight holy wars—there were no Buddhist Cru-
sades or Inquisitions—and the religion did exert a pacifying effect
during certain eras. Yet Buddhists fought each other in Southeast

Asia, Sri Lanka, and Japan. In China, Buddhism acquiesced to belligerent regimes, and in Japan Buddhism repeatedly allied itself with militarism.

Nonetheless, Nelson Foster, one of the founders of the Buddhist Peace Fellowship, argues, "The Mahayana tradition of political inactivity is a result of the restrictive social environment which Buddhism encountered in China and Japan. It is not inherent to the Buddha way." The Pali canon provides evidence to indicate that Shakyamuni Buddha saw individual serenity and social concord as inseparable, and he left guidelines for the development of just social institutions. Nagarjuna, the second-century Indian founder of Madhyamika, also discussed the application of Buddhist principles in the social realm. According to Robert Thurman, Nagarjuna envisioned "the broad outlines of an individualist, transcendentalist, pacifist, universalist, socialist society." Buddhist popular literature can also be interpreted in this spirit. In the Jataka tales, Rafe Martin notes, "the Buddha is shown not as withdrawing from the world, but as acting with compassion and wisdom for the benefit of all living beings."

A second step in developing engaged Buddhism's doctrinal base is an explicit justification of involvement in the social, political, and economic realms. As Burmese statesman U Thant declared, "I have not found the slightest difficulty or contradiction between my Buddhist faith and my duties as Secretary General of the United Nations."

An important touchstone is the Buddhist vision of interdependence, the dynamic oneness of all existence (and nonexistence). In the classic image of Indra's Net, multifaceted jewels reflect one another infinitely. A related Mahayana claim is that "Nothing obstructs anything else." Or, as Roshi Philip Kapleau once joked, "All is one, and one is all, and vice versa." For Buddhists, interdependence is not just a doctrinal tenet but something that can be experienced directly and deeply. Several repercussions of this worldview are of special import for Buddhist activists. If we are not separate from others on a fundamental level, it follows that the suffering of others is also our suffering, that the violence of others is also our violence. In the words of Christopher Titmuss:

People are beginning to see that personal pain and global pain are not two separate factors, but very much interrelated. Some people experience inside of themselves what they conceive of as being the pain of the world, but in a way it's the pain of themselves. There are others who experience inside of themselves what they conceive of as being purely personal pain. In a way, it's the pain of the world.

This somber conclusion has a brighter flip side: the intimate link between personal peace and world peace. If everything is interdependent, then one individual's peace of mind significantly contributes to peace everywhere. That is the basis of the Dalai Lama's assertion that "peace is the responsibility of everyone."

Another justification for involvement in the social realm is that individual enlightenment cannot ripen fully without a corresponding degree of social awareness. This approach echoes the time-honored bodhisattva ideal, in which the salvation of all beings takes precedence over one's own salvation. The Japanese have a beautiful expression, *jiririta-enman,* or "self-benefit and other-benefit, perfectly fulfilled." In the late 1960s and early 1970s, many meditators were preoccupied with their own enlightenment, building a necessary base but not ready to take on larger concerns. Now these same practitioners sense that their spiritual striving embraces a meaningful relationship with the world.

One further justification for Buddhist involvement in politics is that we are all involved in politics anyway. According to peace activist Jim Perkins, "Politics is just our relationships with other people in large numbers. We cannot avoid participating." As individuals, our daily lives involve countless choices in the social realm: not only which candidates we support, oppose, or ignore, but where we choose to live, how we spend our money, and so on. I realized (belatedly) that even buying a light bulb has political implications when I learned that General Electric manufactures MX missile components near where I live. Our group actions, including those of our Buddhist centers, also have a political dimension. From this standpoint, there can be no such thing as *dis*engaged Buddhism.

These arguments lead to the conclusion that a Buddhist's task is not to avoid politics, but to become more politically conscious and responsible. In Nelson Foster's reformulation, "Political action may be a natural result of Buddhist practice, a spontaneous response of wisdom and compassion to the social and ecological problems we face."

A central tenet of engaged Buddhism is that individual transformation is the heart of Buddhist social activism, its *sine qua non*. If a Buddhist social movement is pursued only from a social/political standpoint, without this transformative element, it may fail to achieve real results and may even perpetuate the ills it aims to cure. Thus Joanna Macy speaks of "the inner work of social change." Ultimately, Buddhist social action must come out of enlightenment, or *prajna*. In the broadest sense, enlightenment simply means awareness, inherent in us all, and there is nothing mystical about its application: stopping on the street to pick up litter is an engaged act that comes from awareness. More specifically, spiritual maturity enables one to deal with "opponents" nondualistically, to avoid getting stuck in a particular position, to be involved *and* detached. Engaged Buddhism seeks a genuine integration of the contemplative and the active. In Robert Aitken's words:

> The Buddha did not remain under the bodhi tree, and neither does Mother Teresa neglect her prayers. Prajna and upaya, wisdom and compassion—these are the "head and tail" of religious practice. Stagnation or burnout are the negative results of neglecting one end or the other.

Engaged Buddhism is notable for its lack of attachment to ideology. The first precept of the Tiep Hien Order, founded by Thich Nhat Hanh, is not to be bound to any doctrine, theory, or ideology, even Buddhist ones. "Buddhist systems of thought must be guiding means and not absolute truth." Engaged Buddhists are even willing to dispense with the "Buddhism" label if it becomes a hindrance. Nor is it necessary for an individual to sign on as a Buddhist to partake of the tradition's resources. This nonattachment to ideology is certainly one of the most distinctive and refreshing aspects of engaged Buddhism. It is close in spirit to the "irreverent reverence" of Zen, and a far cry from the fundamentalism that rages through many belief systems. What better antidote than this for today's ideological gridlock, which causes such widespread suffering in the world?

Amid these areas of broad agreement, one also finds issues that require further clarification. For example: Does engaged Buddhism claim that all Buddhists should become social activists? Must everyone leap off the mat and rush into the streets? No, engaged Buddhism is rather an attempt to establish the legitimacy of public involvement for those who wish to move in that direction. A more complex issue is the proper role of Buddhist groups. Should *sanghas* [Buddhist communities] become politically engaged? Different guidelines may be applicable in different situations. But how can a Buddhist take sides? some will ask. Wouldn't it be more correct to remain impartial? Again, the answers may depend on specific circumstances. A helpful tool here is the doctrine of the "twofold truth,"—conventional and ultimate. Taking sides on the conventional level does not necessarily mean that the ultimate has been violated or abandoned. Rather, Buddhist activists strive to take sides with lightness, flexibility, and a natural empathy for other points of view.

Another challenging issue is whether Buddhism demands absolute pacifism. Though the first precept is to cherish all life, the Mahayana interpretation of that precept is not absolutist. For instance, if a rabid dog is chasing children down the street, the dog must be shot for the community's welfare. The question then becomes: Where does one draw the line?

Buddhism never developed a theoretical standard like Christianity's "just war" doctrine. In European history, the Pope was the one who pronounced a war just or unjust, but Buddhism does not have anyone so infallible. Asian Buddhism generally sanctions wars of self-defense against a foreign invader; today Taiwanese monks routinely serve in the army (disrobing temporarily), prepared to fight mainland China if necessary. If the Buddhist nonviolent movement in the West opts to reject all rationales for war, even national self-defense, it will need to offer some viable alternatives. In this regard, Dr. Gene Sharp, nonviolent action theorist at the Albert Einstein Institute, has done valuable work on methods of nonviolent struggle and civilian-based defense.

What are some of engaged Buddhism's current weaknesses or trouble spots? What needs to be done to move the movement forward?

Further exploration and dissemination of key Buddhist tenets would shore up engaged Buddhism's doctrinal base. For example, a better understanding of the twofold-truth doctrine would help clarify some common areas of confusion, such as meditation's role as a response to the world. According to twofold-truth theory, meditation is simultaneously a partial response (conventional level) and a complete response that transcends activity and inactivity (ultimate level).

Buddhist social and political theory, heretofore neglected, is another area in which further work needs to be done. Welsh Buddhist Ken Jones lays a base by stressing the collective dimensions of karma: "It is only some kind of *social* action that can be an effective and relevant response to the weight of *social* karma which oppresses humanity and which we all share." The apprehension of interdependence will be invaluable in Buddhist social/political theory. In our global village, events are no longer domestic or international, but "intermestic." The seminal concept of a Buddhist economics was introduced by E. F. Schumacher in his book *Small Is Beautiful*. And the Dalai Lama has even expressed a willingness to explore the common ground between Buddhism and Marxism; originally, both systems sought the greatest good for the greatest number.

As for engaged Buddhist practice, many potentially relevant Buddhist techniques have yet to be applied. To cite just one example: The *Vimalakirti Sutra*, which predates the common era, offers a formula for conflict resolution in its description of bodhisattvas:

> During the long reign of weapons,
> They meditate on love,
> Introducing to nonviolence
> Hundreds of millions of living beings.
> In the middle of great battles
> They remain impartial to both sides,
> For bodhisattvas of great strength
> Delight in reconciliation of conflict.

Buddhists will continue to develop new forms of nonviolent activism, such as public meditation vigils, that integrate Buddhist and Western approaches. If medieval Japanese masters could devise one-line invocations as routes to salvation, contemporary Buddhists should be able to come up with a few catchy slogans, like, "Live simply, so that others may simply live," or "Think globally, act locally"—phrases now circulating in kindred groups. A bit of ringing rhetoric might even have its place: "And so, my fellow engaged Buddhists, ask not what all beings can do for you. . . ." Engaged Buddhism is also going to need a sacred text or two, something like a "Path of Compassion Sutra" or a "Declaration of Interdependence." Such a work would lead us from the current ideology of mutual assured destruction to a new vision of mutual assured awakening.

Whatever transpires, it will be essential to maintain the spirit of *prajna*, the spirit of enlightenment. In the attempt to reach larger audiences, in the creation of new forms of practice, the nondual insight into True Nature is too easily diluted, especially when budding leaders have not had the benefit of intensive spiritual training. If *prajna* is lost, so is Buddhism.

Originally, I hesitated to refer to engaged Buddhism as a "movement"—the label seemed too substantial to describe an informal network of meditators. But then I began to sense how much *movement* is actually taking place. Engaged Buddhism in the West is a genuine grassroots phenomenon. The absence of a single dominant leader gives many people a chance to lead. The current president of the Buddhist Peace Fellowship, Ruth Klein, describes herself as "well known to my family and friends," adding, "I have never before been president of anything." A ready-made metaphor for a Buddhist grassroots movement is found in the *Lotus Sutra*, which describes bodhisattvas welling up out of the earth.

Historically, Buddhism's ability to change and adapt has been one of its greatest sources of strength. Today we are witnessing and/or participating in another turn in the Buddhist tradition. At the least, the appearance of engaged Buddhism is an important part of Buddhism's indigenization in the West. Is this an event on the scale of a subdivision within a lineage? Or is it something much grander, like the emergence of Ch'an in China, or even the historic shift from Theravada to Mahayana?

Buddhism's contribution to the West may also turn out to be historically significant in a wider sense. Intellectually, Buddhism is offering the West nothing less than a new model of the universe. In place of the prevailing mechanistic view of the world as the sum of separate parts, Buddhism reveals a dynamically organic universe in which everything affects everything else. From this vision of oneness, the principle of nonviolence arises naturally, because to hurt another means to hurt oneself. A Buddhist-influenced paradigm shift in the West would have profound repercussions.

The most effective way to teach and realize the truth, according to the Buddhist concept of "skillful means" (*upaya*), is to use methods appropriate to a particular time and place. This notion is applicable to engaged Buddhism in several respects. First, individual Buddhists now approach social action as a skillful means for deepening their practice. Second, the peace issue seems to be a skillful means for introducing Buddhism to the West. Whenever Buddhism has entered a new culture in the past, it has had to hitch itself to a larger wagon, at least temporarily. What better *upaya* for Buddhism today than nonviolence? Third, Buddhism itself may turn out to be a skillful means for helping humanity out of its present predicament.

We have been looking at engaged Buddhism dispassionately. Peace and nonviolence seem like nice, gentle ideas. It appears that we are conducting business as usual. But these impressions belie a more potent reality. Peace and nonviolence are ideas that transform people and nations. Peacework demands risks and sacrifices and passion. Nonviolence, in a culture as violent as ours, amounts to cultural revolution. In such a revolution the revolutionaries are bodhisattvas, armed with wisdom and compassion.

(1986)

BUDDHIST RESOURCES
FOR DESPAIR

Joanna Macy

To live in the nuclear age is to live on the brink of time. The arms race, the destruction of the environment, the spread of conflict and oppression—these developments render questionable, for the first time in history, the survival of the human species. They summon us to conscious, nonviolent, collective action, if disaster is to be averted. Yet, while the customary forms of social action—from leafleting to lobbying—appear more necessary than ever, they are also by themselves inadequate. For the dangers confronting us, and the horrors they portend, are of such magnitude as to numb the human psyche, building resistance to the very information we most need to convey and to face.

To overcome this psychological numbness and resistance, a new dimension of social action has emerged. Spreading through writings, conferences, and workshops, and known by a variety of names—"despairwork," "interhelp," or simply the "inner work" of social change—it helps us expand our awareness of both the peril and the promise of our time. Tapping our important responses to the current crises, it helps us listen to our pain for the world and transform it into courage, compassion, and commitment to act.

What is significant is that Buddhist teachings have been integral to the genesis of this work. While this is not necessarily evident to many who engage in it, the work draws inspiration from central doctrines of the Buddha and a number of the tradition's meditational practices.

In developing despairwork, I drew on my own Buddhist practice, my doctoral studies in both Buddhist ethics and systems theory, and my experience as a participant-observer with the Sarvodaya Shramadana Movement, a Buddhist social change movement in Sri Lanka. Although the effectiveness of despairwork depends in no way on acknowledgement of these roots, the teachings of the Buddha have been intrinsic to its unfolding.

The Buddhist sources of despairwork are twofold. One is doctrinal or conceptual, through the interrelated teachings of *dukkha* (suffering), *anicca* (impermanence), *anatta* (no-self), and *paticca samuppada* (dependent co-arising). The other is methodological or practical, through the adaptation of Buddhist meditations. Let us see how these teachings function in helping people break through denial and psychic numbing, and transform the experience of pain for our world.

Dukkha

"Suffering is." This constitutes the first Noble Truth and one of the "three marks of existence." The Buddha began not with prescriptions, theories, revelations, or comfort, but empirically with the existential fact of human pain, especially psychological pain. To find our way through the confusion and distress of our time, that is where we begin, too. That is what we know most immediately and incontrovertibly.

At the outset of the despairwork workshops participants are usually invited to share a recent incident or piece of information that caused them pain for our world. In the safe setting that the group provides, these experiences surface quickly—a child's nuclear nightmare, the pollution of a nearby river, reports of war or starvation or expiring species of animal life. As participants hear themselves and each other give voice to their social despair, it ceases to appear as a personal morbidity or an idiosyncratic aberration. Its validity and universality become apparent. And because this pain arises from a level deeper than opinions and partisan allegiances, it undercuts our tendency to engage in debate. Argument often serves as an avoidance mechanism when faced with frightening information, but when the focus is on our feeling response, argument is irrelevant; what emerges is the commonality of our caring. Shared pain for the world becomes the ground on which we rediscover our capacity for compassion and mutual trust.

Anicca

One of the reasons we repress despair is the fear that, if we let ourselves experience it, we will become stuck or mired in it. In despairwork, however, as in insight meditation, we experience that "all dharmas are *anicca*": all phenomena, thoughts, and feelings are transient. It is only our denial of them that lends permanence to our feelings, and freezes us in relation to our pain for the world. Once brought into the light of conscious awareness, the impacted pain begins to loosen and flow. It holds less terror for us when we experience its dynamic quality, its ebb and flow, as we cease holding it at arm's length and let it pass through us. As our resistance against it dissolves, we open to wider currents of knowing—currents of correction and caring.

Anatta

Our inner responses to the world's distress are also blocked by fear that we might fall apart. Prospects of global disaster and knowledge of present destruction and suffering seem too overwhelming for the separate ego to cope with.

If we *are* but separate, self-existent egos, our pain for the world is hard to credit; there is no reason why we should be experiencing it. If all our drives and desires are essentially motivated by individual needs for pleasure and power, whence come our tears for our fellow beings, for those unseen and those yet to be born? Are we sick? Neurotic? Traditional mainstream Western psychology, being largely ego-based, tends to reduce such distress to private pathology, seeking its cause in personal history and personal maladjustment. This tendency, of course, encourages the repression of despair, and increases the sense of isolation and craziness we can feel when it breaks through our defenses.

In despairwork, the sharing and validation of our pain for the world—of our suffering with it—gives the lie to such reductionism. In the process it reveals that our experiencing does not arise from an isolatable, autonomous self so much as from our interaction with the world around us. As we sense the truth of that, experiencing how ever-flowing perceptions, feelings, and knowings interweave us into the wider fabric of existence, we cease to fear that we will fall apart. Our defenses and comforts may shatter, but the self is not an object that can break.

Such inklings are close to the Buddha's teaching of *anatta,* or no-self. Just as the illusion of separate selfhood is seen in the dharma as a chief obstacle to enlightenment, so also, in the context of despairwork, it constitutes a hindrance to our capacity to deal with our feelings of planetary anguish. When we move beyond that illusion, shedding the need to protect a fragile self from painful information, we move beyond denial, avoidance, and numbness as well. The reverse is equally true: The acceptance of our pain for the world validates our interconnectedness and loosens the bars of egocentricity.

Paticca Samuppada

The Buddha's central doctrine of dependent co-arising presents us with a view of reality where all is interconnected and interpenetrating—self and other, thought and deed, mind and form. From such a perspective, the military, social, and environmental dangers that threaten us come from no source external to the human psyche; they are reflections of it. They mirror its fears, greeds, and hostilities, just as the psyche itself is conditioned by the institutional structures in which we live. Self and society are interdependent. This understanding is very close to the systems view that emerges from contemporary science, and also to the holographic model of the universe, in which the whole is reflected in each of its parts.

Despairwork is posited on a similar premise or intuition: that each of us, indissolubly and inextricably interconnected with the vaster web of life, is ultimately inseparable from the fate and experience of other beings. In our time of crisis this mutual belonging is most manifest in our inchoate feelings of pain for the world—of suffering on behalf of the whole.

In the workshops, as participants share this kind of suffering, it is valorized as an appropriate and wholesome response to current conditions and, furthermore, named and seen as proof of our interconnectedness. Breaking out of the isolation in which many have harbored their feelings, participants "come home" to their intrinsic mutuality. The sense of homecoming is so vivid that the response is often one of joy, even hilarity. Feelings of pain for the world are not purged thereby—nor can they be, for each day's news brings fresh signals of distress—but they are taken henceforth as reminders and proof of our interexistence, which in turn serves as a source for resilience and creative action.

To express this wider, interdependent sense of being, a number of images tend spontaneously to emerge in the course of the work. Participants speak of being as interrelated as the cells in a body, or as neurons in a neural net. Such images are appropriate to the synergy experienced in despairwork. Synergy ("power with"), like the power of neural interactions, springs from openness and responsiveness (response-ability), in contrast to the old hierarchical notion of "power over," which is identified with armor, defenses, and invulnerability. The recurrent image of a neural network is very close to that of Hua-yen Buddhism. There, in the Jeweled Net of Indra, all beings are seen as nodes in a limitless web; each reflects all the others and, at each node too, intelligence and compassion can co-arise entire.

Conditioned to conceive of ourselves as separate, competitive entities, we need help to sustain and nourish this sense of interconnectedness and the synergistic power it can give us for social action. Certain practices, adopted and adapted in the course of despairwork, provide this assistance. Useful in groups, they can also serve one's ongoing personal discipline. Geared to be used in the course of the activities and encounters of our daily lives, they remind us that we do not need to withdraw from the world, or spend long hours in solitary prayer or meditation, to begin to wake up to the spiritual power within us.

In summary, the concepts from which despairwork is drawn owe a large debt to Buddhist teachings; yet the work hardly depends on

Buddhist belief for its efficacy. Other traditions as well offer guidance in moving through the dark of our time and in finding, through the acknowledgement and sharing of our pain for the world, the power to redeem it. It is, perhaps, the distinctive gift of the Buddha that the insights and methods he offered are so universally applicable. Refusing to be drawn into debates on the correctness of differing views and opinions, he focused, like a physician, on one fact above all—that there is suffering. Because his teachings preeminently address that fact, they remain ever relevant and can nourish other traditions, other societies.

(1985)

NOURISHING FREEDOM

Five Ways to Provide an Engaged Buddhist
Education for Your Children

Mushim Ikeda-Nash

Celebrate Buddha's Birthday Today

We can communicate to our child, even before birth, and certainly every day thereafter: "You are the Buddha. Happy birthday, baby Buddha!" An engaged Buddhist education, as I define it, begins with transmitting to our baby that all beings have buddha-nature. When our children understand this, they feel bathed in love and trust, just as in some traditions a figure of the baby Buddha is bathed in warm sweet tea each year.

I recently attended instruction in Zen meditation given by Layla Smith, at a North American Buddhist women's conference. Layla, who is a mom and a Zen priest, showed us some stable sitting postures. "Now, sit like a baby," she said, smiling. "Sit like a baby in Buddha's lap."

Teach Children How to Take Refuge

My son Joshua's original home was my body. At nine, he still likes to hug me and pat my tummy. "I came from there," he says. "I was little, like a fish. I liked it in there." Although Josh, my husband Chris, and I have lived in a one-bedroom apartment for seven years, whenever we talk about moving to a larger place, Josh says, "I don't want to leave this house. It's my childhood home. I'm used to the way it smells. I love everything about it."

We establish safe, loving homes for our children, places where they can take refuge from stress and overstimulation. As our children grow, they naturally spend more and more time away from us, developing new skills and testing what they've learned so far. But what happens when they are away from home and "lose it"—fall apart emotionally? As a mother, I try to give my son and other children a way to go for refuge, a way to touch home base in any situation.

The Buddha himself left his "palace" and wife and son to find a new home for himself under the bodhi tree. The home he found was his body, his breath, and his buddha-nature. It was very portable. We can remind our kids, also, from the time they are a few years old, to center their energy in their bodies, to learn awareness of breath, and to visualize the baby Buddha inside themselves, always sitting happily and peacefully, bathed in loving-kindness.

Some years ago I went to pick up Josh from his kindergarten class. A teacher told me that he was in the auditorium, "getting counseling from the principal." Apparently he had been playing with his two best friends, and they had decided to exclude him. "It's two against one," one of his buddies said. Josh was so hurt and angry that he lost control and bit his friend's hand, drawing blood.

The instant I saw my five-year-old, standing next to his friend and the school principal, I felt shocked by how absent he looked, how unlike his normal self. He was pale, trembling, his entire body rigid, and his gaze distant. I brought him home and made him sit in a warm bath to bring him back into his body. Then I told him that the Buddha had given us a special way to heal ourselves when we feel wounded, or have hurt others. Would he like to try it? Josh said yes, so we offered incense at our home altar and he sat in my lap. Then we recited the *Metta Sutra* (sutra on loving-kindess) together, offering wishes for our own happiness and well-being, then wishes for all the people we loved and liked, then for all the people we did not like, then for all beings. We put his friend's name into the sutra, and prayed, "May [my friend] be happy and well. May he be free from suffering."

By the end of the recitation, Josh had relaxed, and looked more like himself. He went to his room and played quietly the rest of the day. Two years later, when I again picked him up at school after an especially chaotic day, I asked him how his day had gone.

"Not good," he said. "I got a bad headache. At recess I sat under a tree and meditated."

"Did it help?" I asked, amazed.

"Yes," he said.

Teach Your Child the Art of Questioning, and Be Open in Giving Answers

A typical second-grade math problem at my son's alternative public school is: "How do you measure a puddle? Write and draw your answer." Children are encouraged to collaborate with one another and to seek multiple ways of finding the "right" answer to a given problem.

Probably the most powerful "Buddhist" tool I feel I can offer children is identical to what is called "critical thinking" in modern education—the ability to formulate questions that can open up new areas of thought and being, and the courage to do so. What greater gift can we give, since surely we do not have all the answers? I believe in spending lots of time talking with kids, asking them questions, joking around, and encouraging them to ask me questions I can't answer, then strategizing ways we might be able to find an answer. As far as I am concerned, no question is taboo, and I never withhold information, although occasionally I will say to my son, "This has to do with adult sort of material. However, if you like I will explain it to you as fully as I can. Would you like to hear the answer?" Sometimes he says yes, sometimes no. In this way we have discussed subjects such as how people can get AIDS, why children are starving in North Korea, and why his birth father does not live with us.

Free and open access to information and the ability to choose what he is ready to learn have given Joshua dignity and inner strength. He and I recently talked again about how, after my father unexpectedly died in the night, I had to decide whether Josh deserved the choice to look at Grandpa's body, not yet embalmed and "fixed up" by the funeral home.

"Some adults thought I shouldn't have given you the choice," I said.

Joshua was indignant. "They're totally wrong," he said. "If you hadn't given me the choice, I would have torn up the house. How could I accept Grandpa's death if I didn't see his body? That's just insane. Anyway, other people don't know what's best for you, me, and Dad. Only we can decide, because we know our own situation."

Be an Activist for Universal Education

When Josh was finishing preschool, several parents said to me, "He's so bright, you should try to find a private school for him. The public schools in Oakland are no good." One mother said, "You might consider a Catholic school. I know you're Buddhist, but all religions are the same because they all say we should love one another." Although these people were well intentioned, and had good points to make, Chris and I wanted Josh to attend a public school where racial, cultural, and socioeconomic diversity would be ensured. I wanted to be an educational advocate for all the children.

If we regard all children as potential Buddhas, I don't think we can say that some children deserve a better education than others. Robert Thurman, arguing for "universal, total, unlimited education of all individuals" in his essay "Nagarjuna's Guidelines" in the *Engaged Buddhist Reader* (Berkeley: Parallax Press, 1996) says:

> [T]he educational system of a society is not there to "service" the society, to produce its drone-"professionals," its workers, its servants. The educational system is the individual's doorway to liberation, to enlightenment. It is therefore the brain of the body politic. Society has no other purpose than to foster it. It is society's door of liberation.

Although admittedly a very American, broad, and democratic take on education, Thurman's comments have for years inspired me. I decided to become an activist parent in support of public education, and I keep finding new ways to express my commitment: participating as a facilitator in antiracism work in the school, volunteering to help with literacy, and lobbying the school district when severe problems remain unaddressed because of bureaucratic red tape. A proactive attitude can lead to surprising results.

Last spring I had taken myself out for a lunch special at a Chinese restaurant in my neighborhood when Oakland mayoral candidate Jerry Brown walked past my table. Emboldened by the fact that he has practiced Zen meditation, I leaped up and shook his hand vigorously, then ran home and found his campaign website, "Oaklanders First." I e-mailed him: "Jerry: If you are elected mayor, what can you do about our public schools? They're falling apart!" About five minutes later the phone rang, and a strange voice boomed, "Hello!"

"Who's calling?" I asked suspiciously.

"Jerry Brown!" the voice said. "I'm quick, aren't I?"

I told the ex-governor of California all about my son's school: the moldy, tattered rugs, vandalized bathrooms, dedicated teachers, lack of supplies, and nearly barren playground. He listened carefully, and at the end of our conversation repeated back to me the points I had made. He assured me that I was not alone. Whether the neighborhood was rich or poor, he said, all Oakland residents had the same two complaints: crime, and the alarming condition of the public school system.

"Please write down an educational policy for the new mayor's office and send it to me," Jerry Brown said in parting. A few months later, Brown was elected mayor in a landslide vote; a newspaper article said he was possibly the first politician to get elected by listening carefully and fully to people instead of talking at them.

Although it may be provocative, I want to argue that a Buddhist education should be a public education—or, as Thurman says, the door of liberation for all: "By giving others the gift of education, they gain freedom, self-reliance, understanding, choice, all that is still summed up in the word 'enlightenment.'" Can we work toward providing this?

Practice "Letting Go"

Practicing nonattachment doesn't mean not loving our children. But if we cling to them and they cling to us, eventually we'll both be limited, distorted by our love.

I've heard some parents express fear of the "outside world" as being full of contamination. They feel threatened by pop culture, and see their children as pure beings who must be sheltered as long as possible from television, video games, the Internet, and fast foods. Imparting a Buddhist education, instilling in my son the ability to fearlessly ask questions, telling him he has the right to seek answers, and showing him how to go for refuge, provide what I feel my child basically needs to deal with the "outside world." When I trust that Joshua's "inside world"—his sense of self, and his trust in innate goodness—is healthy and intact, I trust him. When I trust him fully, I take joy in his growing up and I can let him go. And that's my Buddhist education.

(1998)

ABOUT MONEY

Robert Aitken

We associate money with Mara, the destroyer, who becomes fatter and fatter with each financial deal at the expense of the many beings. We can also associate money with Kuan-yin, the incarnation of mercy, whose thousand hands hold a thousand tools for rescuing those same beings. Money can be one of her tools.

Kuan-yin functions as the Net of Indra; Mara, the destroyer, functions as the Net of Indra too. Each point of the net perfectly reflects each other point. Each point is a hologram. Mara says, "All of you are me." Kuan-yin says, "I am all of you." It's the very same thing, except in attitude. Attitude poisons or nurtures the interbeing.

The ninth-century Chinese master Ta-sui announced that you and I perish along with the universe in the *kalpa* fire, the fire at the end of the aeon that destroys everything totally. Joyous news! Joyous news! *Dukkha*, anguish, disappears in the laughter of Ta-sui. How to find Ta-sui's joy is the question. The path is eightfold, the Buddha said: Right View, Right Thinking, Right Speech, Right Action, Right Livelihood, Right Effort, Right Recollection, and Right *Samadhi*.

Mara hates Ta-sui, for he confirms the demon's worst fears and seems to exult in them. How can Ta-sui joke about the ultimate end! Mara hates the Eightfold Path because it undermines the ramparts of his firehouse. The firehouse itself becomes a hostel and the champion fire fighters become nurses. Who will put out the *kalpa* fire?

Meanwhile Kuan-yin reposes on her comfortable rock by the waterfall, shaded by a willow tree. People say they don't like bowing to Kuan-yin because she is just an icon or an idol. Of course it's nonsense to bow to an idol. Kuan-yin doesn't think of herself as an idol. Her idol is her ideal, her ideal is her Right Views, her Right Views are her blood and guts.

Kuan-yin's practice is elemental too. It is embodied everywhere—as the Earth, for example, exchanging energy with Uranus and Jupiter and Mercury and others together with the Sun as they plunge on course through the plenum. It is embodied as the plenum itself containing the vastly more incredible dynamics of the nebulae. The *dana*, charity, of Kuan-yin is not only a vast chaos of order; you will find it in tiny systems of mutual support as well—the termite, for example, nurturing parasites who digest our foundations in exchange for a dark, wet place to live.

Primal society also embodies the *dana* of Kuan-yin, circulating the gift that nurtures its families and clans. At a single festival, a necklace of precious shells becomes two dozen precious pendants. At a single market holiday, a knife becomes salt and salt becomes a colt. The honor of a new chief is spread by blankets far and wide. Of course, Mara blows his smoke through these exchanges. Did the primal peoples know Mara from Kuan-yin? They'd never heard of it either, of course, but they knew greed when they saw it, and so do we.

Mara isn't an icon either, and he is bowing to himself all day long. He hates the notion of circulating the gift. Instead he circulates the folks. He maneuvers them, lines them up before his machinery, then offers them their own products for their money. He circulates the animals and their products, the grasses and their products, the trees and their products. Broken glass set in cement on the tops of high stone walls protects his treasure from those whose diligence produces it. Gates and armed guards and police dogs protect his children and judges protect his bookkeepers. With his ardent practice the poor get so poor that he must give a little back to keep the arrangement functioning. He is ennobled and great institutions of benevolence bear his name. Bits of nature are conserved. Peruvian musicians are recorded. Yet the karma of wealth can be inspired by Kuan-yin. The wealthy are stewards named Kuan-yin.

All the while Kuan-yin herself sustains the poor. They are her teachers. She doesn't circulate the folks or their products; she leaves them be. She leaves the birds and the fish and the animals be, the stones and trees and clouds be—and does not move them around. The walls with their broken glass and guarded gates hold her in her place, outside. If she keeps the folks entertained, she might even get a grant. You can have a grant, you can do your thing, or you can go to jail. It's up to you, Kuan-yin.

It isn't easy for Mara to manipulate people and things. He practices so diligently that he foregoes golf and the theater sometimes. Kuan-yin foregoes golf and the theater too as she sits in royal ease, delighting in the birds as they dip in and out of the spray. But Mara never finds ease of any kind, not even in the middle of the night. His prostate gives him hell and he sweats with fear.

This Mara mind is the uneasy, primordial mind, arising from the muck, as reptilian as a dinosaur. It is much older than Kuan-yin. How old is Kuan-yin? Don't say ageless. You are just letting Mara do his dirty work unchallenged. Don't say she is the moment. That is Mara's view as well, pouring out the drinks at his villa on Majorca.

Mara can be your fall-back mind. After all, it's a dog-eat-dog world and I've got mine, Jack. Kuan-yin, on the other hand, is always fresh and new. She can come into our time and go out of it freely, a trick Mara never learned. We cannot fall back on Kuan-yin; we have to remember her. With a single Mara thought we are in his reins. Giddiyap horsie! With a single Kuan-yin thought, we are laughing at the puppies. *Namo Avalokiteshvara Mahasattva! Namu Kanzeon Makasatsu!* Veneration to the Great Being Who Perceives Sounds of the World! As the *Ten Verse Kannon Sutra of Timeless Life* declares, "Thought after thought arises in mind. Thought after thought is not separate from mind."

Mara and Kuan-yin create and cultivate many nets within the Net of Indra. Like the stars, the points in these lesser nets survive by exchanging energy, called money by Mara, called money by Kuan-yin sometimes. There are industries and collectives, golf clubs and base communities. In the lesser nets, Mara dominates, Kuan-yin subverts. Mara co-opts the subversion. Kuan-yin chooses to counter with her money sometimes, if it will keep the waterfall abundant and the birds happy. Sometimes Kuan-yin runs an industry. Sometimes Mara runs a collective. Sometimes there are base communities within golf clubs. Sometimes there are golf clubs within base communities.

It is possible to play endlessly with archetypes and metaphors. Mara as the reptile mind can be called the id. Kuan-yin as the Buddha mind can be called the superego. When the id is boss, the forests burn in Armageddon's self-fulfilling prophecy. When the superego is boss, the fires of love are extinguished. But Mara and Kuan-yin are not Mara and Kuan-yin, therefore we give them such names. Wipe away the terminology! Wipe away the archetypes! Let Mara and Kuan-yin disappear!

The anguish of nations and families arises from an anxiety to prove oneself—or oneself together with kin and compatriots. The vow to save everybody and everything brings fun to the dinner table and to international festivals. But proving yourself is the Way of the Buddha, bringing forth your latent pantheon of Manjushri, bodhisattva of wisdom, Samantabhadra, bodhisattva of great action, and the others, as the self. (The archetypes keep popping up anyway!) The shadow side of the vow to save everybody and everything is the imperative to bring Mother Hubbards to heathen Hawaiians.

Checks, bills, bonds—the tokens of power—transport solutions of sugar and salt to rescue infants from dysentery. They prime the pump of life and order eggplant Parmesan at Aunty Pasto's Restaurant. They build the dam of energy. Moose and beavers and primal people die. Checks, bills, and bonds dance to the music of attitude. Attitude poisons or nurtures the interbeing.

We're in it together. You can't hide out and drink from streams and eat from trees. Or if you do, you are languishing at the top of Chinese master Ch'ang-sha's hundred-foot pole, and he'll kick you off. The culture we treasure does not exist apart. The municipal symphony, museums, galleries, theaters, bookshops, even our practice centers are intimately integrated into the acquisitive system. We have to work with this fact somehow. It is not clear to me, as it may not be clear to you, how to go about this. As you go along, your qualms can get worse. You can find yourself in a truly dark night, with many misgivings about the Way and doubts about how to deal with the terrible ethical problems that confront every person in middle or upper levels of management—and that confront every worker, every teacher, every social worker.

I suggest that the way to deal with a lack of clarity is to accept it. It's all right not to be clear. The practice is to clarify. Moreover, you're working always with your ego. You never get rid of your ego. Your ego is just your self-image. Burnish your ego down to its basic configurations. Then it will shine forth. You can forget yourself as your vows take over your practice, like the birds in the spray of the waterfall.

(1993)

IMPOSSIBLE POSSIBILITIES

Norman Fischer

I watch morning television—a practice I would recommend. You can learn a lot from it: what people are buying and selling, what they are thinking and talking about, what they are afraid of, what they hope for. The other day a woman appeared on television who had worked out a good method for achieving happiness. Her idea was that you would write in a journal every day, as a way of keeping track of yourself in various areas of your life, like physical health, relationships, and spirituality. Through the writing there would somehow be an improvement. I was impressed that in the category of spirituality she included forgiveness as a regular daily topic: that every day you would write in your journal about your efforts to forgive yourself for what you had done that was harmful, and to forgive others for what they might have done to you. She had her own personal story to tell, about how her life had changed dramatically for the better because of this practice.

It seemed quite startling to me to imagine that there was so much hurting going on in the world that every day every person would need to spend some time actively forgiving people, including him- or herself. But I quickly saw that yes, this is probably true. There are so many possibilities for hurt! There is the explicit hurting through anger, violence, deprivation, and oppression, but also the more subtle hurting that comes from failing to love enough, failing to acknowledge and appreciate oneself and others—the kind of hurting that goes almost unnoticed and yet is a powerful negative factor in our lives. So yes, it would make sense if you were going to take care of yourself well, take your vitamins, eat a low-fat diet, and so on, that you would also, as a hygienic discipline, take on the daily practice of forgiveness.

But forgiveness is difficult. It's painful.

If you have hurt yourself or someone else, you are responsible for having created pain. Whether conscious or not, that pain is there in you. And if someone else has hurt you, then of course the pain is there. The first step in forgiving yourself or another is to let yourself feel the fullness of that pain. So forgiveness, at least in this first stage, doesn't feel good.

Nobody likes to feel pain. Naturally, we want to distract ourselves from pain, and we will latch onto something else, anything else, to avoid it. Our economy depends on this human tendency—companies that market the drugs that keep us pain-free, the products that distract and amuse us, the entertainment that absorbs our attention so we won't think of anything that matters—all this is essential for our prosperity.

But the most compelling form of avoidance of pain is blaming. When you can't entirely eliminate the pain by distraction or oblivion, you get around it by blaming it on someone or something—even if it is yourself. Blaming is a smoke screen for the pain itself. You focus forcefully on blame so you don't have to notice the horrifying weight of your suffering.

So forgiving has to begin with allowing yourself to drop blame, distraction, and oblivion and actually feel the pain of what has happened. This is hard work, especially since much of the time the pain isn't within the immediate frame of your awareness, and you need to do something to evoke it, to bring it forth into your heart. It's rare that anyone is willing to sit still for this, but forgiveness requires it. This is one reason why meditation practice is sometimes not so peaceful: if you meditate with a sense of openness to what comes in (and this is really the only way to meditate), it does tend to evoke all of this hurt. Meditation practice itself in this way can bring you toward a sense of forgiveness.

The next step toward forgiveness, which comes with the thorough completion of the first step, is to go to the root of the pain, beyond the story that comes associated with it and beyond the dismay and the fear.

Pain's true root is always the same: existence itself. Because you are alive, there is this pain. With being, there is always this pain. You've been hurt, yes, it's true. Someone has done something to you—that may also be true. But if you didn't have a mind, a body, an identity, it wouldn't have happened. Since you do have a mind, a body, an identity, it is guaranteed that you will be hurt when the conditions for your being hurt come together. So the person who hurt you, you yourself, and the story of the hurting are all actually incidental to the ultimate fact of your existence. Forgiving follows naturally when you see that we are all in this together and that we are all victims of hurt.

This is a tall order. This is forgiveness as a profound religious practice.

So I agree with the expert on television that forgiveness must be a daily practice—a path that we have to keep walking, probably for our whole life.

To forgive yourself seems the hardest form of forgiveness. In Zen practice, simply allowing yourself to be yourself, just as you are, is considered the mark of awakening. Short of this, you are at best slightly embarrassed about who you are, and at worst, tortured by it.

Forgiveness of another person is also an internal act—it is something you do, in the final analysis, for yourself. After all, if you harbor resentment for another it is you yourself who will suffer for that. The other person may be just fine, completely oblivious to how you feel about him or her, while you are eating yourself alive with anger. You think: I'll never forgive him—he doesn't deserve it. This is a little like hitting yourself over the head with a hammer and refusing to stop because the other person isn't worthy of your stopping. So forgiveness is for yourself. In a way, it doesn't really affect the other person. If you forgive people, it doesn't get them off the hook for what they have done. They are still responsible for their actions. No one can ever escape the consequences of action; everyone has him- or herself to answer for and live with. When you know that, you can feel free to forgive. And to do so in order to open your own heart, so that maybe one day you can actually learn how to love others completely. Forgiveness is something you do inside yourself and for yourself.

Reconciliation is the effort you make to reach out to those who have wronged you or whom you have wronged. Because reconciliation involves others it is much more complicated. With reconciliation you try to understand things from the other person's point of view, to express that understanding, and to make peace based on that mutuality of understanding. It is like reconciling your checkbook—you balance one side with the other, until there is a sense of mutual identity.

This also is not so easy, and you can't expect too much. When there is pain between two people, or groups of people, there is a risk that more talk will actually lead to more hurting. Sometimes reconciliation is impossible—or at least for now. Maybe a lot of time has to go by. Sometimes the best thing is to agree that nothing can be said without causing more trouble, and to part company for a while.

The other day there was yet another horrible bombing in Israel, at a disco, and the victims were teenagers. And I've been thinking about how it is that Jews and Palestinians persist in hating one another, and hurting one another, over such a long time, at such tremendous cost to all involved. People think it's irrational—just a matter of blind prejudice. Why can't they be more reasonable, more kind, like the rest of us? This is a very naïve view.

The fact is, hatred is not irrational. People have very good reasons for hating each other. They hate each other because they fear each other. And they fear each other because they feel that the other is a direct threat to their identity. And since fear is a disempowering emotion, it is usually covered up with hatred.

Although Buddhism's genius is to deny the reality of identity, and to offer a thoroughgoing path that takes us beyond fixed identity, still, for most of us in this world, including Buddhists, identity is experienced as a fact. Gertrude Stein famously said, "I am I because my little dog knows me." And I am I because of my beliefs and associations. If your beliefs and associations seem to deny mine, then I am frightened for my very lifeblood, and I feel I have no choice but to hate you. Your existence threatens to blot mine out.

And this hatred isn't made up: It is rooted in external events. Members of your group have killed members of mine; my brothers, my sisters, my countrymen. They have taken away our land, forbidden us to speak our language, and withheld our rights. And they have done this not only to some of us but to many of us, and have done it not only once or twice but repeatedly. How can I be who I am, a Jew or a Palestinian, or an Irish Catholic or Protestant, or a Lebanese Christian or Muslim, or a Serbian or Albanian, if I can forgive such things? If I were to forgive you, how could I face myself, and how could I face my community?

When I visited Northern Ireland last year I saw how in some situations, not to hate the enemy is an unthinkable possibility. In Northern Ireland everyone must be either Protestant or Catholic, and if you are one it means you must deny the other. I was there with His Holiness the Dalai Lama, and believe it or not, people wanted to know whether the Dalai Lama was a Protestant Buddhist or a Catholic Buddhist. They accepted that he was a Buddhist—but which kind of Buddhist was he? So, in certain historical situations, it becomes almost impossible to let go of your cultural identity. Some years ago, when I was in Israel, I tried to speak to people there about Zen practice and about the Buddhist sense of reconciliation based on emptiness. I found I couldn't even get the words out because it was simply an inexpressible thought in that culture at that time.

Tremendous emotion builds up over a long time, and myths are created. As we tell the story of what has happened, it becomes not so much the story of what has actually occurred as the story of our pain and our fear. With these stories conditioning our views, how can we ever reach out to one another in reconciliation?

I have seen this happen in personal conflicts among my own friends. Without the practice of forgiveness, which commits us to feeling the naked truth of our pain and simply allowing it to be what it is, the effort to reach out fails every time. In political conflict involving generations and multitudes, the situation becomes far worse. If you listen to what Jews and Palestinians say about what has happened in the past, it is astonishing. They describe events in which both peoples have participated, but the descriptions seem to have nothing to do with one another. Even the very names of the places over which they contend don't jibe. There seem to be no facts whatsoever—only myths that are accepted, almost on faith, as facts. So there is no way to sort things out. And at the root of this tremendous dissonance is the fear of loss of identity.

Years ago, in Israel, I ran into an old settler who said to me, with utter confidence and cheer, "Peace will come. The momentum is always for peace." At the time I was in despair about the situation, and I was astonished by his comment. He was not a naïve, sentimental person but someone who had seen tremendous hardship in Israel, and in Europe before he came to Israel. But now I believe that he was absolutely correct—that the momentum is always for peace.

I suppose this is nothing more than a species of faith. The human capacity for bitterness and hatred and delusion is tremendous, and that energy is by no means played out in this world. And yet, people still fall in love, still have children, and still love those children. People still hope for peaceful homes and neighborhoods. They hope for beauty.

Identity and fear are powerful motivators, and they need to be respected. Probably the single most important realization that would lead to peace in the world would be this one—the recognition that we are all afraid of ceasing to be what we imagine we are. This is what motivates most of our political activity.

So yes, we need to respect fear and identity—they are strong. But stronger still is the desire for peace. Peace is the end of every story, just as it is the end of every life. So peace will come, and people want it to come.

When I was in Northern Ireland at the Way of Peace Conference with His Holiness the Dalai Lama, I listened to a panel of victims of "the troubles." These were people who had all, each in a different way, been devastated by the conflict. There was a man who had been blinded by an English soldier's bullet, a woman who was a paraplegic as a result of a drive-by shooting, and a man who was broken inside spiritually, and said so very movingly, because of the acts of violence he himself had committed.

What was inspiring about their presentations was that each of them had had a change of heart. Each had gone through enormous hurt and bitterness to find that place where hurt is just the hurt of being alive, and there is finally no one to blame and nothing to regret. In a way, for each of these people, the worst had happened. What they had feared and dreaded, with a fear and a dread that had previously motivated them to hatred, had actually taken place, and there was nothing else to do but let go of identity and fear, and accept a new life as a different person.

The alternative is to shut down internally. But these panel members had done the opposite; they had opened instead of closing. And they were cheerful people, natural and at ease with themselves, and every one of them was actively and passionately involved in peace work.

As long as there is more than one of us, there are going to be conflicts and tragedies and the need to work things out in the midst of difficult situations. So we will always need the skills of hard-nosed and realistic negotiation, of tradeoffs and strategy. But I am convinced that real reconciliation depends ultimately on forgiveness, which is internal, spiritual work that all of us have to do.

(2001)

BUDDHA'S MOTHER
SAVING TIBET

Robert Thurman

The following is adapted from a talk given by Robert Thurman at Green Gulch Farm Zen Center in Muir Beach, California, on April 14, 1991.

I'd like to start by reading from the *Avatamsaka Sutra* (Flower Ornament Sutra). Queen Maya, mother of the Buddha, speaks:

> I became the mother of the enlightening being Siddhartha, by the great inconceivable miracle of the birth of an enlightening being. At that time I was in the house of king Shuddhodana, and when the time of the enlightening being's descent from the heaven of contentment had arrived, from every pore the enlightening being emanated as many rays of light as atoms in untold buddha-lands, arrayed with the qualities of the birth of all enlightening beings. . . . Rays of light illumined the whole world, then descended on my body and entered into every pore of my body, beginning with my head. As soon as those light rays, with various names, had entered my body, I saw all the enlightening beings. . .as they sat on the Buddha's lion throne at the site of enlightenment, surrounded by congregations of enlightening beings, honored by the leaders of the world, turning the wheel of the teaching. . . . When those rays of light of the enlightening being entered my body, my body outreached all worlds, and my belly became as vast as space, and yet did not go beyond the

human physical size. The supernal manifestations of the enlightening beings' abode in the womb everywhere in the ten directions all appeared in my body.

[*Entry Into the Realm of Reality*,
translated by THOMAS CLEARY,
Shambhala Publications, 1989]

Apparently, to be the Buddha's mother, to carry the Buddha in your womb, is quite an exercise. While he's in your womb, forty-two trillion different deities come to receive dharma teachings every day. There's this multimedia show going on inside your stomach wall, and Buddha's sitting there in a little pagoda, talking about the dharma instead of being an embryo. You don't want to breathe too heavily, or burp, or gurgle, because you could disturb the dharma teachings for trillions of subliminal beings. The *Avatamsaka Sutra* is an extended evocation of Maya, the mother of the Buddha. It's a fantastic vision of the power of the feminine, where all negativity is harnessed and enfolded within pure love, and formed into beauty, and formed into planets wherein beings can come to their own perfection. This is what it means to give birth to Buddhas at all times.

I want to speak in honor of the Buddha's mother, whose miraculous power is still with us, because otherwise, in our imagination of Buddhist history, we think that Siddhartha Shakyamuni lived 2,500 years ago and that now we have descended into a dark age. We also think that the guys have been doing it all—all the big monks and patriarchs, all the male chauvinist macho enlightened beings—and that the girls have just been making sushi.

Well, this is completely wrong. In the first place, the Buddha is not gone at all. In fact, the death of the Buddha is merely the dissolving of the illusion of the body, and the Buddha is returning to where he has always been, which is in and around us, suffused in every atom of our being. Every one of us, like Maya Devi, has billions of planets in our body, in every cell and atom, and those planets are not just planets where a bunch of morons are fighting nuclear wars, they are planets where Buddhas and bodhisattvas are attaining enlightenment, are giving their lives and benefiting other beings in an inconceivable web of benevolence and beauty.

So we have to start with this miracle level when we talk about Tibet, because Tibet is the place on this planet where the collision of delusions is most manifest. And we are totally connected to it right here and now. Every time you turn on the tap and worry about the water shortage, you are connecting with Tibet. The destruction of the environment of Tibet creates a chimney effect, and it makes the air currents neurotic: they go too far south in the Pacific and too far north on the North American continent, and that's part of what is depriving you of your water.

So Tibet is totally connected to us, and we have to start affirming the miraculous truth that love is in fact powerful. And that evil is stupid and wimpy, screwing things up, but really not the main thing that is going on. We have to start from that because otherwise, when we really look at the horror, we become too depressed. We have to be able to find Queen Maya's belly in order to confront nonviolently the forces of hate and delusion. The force of love is more powerful. Even if they kill us, it's more powerful. Even if we die, if we die loving, the love is more powerful than the physical death.

Only when a whole mass of people understands this will we win the battle. It's the only way we can win it. More people have to be willing to die *not* to hurt others than are willing to die *to* hurt others before the hurting of others will stop.

Do you know the story of the seamless monument? A great Ch'an master in China goes to visit the emperor, who is his disciple, and the emperor says, "Oh master, I like you. After you die, what can I do for you?"

The master says, "Build me a seamless monument."

The emperor thinks about architectural plans, and he notices all the joints in joinery, all the boundaries, all the seams, and he says, "Excuse me, Your Holiness, could you please tell me what such a monument would look like?

The Ch'an master remains silent for quite a while. Then he says, "Do you see it? Do you understand?"

The emperor says, "No I don't—I have no idea."

The master says, "I have a disciple who will tell you fifteen years from now what it's like." And then the master went off and he died.

The poor emperor had to wait. He sent for the disciple, and after about fifteen years the disciple showed up.

The emperor says, "Can you describe for me the seamless monument?"

And the disciple says, "The seamless monument? Sure, I've had that description ready for years!" And then he says this verse which many people meditate on as a *koan*: *The Blue Cliff* Record, translated by J. C. Cleary and Thomas Cleary, Shambhala Publications, 1992.

> South of Hsiang, north of T'an,
> In between there's gold sufficient to a nation.
> Beneath the shadowless tree the community ferryboat—
> Within the crystal palace there's no one who knows.

[*The Blue Cliff Record*, TRANSLATED BY J. C. CLEARY AND
THOMAS CLEARY, SHAMBHALA PUBLICATIONS, 1992]

Now I'll give my commentary. (I guess you're not supposed to comment on *koans*, but never mind. I'm just a woolly Tibetan; I don't know these finer points!) "South of Hsiang, north of T'an"—this is like saying, "South of San, north of Francisco," in other words, everywhere. "In between, there's gold sufficient to a nation." Now, what do you think a seamless monument is? How do you make a monument to enlightenment if you're a ruler? It's nice to make a monument: like giving the Nobel Peace Prize to somebody. You're commemorating their greatness, right? But suddenly you are doing something else when you do that. When you give one person the Nobel Peace Prize you are pointing out that hundreds of millions don't have the Nobel Peace Prize. When you create a monument, you are pointing out that billions of people are not memorialized in that monument. Lincoln got a monument, but Andrew Jackson didn't make it. So a monument creates a distinction between the holy and the unholy. A seamless monument would have to mean somehow that what's being memorialized and the memorializer are nondual. Death and life cannot be different; enlightenment and nonenlightenment cannot be different; Buddhism cannot be different from society.

We think that if we all were enlightened all the time, there would be no economy and we would all starve. We think that only a certain segment can pursue enlightenment and the rest have to work to produce the food, although no matter how much food you eat, you can't live forever. Finally you die anyway.

But the master in the story says no, in between San and Francisco, there is gold sufficient to a nation. He says, "Don't tell me, Mr. President, that you can't afford to support the whole nation's seamless life as a monument to enlightenment! Everything is gold, everything is abundance!"

For example, take Tibet. "We couldn't give up Tibet," says China. "We couldn't afford it. Tibet is so valuable. That's why we invaded and annexed it. It's one million square miles."

And the United States says, "Oh, we can't afford to censure China. We can't afford to stop them from torturing people; it's their internal affair. Besides, think of how much Coca-Cola they're going to drink in the next century!"

We all do this; we all say this "can't afford" justification to ourselves. Tibetan teacher Tara Tulku asks people to do an exercise of counting up the minutes of their lives. Count them up: How many of them were spent trying to achieve the purpose of your life, the fruition that will go on beyond the death that you know is waiting for you? Let's see: I sleep for eight hours, I spend so many hours eating, I spend so many hours making the money to eat, building my house, buying my clothes, keeping up my car and so on. And how much do I spend developing my generosity and wisdom, which is my body of enlightenment, my future house and my future mind? How many minutes of the day do I spend on that? It's a shocking exercise to think about how extremely little time is spent investing in something greater than what we are wrongly misidentifying as ourselves, this personality that is running around busily looking for a cemetery plot. Anyway, all the money we make will be spent by idiots when we're dead.

"Beneath the shadowless tree, the community ferryboat." What is the shadowless tree? The tree that casts no shadow. The tree of enlightenment is nondual. There is no light and shadow. And what is the tree of enlightenment? Is it some tree in India in ancient times? No. It is your nervous system. It is an enlightened nervous system that knows it's not separated from the world around it. It is the Buddha's mother's nervous system. In this *koan*, the Zen master says that beneath the shadowless tree of an enlightened emperor is a community ferryboat. When the emperor is enlightened, society will be a community ferryboat. And what is a community ferryboat? It takes everybody across the ocean of *samsara*.

How do you get across? You can't just get on and have someone else take you across. Buddha cannot take you across. His Holiness the Dalai Lama cannot take you across. Queen Maya cannot take you across. Why can't she? Because you're already there. She can't take you into her own womb when you are in her womb. All you have to do is realize you are in her. And how do you realize that? You have to educate yourself.

Meditating will not get you there either. You can meditate all you want without dislodging your delusion, if you don't educate yourself. You can sit perfectly for twenty years, and your meditation will only build a fortification for your delusion. So Buddhism is not meditation. Buddhism is not a theory. Buddhism is not any particular rules, or actions, or morality. Buddhism is a process of education of the mind and heart through learning, understanding, and meditation, and through loving, virtuous action.

None of us is paid to make peace. It's not our livelihood. Maybe a couple of foundation people, one or two fortunate ones, but mostly not. But the war armies, they have pay! They have hundreds of billions of dollars of budget. They have a giant Pentagon. And it was the same in Buddha's time.

So the Buddha thinks, How do I deal with this? The first thing I'll do is cut all the soldiers' salaries. I'll make them monks and nuns—no need for pay. I'm going to cut down on the clothing budget. How? We'll take some old rags from the corpses in the cemeteries and sew them into monks' and nuns' robes. They can live at the foot of a tree. They can live in old barns. That'll be cheaper. They can beg for a free lunch! In America, too, we could have a free lunch, but they put the surplus food in warehouses to rot, because they are trapped within their Protestant mentality of no free lunch. They underestimate the generosity of their God. God is omnipotent! How can He mind a free lunch?

So the peace soldiers, the monks and nuns, are going to go out and they're going to live for enlightenment. They'll die to the world, shave their hair—no lice, no bugs, no hairdo problems.

That's the Buddha's peace army, the monastic army of peace.

Imagine when Shakyamuni's army arrives here, which will have to happen soon—within a century for sure—what a zendo we can have in the Pentagon! We'll teach people tantric visualization with all those great video displays. It'll be awesome. We can take over the building. It will be just right for us. The *pancharaksha* mandala (the five mothers mandala) has five sides: it's a pentagon.

And you people are the peace army. This Buddhist peace movement originates from people who have learned something, who have sat, who have meditated, who have reeducated themselves. Protestant culture has mixed up the purpose of human life. It is freedom, not just production. Enlightenment, not subservience. Fun, not work. Fun—they have *fun* in Tibet! They have fun in Buddhist countries. They have festivals where they go out and shake giant *lingams* [phallic icons] in Japan, and get drunk. They're not uptight. Because you don't have to be uptight, intrinsically.

You have to be uptight when you live in a militarized society, because some jerk is going to come and arrest you if you have a good time. As His Holiness the Dalai Lama says, when you have a military establishment, the first person to lose his human rights is the soldier. You can't disobey, or they'll shoot you. And when you've lost your human rights, you want to take everybody else's away, too. It's been happening throughout history.

But now you are the soldiers, and you're ready. There is a Buddhist peace movement. If they try another war, we'll all be out there in the streets. You'll all be out there. Thich Nhat Hanh will be out there, interbeing with that nuke. He'll inter-be that railroad train. We'll all inter-be each other at the big be-in. But is it going to be enough? Can we liberate Tibet in that way?

The Buddhist movement needs Tibet, actually. Interbeing needs Tibet. Everyone needs Tibet to fully appreciate what they themselves are. Buddhism in India was a great force. It demilitarized India and de—macho-male-chauvinized it. By the time India was invaded by the Muslims it had become a topless civilization. You know, if women didn't feel like wearing shirts because it was hot, they didn't wear them, and nobody molested them. God was Mrs. God, and she was usually topless. Sexuality was allowable. They played fantastic ragas, and they did fantastic drumming. They ate 2,742 varieties of mangos. And they wrote exquisite poetry. It was a paradise, it was the garden of Eden.

Since then, the dharma *sangha* in Buddhist countries has never controlled the military authority, and social activism has always been countercultural, balanced against a political authority that had responsibility without enlightenment. Particularly in Japan. No one from the East Asian Buddhist traditions has had the experience of having to be responsible for an entire society. There's even a theory that you're not supposed to take responsibility. You're supposed to sit and meditate and drop out from the world, and just sort of avoid it. The Buddhist Peace Fellowship has come up against this. They've had a hard time persuading some meditators that they have a responsibility to be concerned about the injustices in society.

But such dualism has nothing to do with the Buddha's and Mrs. Buddha's view of the world. In that view of the world, enlightenment should be compassion. Compassion is nothing but universal responsibility. There should be no military. There should be no violence; humans don't need it. It's contrary to our programming. But in the United States you're educated to believe that militarism is inevitable on account of the fact that you're a nasty person with nasty, aggressive instincts and you're surrounded by nasty enemies who have nasty, aggressive instincts. The military establishment pays pseudobiologists at M.I.T. to pump out theories about the genetic nastiness of human beings.

Because of its location, Tibet is unique in the Buddhist world. When the great masters of India saw the Muslim cavalry coming, they said, "Hey, let's sneak up in the hills here." It was the closest place. And they just sneaked right up through the passes into Tibet, and they kept their institutions—all of them, they took the whole thing with them. The Tibetan warlords who lived there were very fierce. Tough as hell. But the Buddhists said, "Okay, we're just going to meditate over here in one little corner." And in about four centuries, that little corner was the whole of Tibet. The emperors were meditating, everyone was reeducated, and the Tibetans became tame and peaceful. Their enemies were so far away, they were able to do that. And finally, the monasteries took over the country. Not like the Protestants. The Protestant ethic destroyed monasticism and created the industrial revolution. But in Tibet, it was the opposite: monasticism itself became an industrialized revolution.

Do you know what a monastic industrial revolution would be like? Imagine industrializing Marin County into Zen centers. The industrial product becomes an enlightened person. The whole county government and the taxes are there to support everybody becoming selflessly enlightened. If you want to go on retreat, you just go to the Board of Retreats in the county seat, and say, "I'm going to be on retreat. I want a free lunch, every day. Delivered steaming hot." The industry is enlightenment. The product is free people who care about each other. I'm headed for the cemetery, so in the meantime, I don't want to get off my meditation pillow. I want to attain enlightenment. I really should be using all my time for this, because if I die without being free of greed, hate, and delusion, they will drag me into the *bardo*, into hellish places, with bad plumbing, no climate control. So I want to attain the ability to be free of that situation. A little temporary climate control becomes a very low priority.

That's what happened in Tibet. Tibet became like that. Tibet developed a different sense of responsibility. The Dalai Lama is the head of state. We think that's weird. We expect an enlightened, holy person to be powerless; we almost suspect that if they're not powerless, there's something wrong with them. But the enlightened person has to take responsibility, take power, in fact. And Tibet is the only place on this planet where political power and enlightenment became the same thing. The Tibetans even tamed the Mongolians, and the Mongolians were ferocious. They controlled the largest piece of land that anybody has ever controlled—and without any modern technology, just horses and arrows. And yet they became over several centuries what the Buddhists call "tamed." And don't think tame is bad. "Tame" means loving, selfless, kind, not jealous, not greedy. A tame society is a society that will not blow up the world.

But in the last three centuries we have participated in the destruction of Tibet. China hasn't been doing it alone. We destroyed them by exporting our confused idea of reality, which is that reality is something external. We think we are not real. We threw out the idea of the soul. I'm nothing, and therefore I can do anything I want, because I'm not really here. My brain, my flesh, are just external things. And the planet is external.

Before we infected China with our confusion, they never even tried to conquer Tibet. They used to send huge funds to Tibet. All the Chinese emperors would ask the lamas to pray for them. But we confused them. If Deng Xiaoping were smart, he would say, with the whole world, "Liberate the Tibetans! Train ten million Dalai Lamas, and send five hundred to Iowa, Kansas, Moscow, Paris, Tokyo, Washington, D.C., and teach those people to pray and be tamed before they drop neutron bombs on us." The world should be praying to Tibet to come over here and get us to cool out.

It is time we take action before another holocaust happens. Tibet is the last bastion of Buddha's army of peace. If Tibet's ecology, if Tibet's society, if Tibet's dharma are crushed and destroyed finally by the external-reality, modernizing, militarizing army, the planet is lost. The experiment has failed. Queen Maya's belly was unrecognized by us. We eject ourselves from it.

We will not let the destruction of this people stand. We will take responsibility to see that it does not stand. We will force our governments and the United Nations to protest. And we will have hope, in spite of the fact that we've been taught that good will not prevail. When we sit on our pillow, we will not just sit there blindly, we will sit there until we realize that goodness will prevail.

So please help us save Tibet. His Holiness has spoken about monks in Tibet being tortured and executed. He doesn't like to bring it up. He is committed to being aware of the suffering of all beings everywhere, so he doesn't usually open up about one poor Tibetan who is being dragged to execution. But this is what is going on. When you're sitting on your pillow, you think you have a little pain in the thigh, a little, needlelike pain. You don't know that that little needlelike pain is someone being tortured to death; a fellow believer in enlightenment and love being tortured to death by people whom our government is supporting. His Holiness feels we're ready to think about universal responsibility. Every day Buddhists say, "Beings are numberless; I vow to save them." Now we can make that vow genuine.

Tibet represents an alternative direction for the entire planet, a peace direction that the planet could have gone in four hundred years ago. Tibet is a manifestation of the fact that we can have paradise, we can have Shambhala, we can have Eden again. Easily. But not through "business as usual." When we see that there's something else in the world that the world is pretending is *not* in the world—another possibility—we have liberated Tibet in our mind. And then Tibet will become liberated on the ground. The zone of peace that should be the whole planet will begin in Tibet.

(1992)

CARING FOR HOME

Jack Kornfield

The following is adapted from a talk given at Spirit Rock Meditation Center in Woodacre, California, on January 21, 1991.

It feels wonderful to be home. Coming back after being away, I'm feeling how important home is: having friends, having a sense of community, being connected to the earth in some particular location. We all have this longing in ourselves for home, to find a place where we are connected, where we belong.

In the Buddhist tradition the understanding of home is often expressed in an odd way, in a backward way. The Sanskrit word for someone who becomes a follower of the Way is *anagaraka*, or a homeless person. What does it mean to be homeless? It means in some way to discover that our home is everywhere, that wherever we are is our home. To find our true home is to find in ourselves an unshakeable place in our hearts, in our being, where we belong to all things, where we are connected to the sky and the earth and the plants and the animals and the people around us; it is to care for wherever we find ourselves as our home.

Here is a quote from a Russian astronaut about home: "We brought up some small fish to the orbital space station for certain investigations. We were to be there three months. After about three weeks the fish began to die. How sorry we felt for them! What we didn't do to try to save them! And yet on earth we have great pleasure

197

in fishing, but when you're alone and far from anything terrestrial, any appearance of life is especially welcome. You just see how precious life is."

And another one of the astronauts said, "All I wanted to do when I came back was to take the politicians and bring them up into space and say to them, 'Look at the earth from this perspective—look at the Persian Gulf, look at the Indian Ocean. See the beauty of it.'"

So the question arises in this time of war—can we find home in ourselves, can we find peace in ourselves, in the face of conflict?

Martin Luther King, whose day it is today, says, "Never succumb to the temptation of becoming bitter, no matter what happens. Never succumb to the temptation of using violence in the struggle, for if you do, unborn generations will be the recipients of a long and desolate night of bitterness."

So now, we have our war in the Gulf. I watch television, as most of you probably do, and it's not called the "war," it's called "Desert Storm," the miniseries. It's like the Superbowl. There's a kid down the street from us who asked her parents, "Is our team still winning?" Or it's like some video game, only it's live from the Persian Gulf. And it's really hard to tell if it's just the usual TV violence or some other violence.

I started to watch it and I got really interested. Look at those missiles! They carry a picture in them and they match the picture up, and—they got 'em! Let's wipe out the nuclear power plant, and then we'll wipe out the chemical factories. And we'll do it in a few days. It will be surgical, right? Which means no blood, just clean. It's like a game. The most horrifying thing about it is that they don't show any people and they don't show any blood. It's just machines.

I began to pay attention to my body as I watched the war on TV, and noticed that it was very hard to stay in my body. I was actually very, very tense, and there was a lot of pain. It was hard just to feel, and stay here.

Here's a meditative task for you. Can you watch TV, the war, and stay in your body? Or as Thich Nhat Hanh might suggest, can you make a meditation *gatha,* a poem, to recite to yourself when you turn the TV on?

Watching the war,
It is not far away.
It is people like me.
I send my love.

Make your own poem.

As I feel it and I breathe and I pay attention, then all the things of childhood come, the despair that I carry anyway that has nothing to do with the war, that the war touches, or my own fear and loss and helplessness and depression. And I sense that the war has been here a long time—hundreds, thousands of years. For millennia we have been creating images of conquering nature, conquering one another, and conquering ourselves, putting aside our pain or our fear or our loss or our joy and making war with ourselves.

When I look at the images of the war I sense these enormous contradictions: my safety sitting here in my living room in Marin, and the danger and pain of the war.

I wonder if it's okay to have my problems. I got irritated with my daughter for doing something. Am I supposed to do that? There's a war on. Can I be petty today? Can I do my own thing? Is it all right to make money or to carry on business while the war is happening?

Or you drive around in your car, and maybe it's a little bit smoggy, and you say, "We're fighting a war to get more oil, right, so we can have more smog and drive around more." It's not just somebody else's war, it's the war that we create in living the way we do. It's our country and our culture and our boys, and they are mostly very young.

Make no bones about it, war is a terrible, terrible thing. The way it's packaged, the way it's sanitized on TV, it's hard to really see it. But if you want to be in touch with it, think of the worst day of your life. Think about the day you were mugged or abused or your friends died in a car accident, or you nearly died. Or remember the earthquake last year? That was small—one bridge and part of one highway. Remember how that shook us up? Imagine putting all of those worst days together, and then imagine it continuing day after day after day.

The sickness of our culture is that we've isolated ourselves, that we've lost our feeling, that we've lost our connection to one another and to the earth. And in losing our feelings we lose our sense of our home. To live at home asks a very great and brave thing of us, which is to not pretend but to open ourselves to our feelings and our connection with each other.

In the book *The Wall,* about the Vietnam Veterans' Memorial, a vet says, "I wish I could take them all—all of the lawmakers and the politicians and the generals—by the hand, and walk them by the Vietnam Veterans' Memorial together with the mothers and the husbands and the wives and the children, the parents of the people who died, holding their hands and reading the names. To walk by it and really know."

This is our home and we can learn to care for it in many ways. Put on Mozart instead of the news. I'm serious. Make your home a place of peace. Make a peace garden and tell people that you're doing it. Write letters. We went to a march a few days ago and talked a lot about President Bush. My daughter, Caroline, who's six, wrote a letter to him: "Dear President Bush, I don't want any war. You should stop the fighting wherever it is and use your words. Love, Caroline." That's what she's been told in preschool and kindergarten. When the kids start hitting one another, they're told, "Use your words, now—tell them how you feel."

Is it human nature to fight? Is it necessary that we as a species continue to have wars? Or could we evolve? Is there another possibility for us on earth?

We're here for a short time in this great mystery of being alive, the mystery of becoming conscious, being born out of a woman's body and waking up and saying: Wow! Look at this!

So what is really our home, and what is this mystery that we come to live in? And what are we to do with it for the short time that we're here?

We live in a materialistic, scientific kind of culture that has very few models about how to deal with conflict and difficulty. We just have the old ways.

But gradually we can learn another way. We can embrace the simple principles that life is really precious and that we human beings have the capacity to face the joy and the sorrow. We can do that. That is our birthright. And if we do, we will find that true strength is in love and in forgiveness and in compassion. That's the true strength. Even Napoleon said it. He said, "Do you know what astonished me most in the world? The inability of force to create anything. In the long run the sword is always beaten by the spirit."

American astronaut Edgar Mitchell said, "On the return home, gazing through the black velvety cosmos at our planet, I was suddenly engulfed with the experience of the universe as intelligent, loving, harmonious. After visiting space, it is now our task as humans to fulfill this vision on earth."

So, write letters or sit or walk for peace, or drive peacefully or plant a peace garden or create a sense of community or join a vigil—but realize this is our home and our earth. We can create it in many different ways, and its creation comes out of each of us and out of each of our hearts.

(1991)

SPEED

Diana Winston

"Nearly all American drivers agree that running red lights is dangerous, but more than half admit they've done it. Mostly because they were simply in a hurry, a survey found."

—*San Jose Mercury News*, October 7, 1999

"O Son/Daughter of an Enlightened Family, do not be distracted!"

—*Tibetan Book of the Dead*

In my early twenties, when I was unemployed and living in New York City, I had a ritual for myself. I would go to Grand Central Station at evening rush hour, plant myself in a busy intersection crammed with people running for trains and subways, and simply watch. The giant underground room was a whirl of bodies in dark overcoats zooming past each other with an inexorable sense of importance. They never bumped into each other. Rushing, running, spinning out of control, and I, like a ghost, stood there with nothing to do except watch and wonder.

Years later, immersed in a culture where speed is the order of the day, I too am part of this herd. I too have a datebook that is filled to the brim, and intimacies are bargained into its corners. I hurry from one appointment to the next and the next. I run from planning meetings, to work, to sitting group, to dinner with friends, to the latest movie. Most things I do are "worthwhile," helpful, beneficial to myself and others. I roll into bed at night, exhausted, forgetful. What did I do all day?

Contemporary America: We love fast things. Fast cars, fast meals, microwaves, one-night stands, instant credit, overnight express, cable modems, amphetamines, pizza delivery, McEverything. What did we do before e-mail?

I don't have time to write letters, read books, visit my friend, play with my little brother, kiss touch sigh dance relate eat ice cream make music cook pray smell meditate take a walk my god make it all stop I don't have time and it's running out and I'm running fast and furiously and I want it to stop ouch it's painful why won't it stop can't you make it stop my god what's wrong with this country have we all gone crazy are we insane we've lost touch we've lost touch we've got to stop this endless running about all I want to do is slow down just crawl into bed and rock myself to sleep not this craziness not this crazy running about I am so tired please somebody you have got to help me stop!

A caveat: I am embedded in a particular class, race, nation, and time in history, so my words don't speak for everyone, everywhere. However, for me, I believe it's a subversive act in this historical moment to slow down. The momentum of the culture sends us careening at breakneck speed. We are experiencing a host of physical and psychological illnesses resulting from our addiction to speed. Running at this rate is actually painful. It's causing wear and tear on our nervous systems, on our bodies and familial relations, on the earth. This is not news.

To slow down is to disassociate myself from the consumer culture that deifies acceleration. Say no thanks to the tyranny of the equation that time equals money. No thanks to being a cog in somebody else's wheel. The faster we go, the less we question, and the more we buy. Products/people wear out rapidly and new ones replace them. There's always an upgrade to be had.

I won't take part in that. I refuse. I will slow down. I will take care of myself. I will not buy a faster modem.

I learned a few lessons when I was in India this year. I made a rule for myself: If I accomplished one thing in the day, I rejoiced. A trip to the bank to exchange money could easily be an all-day undertaking.

Mailing a Letter: A Story in Three Acts

ACT I. 1:00 P.M.—I leave my house for the post office, pausing for a game of hopscotch with the little girls next door. "Dinah," shouts my neighbor, Mr. Khaitan, "vait, come have some chai. You must hear my new plan." I have known him three months, and every week he has a new money-making scheme. Last week it was a day-care center, the week before, a shoe store. Today we chat for twenty minutes over a cup of the deliciously too-sweet brown liquid. He tells me of his plan to turn his general store into a restaurant. "Dinah, you like pizza, ice cream. I will serve the most excellent meals for Vestern tastes." We discuss the pros, cons, and recipes for spaghetti sauce.

ACT II. 2:00 P.M.—I jump on my bike and pedal over to the post office. It's still closed for lunch. I wait for the man, on lunch break, whose job is to unlock the postmaster's window. It doesn't matter that there are five other men standing around drinking chai (code term for doing mostly nothing). The man with the key to the window isn't there. So I sit outside on the porch of the G.P.O. chatting with the postal workers, practice sky gazing, walk down the street to play with the beggar kids. I return to see if the window's open. Alas, still not back. I scratch a few mosquito bites, buy the *Times of India,* and read of the latest mob violence.

ACT III. 4:00 P.M.—The man with the key returns. He was in a motorcycle accident but wasn't hurt. The men assume their positions. One man can't find his postage meter. He searches through piles and piles of paper, and finds it at last, underneath his *tiffin* (lunch box) in the left-hand drawer. The man-with-the-key unlocks the window, and one of the chai drinkers becomes the postmaster and sits down on the other side of the window. But my letter won't close. The postmaster hands me the sticky goo that substitutes for glue, and I slop it all over the letter. I rub the excess off my hands, pass the letter to the gentleman, and he stamps it. Finally, I depart victorious. It's

5:00 P.M. and I have successfully mailed my letter before the post office closed. I feel joy.

When my father picked me up at the airport on my return from Asia, we drove up to a tollbooth. He contemplated out loud: "Well, if I go to the left I should make it through faster, well...unless that bastard tries to cut me off...okay, yeah, we're going to take the left booth."

"Dad," I sighed, "I haven't been home in two years, and you're worried about shaving off thirty seconds of time."

"Diana, you know I'm an efficiency expert."

I'm not saying the East is better because things are slow. India has an array of social problems, from overpopulation to religiously motivated violence, poverty, fanaticism, corruption, and illiteracy. But speed is not one of them. I love India's slowness, although frequently it's infuriating. A fourteen-hour train ride from Varanasi to Calcutta once took me twenty-eight hours.

How can I keep track of the multitude of information from TV newspaper dailies weeklies alternative journals web e-mail snail mail commercial radio public radio what my friends say posters flyers billboards advertisements magazines books bookstore windows dreams?

In India, I got an e-mail from Sue asking me to write an article for *Turning Wheel* about my time in a monastery in Burma. She wanted it. I wanted to do it. I had a great angle, the outline was all set, I was sure it was an important piece. But the days passed and I never managed to get it done.

It's almost time to leave for Bodh Gaya for a ten-day retreat. I have just one day to finish the article. I sit on my porch to consider what to do: I could work on the school's computer, but if there's no electricity, I don't want them to start the generator just for me. . . . I could try the university, but, no, I think they're closed again for some religious holiday. . . . My friends have a laptop, but they're German and the keyboard letters are in all the wrong places. . . . I guess I could rent a computer in Varanasi, but that's a forty-five-minute ride into town. And without electricity, how can I e-mail this out? Damn, damn. I could try faxing it but the fax down the road is usually broken.

Finally I realize that the level of anxiety I'm creating for myself has gotten out of control. My stomach is knotting; I feel panicky, sweaty, nauseated. Suddenly a voice pops into my head: "You know, you don't have to do it."

My immediate response: "*Yes I do!!!* This is a very important article. I am an important person with important things to say!"

The first voice repeats, "You don't have to do it." A battle ensues. The self-building voice struggles against the faint, calm voice that urges me to drop it.

Finally I think, "Do you want to write this or do you want to have peace?" At that moment something deep inside me shifts, and I know I have to let go. I take a breath. "I'm not going to write the article," I announce to myself. In seconds I feel a profound sense of peace. The anxiety falls away, and I begin to cry with relief.

All of the things we say we have to do—do we really have to do them?

Here we go restless can't stop now spinning careening wildly out of control faster now faster got to make that date gotta invent something new gotta go can't explain now gotta check my Web site over here over there where no it's not fun anymore on to the next better newer happier yes this is it got it no it's not quite it wait there must be more...

I propose that looking inward as part of a cultural critique is a hallmark of socially engaged Buddhist analysis. One of my credos is that what happens out there is happening in the mind. My Buddhist practice can help me understand how social systems and mental structures reinforce each other.

During my years of meditation practice, I've been investigating restlessness. Of the five classical hindrances to meditation practice—sense desire, aversion, sleepiness, restlessness, and doubt— restlessness is my lot in this life. Early on it was like torture. If my mind was restless I could barely sit still. Eight years ago, on a long retreat, I had so much energy coursing through my body and so many thoughts cascading through my mind that at midnight I ran laps around the parking lot. It didn't help, so I moved into strenuous, advanced yoga poses. Still restless, I took a walk in the woods by moonlight, only to terrify myself with what I took to be a cougar.

(Are there actually cougars in Massachusetts?) I ran inside, crying, but there was nowhere to hide.

When I told my meditation teacher of my horrible night, and how none of my antidotes to restlessness had calmed me down, he cocked his head, hid a smile, and asked nonchalantly, "Why didn't you try sitting with it?"

"Oh, wow," I said, "I never thought of that."

More recently I've learned that when I experience rapid thinking and jarring body sensations, there may be something going on underneath that I don't want to be present with. Usually, it's emotional pain. So when I see restlessness coming, I try to sink deeper, below the spinning mind to the unpleasantness underneath. Sometimes, the restlessness stops. Sometimes I fall into wells of sadness. Sometimes there's a story behind the restlessness, sometimes not. Sometimes my awareness grows spacious enough to be okay with hating the restlessness. Restlessness then becomes an arising just like everything else.

What does this have to do with speed? I believe that American culture is stuck in the "hindrance" of restlessness. The careening speed—the rapid turnover of events, information, relationships, and goods—mirrors my own poor, restless mind.

What's the deeper problem? I'll venture a few guesses. As a society, there's a lot we don't want to look at: ceaseless human suffering, a sense of meaninglessness, political disempowerment, polarization of the rich and poor, loss of community, breakdown of social structures. . .do I need to go on? We have a lot to be sad about. Who wants to feel these things when it hurts so much? Better to rush and run and rent videos. The faster we go, the less we have to feel the pain, at the moment, anyway.

Could we possibly learn to sit with it?

They are now trying to cut the blank spaces out of TV. You know—the moment after the show stops and before the commercial begins, that less-than-a-second of dead space. Networks believe the lag time is too upsetting for viewers.

Is there anything wholesome in all this rushing? Could it be that humans are seeking connectedness, and that it is the urgency of this

Speed

need that makes us hurry? Using new technologies that speed things up, we are trying to overcome boundaries of space and time. Behind the speed, there may be a longing to connect.

In my year in the monastery in Burma, not much really happened, at least on the outside. For a year I never got into a car or left the monastery's walls. I talked very occasionally, to just a few people. I only ate what was put on the plate in front of me. I never went to a restaurant. I spoke on the phone five times in one year. Not once did I watch TV, see a movie, dance, go to a party, have sex, hang out with friends, sing, eat after noon, use hot water, or buy anything. I only wore one pair of shoes for the whole year, which, as my friends know, is a big deal for me.

When external activity is so stripped down, every little event becomes large in the mind. On retreat I discovered that anytime I did anything, there were results in my mind. When I ordained, it took my mind weeks to settle down from the thrill of it. Drop a pebble in a pond; small circles of ripples move outward and outward. When I nearly stepped on a toad I was nervous for three hours afterward. The tiniest action had an effect, like the time a butterfly landed for a second on my toe and I sat transfixed with awe for several minutes. In the silence, there was time for my mind to feel the repercussions of each event, to integrate it, and to settle with it.

I call this time reverberation time.

Last night I went on a sort-of date. When I got home my mind was so excited it couldn't stop spinning. So I crawled into the bath and let the reverberations happen as the hot water enveloped me. I let the rippling thinking run its course; I watched the chills and excitement and planning. Then after an hour or so, the thoughts mostly subsided. Then I went to bed.

We need this time. Events affect us all the time, of course, not just when we are on retreat. But the speed of our culture and the pace of our lives doesn't allow for reverberation time.

Everything affects us.

What happens when we don't give ourselves the silent space to sit, and feel, and move, and transform, and gestate, and integrate? What happens when we no longer have reverberation time?

(2000)

CAN THIS SPIRITUAL
PRACTICE BE SAVED?

Jan Chozen Bays

A Parable

After ten years of hard study, Mojo begins work as a spiritual teacher with only a dozen students. The students have a lot of access to him, both in group gatherings and in private interviews. They spend time with their teacher in his home and work shoulder-to-shoulder in the gardens. Each student feels Mojo knows him or her intimately.

Gradually Mojo's reputation grows and within five years there are more than a hundred students living at the spiritual center and several satellite groups around the country and overseas. Mojo is busy traveling, attending meetings with people who administer the organization, and meeting with public figures to raise money and to oil the political machinery necessary to keep his organization going. Students get to see him once a month in public talks if he is in town. Often they must watch videotaped lectures from the early years.

Students long for a personal connection with the teacher. If he makes eye contact with them or says an individual word in passing, they treasure it for days. People insert "Mojo says..." into conversation to imply they have talked with the teacher. People begin to vie for any tiny bit of personal contact by rushing to be the first to bring Mojo hot tea at a meeting, or remove his shoes and secretly polish them, weed his garden, or tend his children. His wife at first is happy to have a bevy of students cleaning house, cooking, helping entertain guests, and baby-sitting. She secretly enjoys being Queen of the Way, loved and waited on by all her husband's students.

But soon a small unease develops. If her husband sneezes, students rush up with Kleenex, herbal tea, Vitamin C, and offers of therapeutic massage. When will they begin to wipe her husband's bottom for him?

She has no one to go to for advice. Everyone she knows is her husband's student and more loyal to him than to her. She is the only one who sees Mojo at his most ordinary, sneaking a forbidden cigarette, upset when the toilet paper runs out or the children spill their juice. All the other students see his anger as crazy wisdom and try to learn from it. She suspects that some students feel that she and the children are an impediment to Mojo's true mission in life, diverting energy from his ability to teach.

Mojo is surprised at how quickly his popularity has risen. At first he was pleased to have so many students; it confirmed the truth of his understanding and his teaching skill. With legions of students eager to do The Work of the Way, the community was able to get a lot accomplished: building meditation and dormitory halls, maintaining gardens, and doing community outreach projects with the poor.

He has little time to practice himself. He is in such demand that he can't find time to read or to find a source of inspiration. He begins to repeat old talks, and gets tired of hearing himself tell the same spiritual anecdotes.

He used to enjoy long retreats, when everyone put aside their trivial concerns and strove for the same goal: enlightenment. It was then that he experienced true, deep intimacy with students in private interviews. Their hearts were so pure, so open. He felt himself a true teacher, committed wholly to the Way, gently guiding students toward realization.

At the end of retreats when everyone left, he felt lonely. What occurred in the interview room was secret, so there was no one he could talk to about his own insights, dilemmas, doubts, and triumphs. One student showed exceptional promise, and he found himself beginning to confide in her, telling himself it would help her to know these things when she became a teacher one day. When he was tired he found himself wanting to rest just for a moment in her arms.

His student was flattered by the attention she received, and awed by Mojo's statements that she had unusual potential for real-ization. She might even be a teacher herself someday. She treasured each moment with him, and would have been glad to be his daily attendant, doing anything he asked, just to be able to hear a few scraps of his conversations. She learned so much from his every word and gesture! She liked Mojo's wife, but felt she should be more generous about sharing her extraordinary husband with his students.

Lately she had been feeling that she and Mojo shared a spiritual bond that was much deeper than ordinary marriage. He had even said that worldly marriage was only for one lifetime, but a true, pure, spiritual marriage of minds and understanding would last forever. She wondered what kind of child would be the result of a physical union between two clear beings. In certain traditions when a great teacher died, he could reappear in the form of an infant. Perhaps she would be the vessel to bear such a child!

In the words of *Good Housekeeping* magazine, can this marriage (and these spiritual practices) be saved?

Snags to Catch Our Toes

Since I have begun teaching I've become aware of the subtle yet powerful forces that play upon a teacher. These forces can cause difficulties in spiritual communities, from mild upsets to disastrous eruptions. I've stumbled my way through some of these problems. Unable to pack every variety of misadventure into twenty years of being a student and ten years of teaching, I've read books and talked to a number of students from several Buddhist traditions about problems they encountered. I have organized these problems by cause so we can begin to discuss them and diagnose others that may come to light. The parables in this article are composites. The fact that students and teachers from many different practice centers have recognized these accounts speaks to the commonality of the forces and themes.

Abuse of Power

When intensive meditation practice is being undertaken, as in long, silent retreats, the whole world narrows to the meditation hall and interview room. The student becomes intensely bonded to the teacher, the only person he or she talks to in hours or days of silent meditation. When bewildering or unusual phenomena occur, the student is completely dependent upon the teacher for reassurance and guidance. Intense emotions arise during such times, from terror to spontaneous outpourings of love and gratitude. There is tremendous intimacy in the interview room. Even if the student and teacher are so fortunate as to have no difficulties with intimacy under ordinary circumstances, the intensity of the bond in the *daisan* room is intoxicating.

The teacher must not allow a student to attribute the phenomena that occur naturally with intense spiritual practice to the personal abilities or charisma of the teacher. This is an ever present danger.

In its subtlest form, the danger may appear when a teacher thinks, "Well, maybe I was just a bit clever in seeing where that person was stuck. None of her former teachers saw it." Or in not persistently deflecting the gratitude that comes with a spiritual insight back where it belongs: to the buddha-dharma.

In its grossest form, teachers may believe that they have such clear understanding that anything they do with a student is enlightened activity. This has included insulting students publicly, physically injuring or having a sexual relationship with them, exploiting students for free labor, subtly extorting money (for the sake of the dharma), or insinuating themselves between members of a couple and bringing about the end of a marriage.

Idealization and Isolation of the Teacher

Being a teacher is a lonely business. Alone in the midst of clamoring, adoring students, the teacher is seen as the ultimate embodiment of accomplished practice. Personality quirks and flaws may be mistaken for manifestations of enlightenment. The teacher cannot admit doubt or failure lest the spiritual path be questioned. There is a misunder-

standing, encouraged by the hopes of many students and perpetu-
ated by the silence of many teachers, that anyone who is sanctioned
to teach Buddhism must be completely enlightened. Even if this
were true, actualization takes decades of dedicated practice after re-
alization(s).

It is the teacher's responsibility to inform students that he or she
is not a fully enlightened, actualized being, but just another human
being who will make mistakes. The teacher should also be a living
example of the willingness to learn from anyone or any circum-
stance. The Buddha was clearly aware of the problem of spiritual
pride. The gravest lie cited in the Vinaya is to boast about (directly
or even to imply) having reached some higher stage of spiritual development.

Failure to Recognize Archetypal Energies

As more women become spiritual teachers, we will face the
problem of abuse of power by women. Can we predict what this will
look like in advance, and perhaps recognize and interrupt it early?
What are typical feminine archetypal energies that could be distorted and misused? There is the nurturing mother archetype,
which in its distorted form is the smothering mother, involved in
every aspect of her children's lives, unable to let them mature and
leave home. There is the mother-in-law energy that cannot let a favorite son be happy with a female who competes for his affection
and attention. Or a young woman who diverts a male student's attention from pure practice may be characterized by the religious
community as the evil seductress.

What might misuse of power by a female teacher look like?

A Second Parable

Sumaya is a teacher at a large spiritual center. Traditionally the
teacher picks a single promising student to be her personal attendant. This is a position of honor and an unequaled opportunity to
train, since the attendant has intimate contact with the teacher
many hours a day. Sumaya picks Jon, a bright, energetic young man,

and trains him rigorously. As several years go by she comes to depend upon him absolutely.

Jon is available to her any hour she may need him, and carries out her requests more efficiently than anyone else she has trained. She has tested his loyalty during several difficult times at the center. There was a minor but unpleasant episode involving students who were discontent, and who had stirred up unrest in the community. They eventually left. She was more shaken by this than anyone except her attendant knew. When she had Jon transfer funds secretly to cover a blunder by the treasurer, he mentioned it to no one. He was completely discreet about the few times she had slipped, doing and saying things she was not proud of. He is the only one she feels safe in confiding to about her occasional doubts that she is not suited for this work.

Jon has had several significant spiritual "openings," and Sumaya is beginning to hope he will someday be her successor. She has hinted this to him, but not told him outright lest he become "puffed up."

Jon was delighted to be chosen as Sumaya's personal attendant. It is hard work, but more than balanced by what he can learn by watching how Sumaya puts realization into action. He is happy to carry out her wishes, and gains particular pleasure by anticipating her needs a moment before even she is aware of them. Sumaya says he is the best attendant she has ever had, and has hinted that he is making such progress he might be head of the center when she retires.

Jon was upset when a small group of students complained about Sumaya in a community meeting. How could students with so little experience of practice and so little clarity in the Way criticize what the teacher perceives as best for them all? He knew she was not the dictator they portrayed her to be, and that she carefully considered what was best before taking action. It did bother him that she had asked him to put pressure on them in various ways, until they felt it necessary to leave the community. He had tried to translate her exact words, uttered when she was understandably upset, into a more moderate and less hurtful message. It had had the desired effect: the troublemakers were gone, and peace was restored to the community, as Sumaya had wished.

Cultural Differences

There is a myth in spiritual communities that cultural differences can excuse inappropriate behavior. If an Asian teacher gets drunk or is sexual with students, it is attributed to cultural misunderstanding. But in fact, when we consult our elders in the Buddhist tribe, whether the Buddha, Dogen Zenji, or the Dalai Lama, we find that sexual abuse of students and drunkenness have always been recognized as harmful.

To excuse abuse of students by saying that it is a cultural misunderstanding is like excusing child abuse by saying that the perpetrator was him- or herself abused. It may help to raise a more compassionate response to the abuse, but it does not excuse it. The perpetrator is still responsible for exploiting children and the teacher for exploiting students, no matter what his or her background. The majority of men and women who were themselves abused do not go on to become abusers. Many teachers raised in different cultural settings do not go on to abuse students. To use the cultural excuse is a subtle insult to the many teachers from other cultures who do not abuse.

Child sexual abuse is harmful because it disrupts, often permanently, the stages in a child's development necessary for healthy sexuality as an adult. Spiritual abuse of students is similarly disruptive, with the result that some students never mature in spiritual practice and others are turned away from the dharma forever. Is this the outcome we want as teachers?

Some child molesters love the innocence of children, a purity they feel they lack. They try to take this energy unto themselves by sexual union with the child. Similarly, when a dharma teacher becomes harried and jaded, with no time for practice and renewal, the innocent love of a new student for the dharma is a balm. A young student's openings awaken memories of the teacher's own enthusiasm and awakening experiences. The aging teacher may try to replenish depleted spiritual energy vicariously through the student, sometimes in the form of sexual union.

We teachers are vulnerable to our own greed, anger, and ignorance, as well as to our capacity to rationalize what we want to do. But it is our duty to ask, "Am I doing this for the student's benefit or for my own?" Who is being served if a student is French kissed by a teacher in an interview? One good test is whether the teacher would apply the behavior to most or all students. Do the old women, fat women, and male students get French kissed too?

Another good test is whether our acts are consistent with what the Buddha taught. Could our behavior be exposed, as it was in the time of the Buddha, to the scrutiny of the *sangha*? Our misbehavior is no secret from ourselves. And as Buddhist teachers, we must also know that, in the One Mind, there are no secrets at all.

(1996)

IMAGINE LIVING IN YOUR BATHROOM

Diana Lion

Imagine that you live in a room the size of your bathroom, about five by ten feet, with a person of the same gender whom you never met before. This space has two bunk beds, one locker for each of you to store your belongings, and an uncovered metal toilet at one end of the bunks with a small sink beside it. The standing space is so small that one of you must be on the bed if the other is off it. You can't sit up straight on either bed without hitting your head. Imagine that this is your home. And you are both living there for a whole day. Now imagine you are living there for a week . . . a month . . . a year. Or five or ten years.

The only time you have any quiet is between the hours of 2 and 4:30 A.M. You never have privacy: you sleep, go to the bathroom, dress, eat, fart, and everything else with this other person. And with thousands of others in the institution. Each morning, you're woken at 4:30 A.M. and you eat breakfast with hundreds of others of your same gender. The food is often cold, with very little nutrition. You must use plastic utensils.

During the days, you work in shipping and receiving. You remember two friends who you worked with for years, the only people you could be real with. But one got transferred suddenly and you never got to say good-bye; the other got stabbed in the yard. That's when you decided to never again get close to anyone—too painful. You work for twenty-three cents an hour—a raise from seventeen cents.

You have attended twelve-step groups and church services, and you play on the baseball team. You feel proud to have earned your GED while inside, and you even completed a few community college courses: you are the first person in your family to go to college! You've gone to some of the Alternatives to Violence Project groups—partly to meet new people from outside, because how else can you do that behind bars? But also because you've realized that the drug and alcohol problems were sitting on top of some deep pain, and that those groups might provide some healing for the rage that surfaces when things get tight. You've realized for the first time that the beatings your dad gave your mom, your brothers, and you when you were little might have been connected with the fury that explodes out of you at times, like the froth from a Coke that's been shaken vigorously. That insight gave you hope about maybe being able to change.

Imagine you've got only four months left in this place. Excitement and fear are competing inside you. Freedom—you can almost taste it! What a kick to drink a beer when you want, and scratch your butt without anyone watching. To get up in the morning when you like, and earn more than twenty-three cents an hour. To be able to touch your girlfriend or boyfriend with no one else watching. Free— to cross the street, buy a soda, see your kid, and smell the night air. And scared—knowing you're gonna walk out the gate with just two hundred dollars in your pocket and what you've got on your back. With a prison felony record, and the only people you still know outside being your mom and some drug dealers. Your parole officer may keep you on a tight leash. (About 70 percent of ex-cons are back within a few months for some "serious" parole violation, like being in the wrong neighborhood, or calling their parole officer five minutes late.)

You're worried that the stress may get to you, and it's a short ride back down if you turn to the relief of that sweet feeling—mellowed out, smooth, energized, confident, unafraid—and who wouldn't want that? Still, that choice you might make to go back to drugs is nothing more than your one-way ticket back to the pain and the pen.

Imagine being told to find a job when you have no clothes to interview in, no home address to give, no phone number people can reach you at. Imagine trying to find an intimate relationship. Trying to accept someone and love him or her in a way you've never had a chance to learn. Imagine trying to be cool about all the changes since you were last on the streets: pagers, cell phones, clothes, music, street names, freeway exits, even area codes.

You're out of prison but you're afraid of the prison that still resides in your mind—which, of course, is totally portable. You need all the help you can get.

(2000)

VOWING PEACE IN
AN AGE OF WAR

Alan Senauke

The following is based on an address delivered at the Dogen Symposium at Stanford University in October 1999. Eihei Dogen (1200–1254), poet and scholar, was the founder of the Soto school of Zen in Japan.

> Awake or asleep
> in a grass hut,
> what I pray for is
> to bring others across
> before myself.

> —Zen Master Dogen, from *Moon in a Dewdrop*,
> ed. by Kaz Tanahashi, North Point Press, 1985

San Quentin Prison sits on a bare spit of land on San Francisco Bay. This is where the state of California puts prisoners to death. The gas chamber is still there, but for the last five years executions have been done by lethal injection in a mock-clinical setting that cruelly imitates a hospital room. About 550 men and eleven women now wait on California's death row; the usual wait is fifteen or twenty years. The voting public supports this state-sanctioned violence. In fact, no politician can get elected to higher office in California without appearing to support the death penalty.

On a stormy evening in March of 1999, several hundred people came to a vigil and rally to protest the execution of Jay Siripongs, a Thai national and a Buddhist, convicted of a 1983 murder in Los Angeles. Sheets of rain and a cold wind beat on everyone gathered at the prison gates: death penalty opponents, a handful of death penalty supporters, press, prison guards, and—right up against the gate, gazing at San Quentin's stone walls—seventy-five or more Buddhist students and meditators bearing witness to the execution, sitting in the middle of anger, grief, painful words, and more painful deeds.

My robes were soaked through and my *zafu* [meditation cushion] sat in a deepening puddle. Across a chain link fence, ten feet away, helmeted guards stood in a wet line, rain falling as hard on them as on ourselves. I felt a moment of deep connection: black-robed meditators sitting upright in attention in the rain, protecting beings as best we know how; black-jacketed police officers standing at attention in the rain, protecting beings as best they know how. Is there a difference between our activities? Yes, of course. But recognizing unity, even in the midst of difference and turmoil, is the essence of peacemaking. I imagine there were guards who were aware of this unity.

Our witness at San Quentin is part of a great vow that Zen students take. Bearing witness is the bodhisattva's radical act of complete acceptance and nonduality. In this time and place it leads me to active resistance and social transformation. We vow to bear witness where violence unfolds. We vow to recognize the human capacity for violence within our own minds. We take true refuge in the buddha-dharma, and seek to resolve conflicts. We vow never again to raise a weapon in anger or in complicity with the state or any so-called authority, but to intervene actively and nonviolently for peace, even where this may put our own bodies and lives at risk.

Who will take this vow? Am I ready? Are you?

Carrying Forth Realization into the World

Meditating on peace, echoes of Dogen ring in my ears. In "The Bodhisattva's Four Methods of Guidance" Dogen writes, "You should benefit friend and enemy equally. You should benefit self and others alike." His radical language cuts to the heart of peace. His thirteenth-century world was different from our own, but the conflicts and twisted karma of suffering beings are the same.

In every age, the dream of peace and the practice of peace arise together with war and conflict. They are deeply related. In every age, war compels people to cover their hearts and to act in unimaginably cruel ways. No other animal is capable of such cruelty. The color and shape of the victims, heroes, and perpetrators may differ, and the landscape itself, but the face of war is always ugly. The victims need our help. So do the perpetrators.

"Because there is the base, there are jewel pedestals, fine clothing." This is Shakyamuni Buddha's great teaching of "dependent origination": Because this is, that is. In an age of war this is an encouraging fact. Because there is war, I know there is also peace. But if I create a concept called peace and cling to it, conditions for war arise. So what am I to do? How can I sustain upright sitting in the midst of grief and conflict?

Let me offer three approaches to Buddhist peacemaking: giving, fearlessness, and renunciation.

Giving

The essential practice of peace is giving, or *dana paramita*. Giving attention, friendship, and material aid. Giving spiritual teachings and community. Giving is the first perfection and the first of the bodhisattva's four methods of guidance. It includes all other perfections. In "Bodaisatta Shisho-ho," Dogen advises us that:

> Giving means non-greed. Non-greed means not to covet. Not to covet means not to curry favor. Even if you govern the Four Continents, you should always convey the correct teaching with non-greed.

Giving begins with oneself. I give myself to practice and practice offers itself to me. In my search for peace and liberation, I find there is always the smell of war. The taste of tears, corrosive doubt, and decay fall within the circle of my own body and mind. The war is here, right where I hide behind a mask of self-attachment, a shelter of privilege, cutting myself off from others. True giving is receiving the gift of *zazen* mind and passing it to others in words and deeds. It means not hiding.

We offer gifts and guidance in many forms. Dogen's four methods of guidance—giving, kind speech, beneficial action, and identity action—expand on the Buddha's own teaching of peace and the foundations for social unity: *dana* (generosity), *piyavaca* (kindly speech), *atthacariya* (helpful action), and *samanattata* (impartiality or equal participation). At the heart of these teachings is the understanding that peace is making connection. On a simple level, material goods are given. On a higher level, teaching is shared. And on the highest level, there is just connection, the endless society of being, the vast assembly of bodhisattvas. In Lewis Hyde's wonderful book *The Gift*, he describes dinner in a cheap restaurant in the south of France:

> The patrons sit at a long communal table, and each finds before his plate a modest bottle of wine. Before the meal begins, a man will pour his wine not into his own glass but into his neighbor's. And his neighbor will return the gesture, filling the first man's empty glass. In an economic sense nothing has happened. No one has any more wine than he did to begin with. But society has appeared where there was none before.

When we really embody the bodhisattva vow to save all sentient beings, then *zazen* itself is a quiet and transformative gift. We receive it in gratitude from the Buddha ancestors and from our all-too-human teachers, and we pass it on. Again, Lewis Hyde:

> I would like to speak of gratitude as a labor undertaken by the soul to effect the transformation after a gift has been received. Between the time a gift comes to us and the time we pass it along, we suffer gratitude. Moreover, with gifts that are agents of change, it is only when the gift has worked in us, only when we come up to its level, as it were, that we can give it away again. Passing the gift along is the act of gratitude that finishes the labor.

During the NATO bombing in Serbia last year, a friend of mine proposed that the United States offer a four-year university education in the United States to every Serbian and Albanian youth of military age. This would provide them with intellectual and technical tools for peace. It would be much cheaper than the billions of dollars spent on weaponry and death.

Such proposals are usually dismissed as naïve. They fail to reckon with the power of arms dealers, the greed of corporations, and the fears of politicians that are sold as truth to ordinary people. But shouldn't we dare to be naïve? What is there to lose in speaking obvious truths? Can we skillfully speak the truth of *dana* to those in power?

Fearlessness

The practice of peace is fearless. Again this comes back to *dana*—giving, and giving up. To give anything to an enemy or opponent, one must be fearless. There is a story in Trevor Leggett's *The Tiger's Cave and Translations of Other Zen Writings* that has stayed with me for years.

> When a rebel army swept into a town in Korea, all the monks of the Zen temple fled except for the Abbot. The general came into the temple and was annoyed that the Abbot did not receive him with respect. "Don't you know," he shouted, "that you are looking at a man who can run you through without blinking?" "And you," replied the Abbot strongly, "are looking at a man who can be run through without blinking!" The general stared at him, made a bow, and retired.

Peace is not just quiet words and gentle demeanor. There is strength and sinew in it. I often think about Maha Ghosananda of Cambodia simply deciding to walk across his country in the midst of a violent civil war. His saffron robes were both refuge and target. I also think about Thich Nhat Hanh, whom Richard Baker described as "a cross between a cloud and a piece of heavy equipment." I have met these inspiring teachers and felt the steel of intention at the heart of their actions.

In meditation we become intimate with all kinds of fear. We come to see that fearing death or great loss is not so different from fearing more humble events like meeting one's teacher face-to-face or performing a new ceremony. Fear itself provides an opening into the unknown. If we continue to make peace in awareness of our own fear, there is room for everyone's fear to fall away. Mutual respect arises.

Renunciation

A third element is renunciation, or relinquishment. Of course this is also inseparable from giving. Dogen writes, "If you study giving closely, you see that to accept a body and to give up the body are both giving."

Renunciation is a difficult principle for today's Western Buddhists. The Buddhist path, as it exists in our materialistic world, gives mere lip service to renunciation. After mind and body drop away, the work has just begun.

The second bodhisattva precept is "not stealing," or "not taking what is not given." For people in the so-called developed world—America, Europe, Japan—this is almost impossible. Many of us, even priests, lead privileged lives in rich countries whose economies are built on stealing the limited resources of the earth and the labors of poor people around the world. The injustice of poverty and wealth is itself a kind of violence. Really, we can't step outside of this system. But if each of us cultivates awareness of the links between consumption and violence, we can begin to make choices about what is of true value in our lives and how much we value the lives of others. Just at that point of relinquishment, renunciation is possible. But our efforts need to go further.

There is an old Quaker adage: "Speak truth to power." The truth is that global corporations and armed nations further theft and oppression in the world. As renunciates, we must link up with each other, just as we join with and support each other in the zendo. Together we can deconstruct institutions built on greed, hatred, and delusion, and build new structures of liberation and spiritual value that belong to everyone. I honestly don't know what this will look like, but I know it is the responsibility of all communities of faith to be present right in the middle of these changes.

An Army of Peace

There is a movement among socially engaged Buddhists and people of all the faith traditions to create a nonviolent army of peace. How many lives might have been spared in Serbia and Kosovo if we had provided ten thousand witnesses instead of billions of dollars of bombs? How many people would benefit if we stood up to corruption, violence, and drug dealing in our own neighborhoods? The practice of "active nonviolence" includes bearing witness and peaceful intervention. In the midst of local, regional, religious, and national conflicts and wars, this peace army could replace armed soldiers, land mines, tanks, and jet fighters.

A peace army's tools would be ears to hear, words to share, arms to embrace, and bodies to place in opposition to injustice. This army would be trained in meditation, mediation, reconciliation, and generosity. Its discipline would include patience, equanimity, selflessness, and a deep understanding of impermanence. Its "boot camp" would be very different from military training, but every bit as rigorous. Its social organization would include supply lines of food and medicine and clothing that could be shared with others.

A peace army might sit down on the battlefield, right in the line of fire, in order to save others. It is necessary to take risks in Buddhist practice. It is just as necessary to take risks in peacemaking. I think of this as a true expression of identity action: identifying with soldiers, guerrillas, and displaced people, identifying with the bombed and shattered earth itself. Is this suicidal? Maybe so. In an extreme way Thich Quang Duc was practicing his vision of identity action when he publicly immolated himself in Vietnam in 1963, while his fellow monks and nuns were being targeted for repression and his country was in flames. Even today, this image shocks us and raises challenging questions. But I am not advocating suicide. Peace is the point. Identity action, as Dogen renders it, is the peace army's rule of training.

Bodhisattvas Walk among Us

In any single breath, each of us can become an enlightening being. In the next breath we might fall into our old habits of thoughtlessness and violence. Our meditation reveals that this choice is always with us. Our deluded actions contain seeds that can flower as either wondrous peace or terrible harm. Our vision can sustain the world if only we dare to look deeply. Our great ancestor, Layman Vimalakirti, described the bodhisattva path this way:

> During the short eons of swords,
> They meditate on love,
> Introducing to nonviolence
> Hundreds of millions of living beings.
>
> In the middle of great battles
> They remain impartial to both sides;
> For bodhisattvas of great strength
> Delight in reconciliation of conflict.
>
> In order to help the living beings,
> They voluntarily descend into
> The hells which are attached
> To all the inconceivable buddha-fields.

from *The Holy Teaching of Vimalakirti*
(trans. by Robert Thurman,
Pennsylvania State University Press, 1976)

Two thousand years later we are still living up to the challenge, falling short, and vowing again. Let us take our vows seriously and be bodhisattvas. Let us respect our dharma traditions and Buddha ancestors, but be truly accountable to all beings. Please bring peace and *zazen* mind right into the middle of our messy, grieving, wondrous world. Watch your step.

(2000)

Resources

Compiled by Donald Rothberg

This listing of resources is limited to the main English-language socially engaged Buddhist books, journals, and organizations. A more comprehensive list may be found in the Spring 2004 issue of *Turning Wheel*. Books marked with an asterisk are excellent introductory books.

Books on Socially Engaged Buddhism

ADAMS, SHERIDIAN, MUSHIM IKEDA-NASH, JEFF KITZES, MARGARITA LOINAZ, CHOYIN RANGDROL, JESSICA TAN, and LARRY YANG, eds. 2000. *Making the Invisible Visible: Healing Racism in Our Buddhist Communities.* 2nd ed. Available online at http://www.spiritrock.org/html/diversity_2invisible.html or from Buddhist Peace Fellowship.

AITKEN, ROBERT. 1984. *The Mind of Clover: Essays in Zen Buddhist Ethics.* San Francisco: North Point Press.

AUNG SAN SUU KYI. 1995. *Freedom from Fear and Other Writings.* Rev. ed. New York: Penguin Books.

BADINER, ALLAN, ed. 1990. *Dharma Gaia: A Harvest of Essays in Buddhism and Ecology.* Berkeley: Parallax Press.

_____, ed. 2002. *Mindfulness in the Marketplace: Compassionate Responses to Consumerism.* Berkeley: Parallax Press.

*BLOOM, PAMELA, ed. 2000. *Buddhist Acts of Compassion.* York Beach, ME: Conari Press.

BOUCHER, SANDY. 1993. *Turning the Wheel: American Women Creating the New Buddhism.* Rev. ed. San Francisco: Harper & Row.

BRAZIER, DAVID. 2002. *The New Buddhism.* New York: Palgrave Macmillan.

CHAPPELL, DAVID, ed. 2000. *Buddhist Peacework: Creating Cultures of Peace.* Somerville, MA: Wisdom Publications.

CHAVIS, MELODY ERMACHILD. 1997. *Altars in the Street: A Neighborhood Fights to Survive.* New York: Bell Tower.

*DALAI LAMA, THE. 1990. *A Policy of Kindness: An Anthology of Writings by and about the Dalai Lama.* Ithaca, NY: Snow Lion Publications.

———. 2000. *Freedom in Exile: The Autobiography of the Dalai Lama.* San Francisco: HarperSanFrancisco.

DRESSER, MARIANNE, ed. 1996. *Buddhist Women on the Edge: Contemporary Perspectives from the Western Frontier.* Berkeley: North Atlantic Books.

*EPPSTEINER, FRED, ed. 1988. *The Path of Compassion: Writings on Socially Engaged Buddhism.* 2nd ed. Berkeley: Parallax Press.

FRIEDMAN, LENORE. 2000. *Meetings with Remarkable Women: Buddhist Teachers in America.* Rev. ed. Boston: Shambhala Publications.

GHOSANANDA, MAHA. 1992. *Step by Step.* Berkeley: Parallax Press.

*GLASSMAN, BERNIE. 1998. *Bearing Witness: A Zen Master's Lessons in Making Peace.* New York: Bell Tower.

GLASSMAN, BERNIE, AND RICK FIELDS. 1996. *Instructions to the Cook: A Zen Master's Lessons in Living a Life That Matters.* New York: Bell Tower.

GROSS, RITA. 1993. *Buddhism after Patriarchy: A Feminist History, Analysis, and Reconstruction of Buddhism.* New York: Continuum.

———. 1998. *Soaring and Settling: Buddhist Perspectives on Contemporary Social and Religious Issues.* Albany: State University of New York Press.

JOHNSON, CHARLES. 2003. *Turning the Wheel: Essays on Buddhism and Writing.* New York: Scribner.

JONES, KEN. 2003. *The New Social Face of Buddhism: A Call to Action.* Somerville, MA: Wisdom Publications.

KAZA, STEPHANIE, and KENNETH KRAFT, eds. 1999. *Dharma Rain: Sources of Buddhist Environmentalism.* Boston: Shambhala Publications.

*KHONG, CHAN. 1993. *Learning True Love: How I Learned and Practiced Social Change in Vietnam.* Berkeley: Parallax Press.

*KOTLER, ARNOLD, ed. 1996. *Engaged Buddhist Reader.* Berkeley: Parallax Press.

KRAFT, KENNETH, ed. 1992. *Inner Peace, World Peace: Essays on Buddhism and Nonviolence.* Albany: State University of New York Press.

———. 1999. *The Wheel of Engaged Buddhism: A New Map of the Path.* New York: Weatherhill.

LEIGHTON, TAIGEN DAN. 2003. *Faces of Compassion: Classic Bodhisattva Archetypes and Their Modern Expression.* Rev. ed. Somerville, MA: Wisdom Publications.

LEYLAND, WINSTON, ed. 1998-2000. *Queer Dharma: Voices of Gay Buddhists.* Vol. 1–2. San Francisco: Gay Sunshine Press.

LOY, DAVID. 2003. *The Great Awakening: A Buddhist Social Theory.* Somerville, MA: Wisdom Publications.

MACY, JOANNA. 1985. *Dharma and Development: Religion As Resource in the Sarvodaya Self-Help Movement.* Rev. ed. West Hartford, CT: Kumarian Press.

*_____. 1991. *World As Lover, World As Self.* Berkeley: Parallax Press.

_____. 2000. *Widening Circles: A Memoir.* Gabriola Island, British Columbia: New Society Publishers.

*MACY, JOANNA, and MOLLY BROWN. 1998. *Coming Back to Life: Practices to Reconnect Our Lives, Our World.* Gabriola Island, British Columbia: New Society Publishers.

MASTERS, JARVIS. 1997. *Finding Freedom: Writings from Death Row.* Junction City, CA: Padma Publishing.

*NHAT HANH, THICH. 1987. *Being Peace.* Berkeley: Parallax Press.

*_____. 1993. *Love in Action: Writings on Nonviolent Social Change.* Berkeley: Parallax Press.

_____. 1998. *Interbeing: Fourteen Guidelines for Engaged Buddhism.* 3rd ed. Berkeley: Parallax Press.

_____. 2003. *Creating True Peace: Ending Violence in Yourself, Your Family, Your Community, and the World.* New York: Free Press.

HANH, THICH NHAT, et al. 1993. *For a Future to Be Possible: Commentaries on the Five Wonderful Precepts.* Berkeley: Parallax Press.

_____. 2002. *Friends on the Path: Living Spiritual Communities.* Berkeley: Parallax Press.

*PILCHICK, TERRY. 1988. *Jai Bhim! Dispatches from a Peaceful Revolution.* Glasgow/Berkeley: Windhorse Publications/Parallax Press.

*QUEEN, CHRISTOPHER, ed. 2000. *Engaged Buddhism in the West.* Sommerville, MA: Wisdom Publications.

*QUEEN, CHRISTOPHER, and SALLIE KING, eds. 1996. *Engaged Buddhism: Buddhist Liberation Movements in Asia.* Albany: State University of New York Press.

QUEEN, CHRISTOPHER, CHARLES PREBISH, and DAMIEN KEOWN, eds. 2003. *Action Dharma: New Studies in Engaged Buddhism*. London: RoutledgeCurzon.

SENAUKE, ALAN, ed. n.d. *Safe Harbor: Guidelines, Process and Resources for Ethics and Right Conduct in Buddhist Communities*. Berkeley: Buddhist Peace Fellowship.

SIVARAKSA, SULAK. 1992. *Seeds of Peace*. Berkeley: Parallax Press.

SNYDER, GARY. 1990. *The Practice of the Wild*. San Francisco: North Point Press.

THURMAN, ROBERT. 1998. *Inner Revolution: Life, Liberty, and the Pursuit of Real Happiness*. New York: Riverhead Books.

VICTORIA, BRIAN. 1998. *Zen at War*. New York: Weatherhill.

WATTS, JONATHAN, ALAN SENAUKE, and SANTIKARO BHIKKHU, eds. 1997. *Entering the Realm of Reality: Towards Dhammic Societies*. Bangkok: Suksit Siam. Also available from Buddhist Peace Fellowship.

WHITMYER, CLAUDE, ed. 1994. *Mindfulness and Meaningful Work: Explorations in Right Livelihood*. Berkeley: Parallax Press.

WHITNEY, KOBAI SCOTT. 2002. *Sitting Inside: Buddhist Practice in American Prisons*. Boulder, CO: Prison Dharma Network.

WILLIS, JAN. 2001. *Dreaming Me: From Baptist to Buddhist, an African American Woman's Spiritual Journey*. New York: Riverhead Books.

WINSTON, DIANA, and DONALD ROTHBERG. 2000. *A Handbook for the Creation of the Buddhist Alliance for Social Engagement (BASE)*. Berkeley: Buddhist Peace Fellowship. Also available online at http://www.bpf.org/html/current_projects/base/base.html.

Journals on Socially Engaged Buddhism

Bearing Witness: The Online Magazine of Spiritually-Based Social Action and Peacemaking http://www.bearingwitnessjournal.com/archive.html.

Indra's Net (journal of the Network of Engaged Buddhists) http://www.engaged-buddhist.org.uk.

Journal of Buddhist Ethics http://jbe.gold.ac.uk.

The Mindfulness Bell (journal of the Community of Mindful Living) http://www.iamhome.org/cml_mindful.html.

Seeds of Peace (journal of the International Network of Engaged Buddhists) http://www.bpf.org/html/resources_and_links/think_sangha/ineb/ineb.html.

Selected Organizations

BUDDHIST AIDS PROJECT (United States)
http://www.buddhistaidsproject.org/.

BUDDHIST PEACE FELLOWSHIP (United States)
http://www.bpf.org/html/home.html.

COMMUNITY OF MINDFUL LIVING (International)
http://www.iamhome.org/index.html.

GAY BUDDHIST FELLOWSHIP (United States)
http://www.gaybuddhist.org/.

INTERNATIONAL NETWORK OF ENGAGED BUDDHISTS (Thailand)
http://www.bpf.org/html/resources_and_links/think_sangha/ineb/ineb.html.

KARUNA TRUST (India) http://www.karuna.org/.

NAROPA UNIVERSITY (United States): MA Program in Engaged Buddhism http://www.naropa.edu/engagedbuddhism/index.html.

NETWORK OF ENGAGED BUDDHISTS (United Kingdom)
http://www.engaged-buddhist.org.uk.

PEACEMAKER CIRCLE INTERNATIONAL (International)
http://www.peacemakercircle.org/bw.htm.

PRISON DHARMA NETWORK (United States)
http://www.prisondharmanetwork.org/.

SAKYADHITA: THE INTERNATIONAL ASSOCIATION OF BUDDHIST WOMEN (International) http://www.sakyadhita.org/.

SARVODAYA (Sri Lanka) http://www.sarvodaya.org/.

THINK SANGHA (International) http://www.bpf.org/think.html (journal available through Buddhist Peace Fellowship).

TZU CHI FOUNDATION: BUDDHIST COMPASSION RELIEF (Taiwan)
http://www.tzuchi.org/.

ZEN HOSPICE PROJECT (United States) http://www.zenhospice.org/.

Contributors

MICHAEL ACUTT has been a Buddhist practitioner for many years. He has also been a housepainter, songwriter, and psychologist. He left California and returned to live in his native Britain in 1991.

ROBERT AITKEN, retired founder and teacher of the Diamond Sangha, now lives and writes on the Big Island of Hawaii. He is the co-founder of the Buddhist Peace Fellowship and the author of ten books on Buddhism, the most recent of which is *The Morning Star: New and Selected Writings* (Shoemaker & Hoard, 2003).

JAN CHOZEN BAYS is a wife, mother, and pediatrician working in the field of child abuse. A dharma heir of Maezumi Roshi, she is teacher at the Zen Community of Oregon, and is the co-founder, with her husband Hogen Bays, of Great Vow Monastery in Clatskanie, Oregon, where they teach and reside.

TREVOR CAROLAN is a poet, translator, and media advocate on behalf of international human rights. A longtime student of Buddhism, he lives in Vancouver, Canada. His most recent book is *Return To Stillness: Twenty Years with A Tai Chi Master* (Marlowe & Company, 2003), and his Web site is www.trevorcarolan.com.

MELODY ERMACHILD CHAVIS is a private investigator and a Zen practitioner. She is the author of *Altars in the Street* (Belltower, 1997) and *Meena, Heroine of Afghanistan* (St. Martin's Press, 2003). She lives in Berkeley, California.

SALLY CLAY has been a leader in the mental health consumer/survivor movement for over twenty years. She has worked as a therapist for Windhorse Associates, a holistic treatment community in Massachusetts. A copyeditor and writer, she makes her home in central Florida. Her poems and essays are posted at her Web site: http://home.earthlink.net/~sallyclay/.

LYNN DIX lives in Berkeley, California, and practices Buddhism. Partly as a result of Lynn's lawsuit against the gun manufacturer Beretta, the governor of California, in 2003, signed the strongest gun safety law in the nation, saying that handguns sold in California must have a load indicator.

MARIANNE DRESSER edited the anthology *Buddhist Women on the Edge: Contemporary Perspectives from the Western Frontier* and is former associate editor and book review editor for *Turning Wheel*. She serves as Editor for the Numata Center for Buddhist Translation and Research, publisher of new translations of classical Buddhist texts from the Taisho Tripitaka, based in Berkeley, California.

MAIA DUERR is currently research director at the Center for Contemplative Mind in Society, based in Northampton, Massachusetts. Before that, she was the associate editor of *Turning Wheel*, an anthropology researcher, and a mental health professional. She received lay ordination from Roshi Joan Halifax and has lived and practiced at the San Francisco Zen Center.

NORMAN FISCHER, former abbot of San Francisco Zen Center, is now the teacher of the Everyday Zen community, a sangha without walls, through which he leads seminars and retreats in the United States, Canada, and Mexico (www.everydayzen.org). His most recent books are *Opening to You: Zen-Inspired Translations of the Psalms* (Penguin USA, 2003), and *Taking Our Places: The Buddhist Path to Truly Growing Up* (HarperSanFrancisco, 1993).

ROBIN HART is a corporate attorney practicing in San Francisco. She has a Master of Arts in theology.

After a career as a college teacher and linguist, ANNETTE HERSKOVITS did volunteer work for an immigrant rights organization. She is currently writing on human rights and political issues. Annette practices at the Berkeley Zen Center.

MUSHIM IKEDA-NASH is a writer, diversity trainer, and Buddhist practitioner. She lives with her husband and son in Oakland, California.

LIN JENSEN is resident teacher of the Chico Zen Sangha in Chico, California, where he writes and works in defense of the earth. He is the author of *Bowing to Receive the Mountain*, with Elliot Roberts (Sunflower Ink, 1997), and *Uncovering the Wisdom of the Heartmind* (Quest Books, 1999).

Along with her full-time job caring for her home and children, JENNA JORDISON hosts a weekly Vipassana/Metta meditation group in Vancouver, Canada. She regularly speaks to church and community groups on dharma-related topics. More than a year following her meeting with Victor Whiteman, Jenna found within herself the ability to release Victor from any sense of indebtedness to her, and the willingness to wish him freedom and happiness on his journey.

JACK KORNFIELD, Vipassana teacher, cofounded the Insight Meditation Society in Barre, Massachusetts, and Spirit Rock Meditation Center in Woodacre, California. He lives near Spirit Rock, where he is a guiding teacher. His books on dharma practice include *A Path with Heart* (Bantam Books, 1993) and *After the Ecstasy the Laundry* (Bantam Books, 2001).

KENNETH KRAFT is a professor of Buddhist studies at Lehigh University in Bethlehem, Pennsylvania. He is the author or editor of six books, including *Eloquent Zen* (University of Hawaii Press, 1997) and *The Wheel of Engaged Buddhism* (Weatherhill, 2000).

DIANA LION is the founding director of the Buddhist Peace Fellowship's Prison Project. She is a longtime Buddhist practitioner, and recently completed the training for Community Dharma Leaders at Spirit Rock Meditation Center. She is a certified trainer of Nonviolent Communication and is now teaching in a Buddhist chaplaincy program.

BOB MAAT works with the Coalition for Peace and Reconciliation (CPR) and the Dhammayietra Center for Peace and Nonviolence, both based in Phnom Penh, Cambodia. A close associate of Maha Ghosananda, he works on the International Campaign to Ban Landmines, and the annual Dhammayietra (peace walk) in Cambodia.

JOANNA MACY is a Buddhist scholar, eco-philosopher, writer, teacher, and peaceworker. Her many books include *World As Lover, World As Self* (Parallax Press, 1991) and her memoir, *Widening Circles* (New Society Publishers, 2000). One of the founding members of the Buddhist Peace Fellowship, she has served on its international advisory board for many years. She lives in Berkeley, California, with her husband Fran Macy, near her children and grandchildren.

JARVIS JAY MASTERS lives on San Quentin's death row, where he writes and practices yoga and Tibetan Buddhism. He is the author of *Finding Freedom: Writings from Death Row* (Padma Publishing, 1997).

FLEET MAULL founded both the National Prison Hospice Association and the Prison Dharma Network. He is a meditation teacher in the

Shambhala Buddhist tradition and a Zen Peacemaker priest. He was released from prison in 1999 and now lives in Boulder, Colorado, where he teaches socially engaged Buddhism at Naropa University.

SUSAN MOON is a longtime Zen practitioner. Besides being editor of *Turning Wheel*, she is the author of *The Life and Letters of Tofu Roshi* (Shambhala Publications, 2001), and co-editor, with Lenore Friedman, of *Being Bodies: Buddhist Women on the Paradox of Embodiment* (Shambhala Publications, 1997).

WENDY EGYOKU NAKAO is the abbot and head teacher of the Zen Center of Los Angeles. She was ordained by Taizan Maezumi Roshi and received dharma transmission from Roshi Bernard Tetsugen Glassman.

VENERABLE THICH NHAT HANH, Vietnamese Buddhist teacher, lives in Plum Village, a Buddhist monastery in southern France, and travels widely, teaching peace. Scholar, poet, peace and human rights activist, he was exiled from Vietnam because of his peace work there during the war. He has published more than 100 titles, including *Peace Is Every Step* (Bantam Books, 1992), *Being Peace* (Parallax Press, 1988), and *Touching Peace* (Parallax Press, 1992). His inspiration and support have been essential for the Buddhist Peace Fellowship from its inception, and he has served on the international advisory board for many years.

TONY PATCHELL is a Zen priest. He stopped working at the Tom Waddell Clinic in San Francisco in 2002, and moved to Sonoma County, California, with his wife, Darlene Cohen. Currently enjoying a respite, he expects to return to work after a period of recuperation.

DONALD ROTHBERG is on the faculty at Saybrook Graduate School, where he has developed a program in Socially Engaged Spirituality. He has written and taught widely on socially engaged Buddhism, and is the co-editor with Sean Kelly of *Ken Wilber in Dialogue: Conversations with Leading Transpersonal Thinkers* (Theosophical Publishing House, 1998).

MAYLIE SCOTT was a Zen priest and teacher at the Arcata Zen Center in Arcata, California, and a lifetime peace activist, deeply committed to socially engaged Buddhism. She died in May 2001.

ALAN SENAUKE was executive director of the Buddhist Peace Fellowship from 1991 through 2001 and continues to be active as BPF's senior advisor. A Soto Zen priest, he received dharma transmission from Sojun Mel Weitsman Roshi. He lives with his wife, Laurie, and their two children at the Berkeley Zen Center in California. In another realm, Alan is well known as a performer (singer and guitarist) of American traditional music. His recent album is *Wooden Man* (Native and Fine Records, 2002).

GARY SNYDER is a poet and friend of the wilderness, who lives on San Juan Ridge in the Sierra foothills, in the Yuba watershed of California. He has published sixteen books of poetry and prose, and received the Pulitzer Prize for poetry for *Turtle Island*, in 1974. One of the founding members of the Buddhist Peace Fellowship, he has served on its Advisory Board for many years.

ROBERT THURMAN is a professor of Buddhist studies at Columbia University, and a translator of Buddhist texts from Tibet and India. He is a lay disciple of His Holiness the Dalai Lama, founder of the American Institute of Buddhist Studies (for the translation of Tibetan Buddhist texts into English), co-founder of Tibet House, and an advocate for the preservation of Tibetan culture.

JOAN TOLLIFSON writes and talks with people about the nature of reality. She has an affinity with Zen and Advaita but belongs to no formal tradition. She is the author of *Awake in the Heartland: The Ecstasy of What Is* (Trafford, 2003), and *Bare-Bones Meditation: Waking Up from the Story of My Life* (Three Rivers Press, 1996). Her Web site is: www.joantollifson.com.

DIANA WINSTON is the founder of the Buddhist Alliance for Social Engagement (BASE) program, and the former associate director of BPF. She is a writer and activist, and teaches dharma and socially engaged Buddhism to youth and adults internationally. She is the author of *Wide Awake: A Buddhist Guide for Teens* (Perigee, 2003).